Endorsements for Discovering Your Authentic Truth

"Those who know me know that the military has played a pivotal role in my life. As a former Marine, I have sincere respect for the military and how military service and training can build both character and strength. Lt. Col. Guy Brilando, USAF, Ret. is a credit to his generation and the United States Air Force. His commitment to sharing the stories that have shaped his life is commendable. I certainly agree with his premise in *Authentic Truth*: the mind is an incredible machine. And it is up to each of us to use our mental resources and strengths… and use them well."
~ **Robert Kiyosaki**, author of the *New York Times* bestseller *Rich Dad Poor Dad*

"**Discovering Your Authentic Truth** is a delightful guide packed with incredible information and practical solutions for those who want to understand the power of the subconscious mind and how it affects the spoken words which in turn affect one's quality of life. Guy, whom I had the pleasure of first meeting two-and-a-half-years ago, is one of the most authentic, credible, knowledgeable, loving, inspiring, gentle yet powerful man I have ever met. Witnessing his own transformation, his understanding of the power of energy healing, and his love and desire to help people, Guy is the right person who can take you on a journey of raising your level of self-awareness to uncover life's challenges and use them as an opportunity for self-transformation and discovering your authentic self. This book is a must read for all."
~ **Master Marilag Mendoza – Master Pranic Healer,** a direct disciple of Grand Master Choa Kok Sui (Founder of Modern Pranic Healing), International Lecturer

"Discovering Your Authentic Truth is simply a MASTERPIECE! This is a book that every person should read and internalize. I've read many books and this is one that will go down in history as a game-changer for those who want to see a real transformation. When you finish this book, share it with your friends and family so that they can experience the same incredible transformation that you will!"

~ **Rob Shallenberger,** CEO of Becoming Your Best Global Leadership, Best-selling Author, and Former F-16 Pilot, BecomingYourBest.com

"In my capacity as a communications professional I thought I knew the playbook. After all I had co-founded BWR, which at the time of its sale to legendary advertising juggernaut, Young & Rubicam, was among the largest entertainment public relations firms in the world. My life changed with this event and the first meeting with Niurka, where the author assisted her in taking me further and deeper into those limiting thoughts of self doubt and irrational fear that I've worked a lifetime to contain, process and discard. Guy has written a primer that encapsulates the Niurka experience and gives readers some of the magic we have all discovered."

~ **Larry Winokur,** Co-founder, BWR Public Relations

"This book is so engaging and eye-opening! Guy Brilando, you've been a dear friend for more than a decade. It's been an amazing experience to witness you go from an analytical mind set of a USAF Fighter Pilot to "Dream Catcher and Vision Stretcher"! I am so very proud of you for learning to "Live your Passion" and having the courage and commitment to write this book so that others have the opportunity to know what is possible when they live their purpose. I am certain this book will have a huge positive impact on every person that devours it! Congratulations, Guy!!!"

~ **Susan Walsh,** Professional Marketing Leader, 24/7 SERIOUSLY!

"I have known Guy Brilando for over 10 years. We met as fellow pilots and immediately became friends. We share a love of country, music, as well as inspiring our youth to become the best they can be. Our values and ideas are so similar. I devote my creative energies to inspiring kids all over this country as the leader of CTS rock band and creator of The Freedom Rock Experience for high school students.

For them to find their passions and live their dreams in life while honoring our real American heroes like Guy, who have served our country. Guy understands this importance of investing and inspiring our youth as well for they are truly our future. I am very honored to know Guy and proud to endorse his incredible new book. I personally know the passion he put into writing it and know you will feel is as well as you read it. I can assure you after reading it, you too will have a renewed excitement about life and reaching inside yourself as well to make your journey the best it can be and live each day to the fullest."

~ **Jeff Senour,** Leader of CTS, the Freedom Rock Experience, and Southwest Airlines Captain

---

"An outstanding read!!! This book is moving, engaging and profound. A REAL life changer. Guy's passion and writing style is rich with insights and experiences that will have a positive impact on anyone's life, both personality and professionally. If you want a break-through in thinking this is a MUST READ."

~ **Brad Hager,** founder Hager Marketing Group

Dear Mark,
Thank you for the friendship, inspiration and belief! Remember: You are precious, a precious gift for the world to know!

Guy Brilando

24 MAR 2022

DISCOVERING YOUR AUTHENTIC TRUTH

Guy Brilando

DISCOVERING YOUR ATHENTIC TRUTH Copyright © 2017 by Guy Brilando.

All rights reserved. Printed in the United States. No part of this publication may be reproduced, distributed, or transmitted in any form or by any means, including photocopying, recording, or other electronic or mechanical methods, without the prior written permission of the author. www.guybrilando.com

Jones Media Publishing
10645 N. Tatum Blvd. Ste. 200-166
Phoenix, AZ 85028
www.JonesMediaPublishing.com

Book Cover Design: www.YourBookBlueprint.com
Interior Layout: Claudia Jones
Editing by: Tara Majuta

ISBN: 978-1-945849-04-6 paperback

DEDICATION

To all those searching for hope and a better life.
The answers reside within you. Infinite possibilities await you now.

CONTENTS

DEDICATION vii
FOREWORD 1
EDITOR'S NOTE: AUTHENTIC TRUTH 3
AUTHOR'S NOTE 5
ACKNOWLEDGEMENTS 9
INTRODUCTION 11

SECTION I   Let's Begin

   Chapter 1:   Welcome… 15
   Chapter 2:   How Did We Arrive Here? 25
   Chapter 3:   Take Flight 35
   Chapter 4:   Awakenings 45
   Chapter 5:   The Secret To Happiness (getting unstuck) . . . 57

SECTION II   True Stories

   Chapter 6:   Catalaya Was Shackled - Part 1 69
   Chapter 7:   Catalaya Was Shackled - Part 2 81
   Chapter 8:   Mom's Turn 93
   Chapter 9:   A Plane Ride To Freedom 105

Chapter 10: An Inner Battle 117

Chapter 11: The Power Of A "Reframe" 129

Chapter 12: Connie Was Addicted 143

SECTION III   Deeper Understanding

Chapter 13: Tuning Up 157

Chapter 14: Introduction To Core Values 169

Chapter 15: A Personal Story 181

Chapter 16: Awareness 193

Chapter 17: Language - Part 1 205

Chapter 18: Language - Part 2 217

SECTION IV   Everyday Use

Chapter 19: Putting It Together 231

Chapter 20: Authentic Communication 243

Chapter 21: Relationships 255

Chapter 22: Intimate Relationships 269

Chapter 23: The Challenge With Affirmations 285

Chapter 24: Empowering Questions 293

Chapter 25: Final Thoughts 307

AFTERWORD 319

ADDENDUM 331

APPENDIX 341

FOREWORD

You're about to embark on a journey of wonder and discovery into your infinite Self. And Guy Brilando is a trustworthy guide who will ignite your inspiration and bring you home into the depths of *you*.

I met Guy in 2014. He came to an event I was leading in Los Angeles. At the time, he was feeling "stuck," desiring change, and searching for a new purpose.

Having realized the zenith of accomplishment in his former life as an F-16 fighter pilot, his work had become his identity. Flying jets wasn't what *he did*, it was *who he was*. When that chapter of his life was complete, he found himself lost... disconnected from his authentic Self, and higher intuitive calling.

Despite these gnawing frustrations, he was sincere and resolved to find answers, to discover *his* Authentic Truth, and create a life brimming with joy, purpose, and meaning. Trusting his intuition, he made a decision that changed his life forever. He and his wife joined me for a retreat I lead in Sedona. Soon, the door to his destiny would be revealed, and reality would never be the same again!

This experience in Sedona (known as NeoGenesis) awakened Guy to aspects within his psyche that had been in conflict. As the light of awareness shined on his inner struggles, old patterns instantly began dissolving in the presence of new angles of observation. He was experiencing the world through enlightened eyes!

FOREWORD

Blown away by this moment of Satori (instant awakening), and experiencing the power of transformation firsthand, (not just within himself, but the profound ripple effect it had on his family and friends) Guy committed to attend all my courses (multiple times). Then, he joined my crew, continually showing up in service to this great work.

Bringing nothing less than the fullness of his inspired totality, and with the endearing zeal of a child on Christmas morning (who's received the ultimate present... *a toolbox for transformation!*), Guy devoutly studies, practices, and generously shares. People come to him for help; he graciously, and masterfully, guides them to break through the greatest challenges in their lives.

His story—and the stories of the wonderful people he's guided—contain key codes that will illuminate your path, empowering you to create your most magnificent life. Fasten your seatbelt and prepare for an adventure of a lifetime!

This book will speak to you, like a wise friend. You will see your own life mirrored in the stories shared. It will shed light on the underlying root causes of your dissatisfactions. It will empower you with insight to reconstruct old limiting habits, so you come to know your true Self and live a life of freedom…the life you deserve …the life you are truly meant to enjoy.

This book is a testament of the power of rapid, radical transformation in action. It is the account of one man's journey of discovery into the embodiment of *his* Authentic Truth, and how sharing his love and knowledge, in service to others, has paved the way for his grandest dreams to become real. And so it is with you.

NIURKA
Creator, The Art of Supreme Influence
www.niurkainc.com

EDITOR'S NOTE: AUTHENTIC TRUTH

Have you ever experienced something so profound, you almost couldn't believe it happened to you? It was like a whisper that passed by your ear, so soft and lovely, you nearly missed it. But you didn't. The moment it touched you, grazing your spirit with its warm embrace, your weary soul came to life all at once.

That's exactly what happened to me when I discovered my Authentic Truth.

I was just like you: curious and seeking something more. The world had given me many opportunities to find myself, and I took them all. Every single experience I had prompted the same important question within me, "What exactly do you have in store for me?"

The answers varied. For thirty-three years, I examined, re-examined, added meaning to, and made modifications to myself, depending on what *I thought* was being told to me. At first it was a glorious adventure, but over time, the journey became overshadowed by doubt and fear.

"Who am I, really?" plagued my mind on countless, sleepless nights. Everyone I knew had their own personal definition for me. And please, don't get me wrong, the things they had to say were beautiful and somewhat fulfilling. But I couldn't stop searching, knowing I hadn't found the answer I was looking for.

Then I found Guy—and this book—and everything changed.

EDITOR'S NOTE: AUTHENTIC TRUTH

When I encountered this book, I was not in a good place. I felt the world had been unkind to me. I didn't blame anyone in particular for my short-comings, but I felt no one could hear me screaming inside. I wanted more. I wanted to feel something, anything that would remind me that I was alive. I needed hope. Search after search left me empty-handed and desperate to quench my ever-growing thirst. And then it happened—the whisper.

Finding your Authentic Truth isn't about *fixing* you. It's not about *handing* you an answer, either. It's so much more than that. It's a much-needed break when you've thrown too much of yourself into the world and received absolutely nothing in return. It's a flowing dance, between you and your inner self, which is designed to help you move together as one. It's an understanding that comes only when you are at ease with knowing that God created you exactly the way you were supposed to be. And, of course, it's only the beginning of a life that you always dreamed of but may have thought impossible.

This book was a blessing in disguise. Every story, every word, brought something new and exciting to me. And as I continued forward, I found *myself*, hidden deep inside the love and compassion present on each and every page. I came to life, stronger and more confident than before, eager to share with everyone I knew the most power realization I had discovered.

I had found myself, again. And this time, I was here to stay.
If you let it, this book will perform the most amazing transformations in your life. So, I invite you to ask this book, and this work, a very specific question: What do you have in store for me?

~ Tara Majuta, Writer, Editor, Storyteller, and Whale Saver

AUTHOR'S NOTE

How does this book differ from others in this field? Although much of the content itself is not new in the world of communication, if unfamiliar with Neuro-Linguistics Programming (NLP), much of it will more than likely be new to you. In a nutshell, NLP is a science of neurology and language that allows a person to transform unwanted behaviors and results quickly. It is extremely effective as well as powerful.

New terminology and depths of understanding into language patterns and internal programming can become overwhelming. Therefore, I purposely designed the delivery of this information to be uniquely different from any other book I'm aware of on this subject. I wish to *involve you*, the reader, not just talk at you.

The stories you'll read are firsthand accounts of my actual experiences with real individuals. To protect their identities, some of their names have been changed. However, the extraordinary results these ordinary people experienced unfolded as described.

Also, when I began writing on this topic, the direction and how to deliver the message was not exactly clear. The path didn't develop until the words flowed through and out of me. As you read this book, you may feel yourself drift away into the soul of this topic in a way that differs from other conventional writing styles.

Why did I do this? During my research on how to write a book, I discovered why so many books out there read the same and decided that I wanted something different. I wanted a book where the more you

AUTHOR'S NOTE

read it, the deeper the understanding of the information naturally flowed and the more comfortable you become with it.

In other words, I didn't want a book that delivered an A-Z approach. Nor did I want to lay out lists (7 Ways to… or 10 Easy Steps Toward…) for you to digest. "Just do this or do that and all your worries and concerns will be taken care of."

Instead, this book will get your mind to think in new ways. Intriguing books are much more than black and white lists or recipes for success. If your mind is not involved on a deeper level, you may not receive the full benefits from what you have read. Allow your thoughts to engage. Open a doorway within your mind for new perspectives to emerge. And if you find yourself confused at times, that's okay. Confusion is necessary first before any true change can commence.

I learned long ago that little lasting change happens without such engagement. Most of my reading is still in the self-help genre. I love what they offer, and I certainly learn from them. However, many of these books today also seem to be written in a way that is, at times, a bit stale. In my opinion, they fall short of actually reaching that deeper level of human consciousness that creates creative thought and integrated learnings. Maybe you too have experienced this.

Yet, when I read older books, say 30, 50 or 150 years old in this same area of self-help, they have a different flavor to them and *engage* the reader to use creative thinking. The reader is challenged to go outside the pages to search for the deeper meaning and understanding within.

This is where my book comes in. Where we are about to go will provide you with the opportunity to *see* yourself, those around you, and the world from new perspectives. If open to it, you will begin asking yourself questions in new ways, gaining new understandings. That may seem like a tall order, but this is why I wrote the book; for you to see new possibilities that you were previously unaware of. That's what a good book does, and that is what we're going to do.

I promise this book will get your mind to think in new ways. At times, you may wonder where I am going with certain thoughts within a chapter or even this book. But in so doing, you will actually be learning new material in a different way that will stick. Quite possibly, you may not even realize this as it is happening! An additional objective is for you to activate more of your senses, such as auditory, visual, and kinesthetic, as you read. The more I can help you engage and get *into* the material, the greater the understanding and lasting results will be.

My intention is for us to *flow* through it together from a position of love and compassion. Pause and close your eyes, imagining us sitting beside one another on an airplane. We're traveling from Los Angeles to New York and have a lot of time to kill. Being cordial and open to learning, you lean over and ask, "So, what do you do?" and I respond with, "I help people discover their *Authentic Truth*."

You become curious and ask several follow-up questions. Pretty soon, a real conversation develops. What you hold in your hands is such a conversation. It is not an allegory but a vehicle to enlightenment of Authentic Truth and the creation of new pathways for your mind.

Even though we are not sitting next to each other at this moment, ask yourself the same type of questions you would if we actually were. Allow yourself to become lost in your own inner world of deep reflection and inquisitiveness, always coming back to these pages with new questions and new understandings. I encourage you to read this book with a red pen and mark it up with questions, highlights, and even areas you may disagree with.

Allow your mind to **engage** with the material. If you do, I believe you'll find it extremely entertaining, educational, meaningful, and thought-provoking, with the advantage of raising your curiosity. If you play full out, you will even begin creating new pathways for your mind. If you allow it, this book will speak to you, and hopefully, you will realize, understand, and feel even more connected to your *Authentic Truth*.

AUTHOR'S NOTE

Finally, I look forward to hearing from you. As you read and have questions or wish to forward your thoughts, please reach out and do so. I will do my best to respond personally in a timely manner. My web site is simply, www.guybrilando.com.

Blessings to you and your loved ones. Namaste.

Guy Brilando

Guy Brilando

ACKNOWLEDGEMENTS

Each soul that has been a part of my life has impacted in some way the creation of this book. So grateful am I to all.

Mr. Murphy, long since passed, believed in me and provided more guidance than any other teacher or authority figure in all of my schooling. I loved him dearly and he was my primary mentor outside of my dad during sixth through eighth grades. His love for us kids, his mannerisms, philosophy, and teachings provided a grounding and moral basis that shaped me during those childhood years. That foundation has carried over throughout my life.

To each of my mentors along the way, so many of you, I thank you all. Of note are a few I wish to highlight. Their influence directly affected my life's path. Janielle and Adrian Vashon who inspired the entrepreneur within me. Brad Hager, who encouraged me to read. Brad's wife, Marcia, who demonstrates how to behave as the swan on the surface while the feet below paddle away. Susan Walsh who taught me how to uplift others. Robert Kiyosaki who taught me the concept of leverage. Orrin Woodward and Chris Brady who taught me what true leadership is. Niurka (and Crew) who affected the greatest awakening within me in the shortest period of time of anyone I've known. To all of you, and those not mentioned, thank you.

To the authors of every uplifting book I've read – the life lessons, wisdom, and knowledge you bless us all with, including the Bible, I express sincere appreciation. Of a special place in my heart is Leo

ACKNOWLEDGEMENTS

Buscaglia who taught me the meaning of loving others during my teenage years with his PBS specials and books. To all my friends throughout the years, thank you. To my loyal followers from Facebook who consistently support me, thank you for your inspiration.

To those who believed in me enough to provide valuable input throughout this book's creation, including my editor, Tara, and publisher, Jeremy, and numerous proof readers—without each of you, this book would not have achieved my desired goal.

And of course, my spiritual guide, Jesus, and my immediate family of endless love, care, and authenticity who give me continuous grounding and support. A warmth of blessings to my daughter, her husband and grandchildren who are the breath to the evolution of life. Finally, to my wife, Elke, who fuels my soul at its deepest levels. Thank you all.

INTRODUCTION

I am honored this book has arrived in your hands. Throughout its writing, my sole focus was ensuring the delivery of this message in a manner that best enables you, the reader, to see, attain, and retain its true inherent value.

If you are ready, this book will give you so much. What you are holding can change your life in several ways. It will open your awareness: how you think, how you see yourself, others around you, the environment, and your circumstances. It will bring a basic education in the field of Neuro-Linguistics Programming or NLP. If this is your first exposure to this subject area, prepare to be blown away by its power. If you are already familiar with NLP, it will strengthen your understanding.

Contained within these pages are a few tools to incorporate into your daily life, such as Empowering Questions, that will absolutely and genuinely connect you to manifesting that which you wish for through the Law of Attraction. And this book will definitely increase your knowledge and skills as a communicator with yourself and those you encounter.

As you read, you will notice certain words in quotations, such as "Secondary Gain." For standardization, these words in quotations relate to NLP terminology. At other times, where quotations would typically be used, you will see words in italics, such as *alignment*, to provide emphasis or in reference to book titles.

INTRODUCTION

To add clarity, the book is laid out in four sections as a building block approach. Below you will find a description of each section including the Afterword. In the Afterword, those chosen in Section II will give you an update to their story in their own words.

Section I—builds rapport between you and me, and introduces new terms and concepts.
Section II—stories of actual transformations of those I've worked with.
Section III—content specific on awareness and language.
Section IV—application of this knowledge in your daily life.
Afterwords—those from Section II share their perspective in their own words.
Addendum—one last powerful story that sums up many facets of this book.
Appendix—contains a list of exercises explained throughout the book.

May you enjoy this journey more and more with every page turned!

DISCLAIMER: The chapter on Empowering Questions is written in a complete format. All other exercises as described in this book are incomplete. As presented here, they are not to be used as a method of working with another individual. They provide an overview, at best, of that which requires extensive training from a professional. I do not diagnose, treat, or mitigate any disease in the work I've done with others. I am simply present with them and utilize what I have been trained in.

SECTION I
LET'S BEGIN

POSSIBILITIES татто NEW PATHWAYS

WELCOME... 1

"Drench yourself in words unspoken, Live your life with arms wide open, Today is where your book begins, The rest is still unwritten."

NATASHA BEDINGFIELD

From the moment of conception, life evolves from the engagement of two individual cells: the creation of a new human being begins. A new heart, a new soul, and a new mind develops. We now know the heart begins to beat around six weeks, and the brain begins to form at six to seven weeks. Feeling, including pain, is felt as early as eight weeks. This is also when limbs begin to form and the first movements happen. Some seven months afterwards, this new life emerges from the mother's womb and is introduced into this world. How fascinating! How miraculous! A magnificent creation of life born into a world of infinite possibilities.

Guess what? You *are* this magnificent creation. You were not made by the hands of man—you were created from life's energy itself. From two separate microscopic parts, you became whole and complete. This biological event is intricate and magical, but none is more fascinating to me than the developing mind—the gateway to interpreting ourselves, the world around us, and beyond.

WELCOME...

The Incredible Mind

It begins with the human brain—the physical, most amazing computer alive. We know our brain exists inside our head. But somehow, **somewhere**, associated with our brain, the **mind** (including the subconscious mind) exists.

The mind encompasses far more than the physical realm. Scientists, to this day, have yet to uncover all that the mind can do. Even more perplexing, they cannot pinpoint *where it is*. It is acknowledged that there is more to the story than just the brain, a collection of fat cells firing off messages that run our bodies. Could it be that the brain is a conduit to the mind? That we are spiritual beings guided by our minds?

Our mind drives how we think, how we behave, our decisions, and our interpretations of the world. It allows us to feel, create, contemplate, and imagine like no other living creature on this planet. And no two people think exactly the same. We are each a unique creation. As my friend, Niurka says, "There has never been, nor will there ever be, another exactly like you."

For each of us traveling through life's experiences, we are bombarded with incredible volumes of input, requiring interpretations of the external world, resulting in specific programming, thus creating individual maps of the world. The result is that no two people *see* the world exactly the same. This is referred to as the individual's "map of the world."

Therefore, this map is *not* reality but an individualized interpretation of the real world. This map is *incomplete* due to deletions, distortions, and generalizations of the reality beyond the individual's mind. As our journey through life evolves, our minds undergo specific interpretations and programming.

For example, in terms of a significant emotional event, this programming is locked into place the moment the event happens. These, along with all the other experiences and learnings we encounter, especially early on, lay the foundation for developing our core values, personalities, and decision-making processes; our Identity.

Regardless of whether a conscious memory of an original event is present or not, certain traits unique to the individual take shape and form within the subconscious mind. Experts in this field tell us the subconscious mind remembers everything; it forgets nothing. *All* is there, somewhere, and much of it is accessible.

The Developing Mind

Included within this wealth of information are our significant emotional events that aid in the creation of our "Meta-Programs." Meta-Programs are basically how you form your internal representations; your "map" that directs your behavior.

An extreme example of a significant emotional event is a learned-phobic response. I use the word *learned* because it is widely accepted that we are born with only two innate fears: loud noises and falling. Everything else is learned, such as from cases of trauma or extreme negative experiences.

Consequently, when a previous trauma is stimulated later (a trigger), a neurological and thus, physical reaction occurs in that person. The trigger fires off internal programming, creating the conditions for the individual to ***experience*** the past trauma again.

In the case of a phobia, a systematic programming gets inserted that acts like an alarm mechanism. The mind does not want you to experience that trauma again so it wards it off before it happens through avoidance.

Take fear of flying, for example. Many people won't step onto an airplane because of this imprint gained at some point in their life (not born with it). The phobic response is there to prevent the person from reliving the past trauma. "If you don't get on that airplane, you will be

WELCOME...

safe." This is one of the "prime directives" of the subconscious mind; to *keep you safe.*

This is the power of our minds at work. Understanding how this fits together with our *language* and overall communication is what changed my world almost three years ago. Although I had heard it over and over again, it wasn't until my mind was ready to absorb its significance that I was truly able to understand communication's impact and how to effectively apply it. The old adage, "When the student is ready, the teacher appears," came during this stage.

As that student, I learned in order to effectively create true transformation and change, we need to be able to step out of our old "frame" and see our situation from new perspectives. Once that happens, the old programming can be replaced with new, more ecological and loving neuro-pathways within the mind. The result from this process frees you from the old, unwanted behaviors and patterns of the past, so you can create your new life in the direction of your sincerest desires.

Seeking Something New

Have you ever gotten all fired up with a new idea from a book or seminar? Or have you experienced an emotional high that you *wanted* and just knew was possible*? Perhaps a new career, new health and vitality, entrepreneurship, or relationship? Or maybe it was a behavior—waking up vibrant, having a positive attitude, eating healthy foods, or the desire to curve or eliminate excess weight, smoking, or alcoholism.

> *A "want" falls in line with a wish and is disempowering language. It is abstract and usually filled with deletions, distortions, and generalizations in the conscious mind from the deeper context within the subconscious mind. As a result, once on the journey, hidden resistances surface. These are what stops a person from achieving their goal or vision. The resistances were there all along but without awareness to them! The person is left wondering, "Why did I fail again?"*

At that moment, your *conscious* mind desired this new you, yet one month, six months or a year down the road, you found yourself having the same repetitious results as in the past, repeating old behaviors. Consciously, you were fired up about the change. You were ready for the change. You wanted the change. You made a decision to change. From this desire, you welcomed the change and the world of infinite possibilities to make it happen. But then, much to your frustration, the old patterns of behavior surfaced again. Managing the decision became more painful than reverting to old ways.

Change is possible at any moment, at any second of any day, right? So, why didn't the transformation happen? Why did you fall back into your old ways when you wanted the change so badly? What was wrong with you? "Other people were able to do it," you say. "Other people can go out there and accomplish their dreams, their goals, and their vision. My vision and goals are just as important. Just as real. Just as achievable. Why are they able to achieve them, and I can't?" So, you read, go to seminars, and take courses, knowing change is possible because others have done it. Then you realize the truth; you are stuck in an unwanted pattern.

My dear friend and mentor, Brad Hager said it best, "For things to change, I must change. For things to get better, I must get better." This is a powerful truth, but what does it really mean? How in the world do you create a *real* change within your mind? It's more than just your thinking—it's your programming, beyond the thinking, that creates the change.

The Essence of NLP

Why do the tools of NLP work? Imagine you live on the other side of a fifteen-minute walk through a forest of trees from a local store you frequent. For years, you travelled the same zigzag pathway through the forest to the store and back. Let's say this represents the old programming, the problem you are stuck in.

One day, a neighbor decides he can shave five minutes off the time of this walk by cutting a new, more direct path through the forest to the store. After doing this, you now travel this new path only. In fact, the old path you had travelled for years is not even an option—you don't even see it any longer. This new path is the only path for you. It's as if the old path was immediately covered in overgrowth and no longer even there.

Change Your Programming

Through hundreds of books read and seminars attended, I fully understood the power of changing my thinking. I began to realize it was more than finding a fast and easy way to change through creating vision boards, reciting affirmations, and thinking new thoughts. I had to dig deeper.

I didn't want to just scratch the surface—I was searching for the secret to true transformation. This search eventually led me to Niurka, Evolved NLP, and ultimately the desired change I sought for so long.

What I discovered was a whole new way of looking at the world, not only from my own eyes, but all that exists around me.

Programming makes you think a certain way. When something happens, you contemplate the situation and develop a thought. And then that thought creates the behavior which expands into decisions and actions which leads to your results.

So, to put it simply, your programming, beyond everything else, creates the results you are getting. It is your "I Am," your Identity, your essence, your true core values, which are at the heart of it all.

And where does this programming come from? How easily can this be changed? The answers are simpler than you might expect! This is the gift Evolved NLP provides.

Once you understand these truths, the veil of your behaviors, values, and programming will be pulled back. You will begin to not only see the world in a new light but also yourself. You will understand why you do the things you do. Even more enlightening, you can *see*, for maybe the first time, how the results you've created up until now have shaped your life.

You get in touch with yourself on a deeper level than you've ever experienced. This permits your "I Am" to emerge from your depths and into your conscious mind with new understandings. A new-found freedom, possibly unlike anything felt before, releases you from your old, unwanted patterns and behaviors, fully and completely. You have a feeling of peace; a feeling of connectivity to your soul. It is this connection that brings forth your *Authentic Truth*.

What This Book Is

The above is just a portion of what this book will uncover for you. As this adventure unfolds, you will develop a curiosity that is the first step necessary for growth and evolution. You'll also receive powerful tools to significantly raise your level of awareness for true empowerment.

This book is not intended to be a scientific book on NLP but rather a sharing of my learned knowledge and useful application of it. Although I'm not a doctor or licensed professional, I am Master Certified in Evolved NLP, a unique hybrid of the NLP model. This book is not intended to replace formal therapy from licensed professionals in any way.

Rather, this book is informational in hopes to open your mind to possibilities that do exist. I learned from Masters in the field of transformation and healing and have read in excess of five hundred books in this and other areas of personal growth. The results I get with others are real. Everything that I am passing along to you here is simply a shortcut from my years of study.

NLP, in its purist form, is a science, removed of emotions. Evolved NLP brings in love and compassion as well as the spiritual aspect all around us. Although I am a born-again Christian, most people I work

WELCOME...

with in this field are not. In other words, this vital information is for everyone, from any spiritual or religious belief structure, to the atheist. This content is important. It is about raising awareness to the miracles all around us and especially within you.

Prepare to be Challenged

Most of us have been challenged by life every now and then. I certainly have! If you find yourself in this situation, remember, there is nothing *wrong* with you. Chances are your behaviors or repetitive patterns have to do with your original programming from childhood. With an update to the old programming, navigating these challenges in a healthy way that provides new possibilities with real solutions, becomes your new reality. That's where the power of this book comes in.

This is not to a recipe to *fix* you; rather, it is a proven construct to help unlock your inner world so you can see that you already have within you everything you need to create the life you desire. The greatest gifts I received in my journey was falling in love with myself again, connecting with my love core center in a completely new way, and discovering my definitive purpose.

I'll share that journey with you, but it is my sincerest hope that this book brings you closer to your Authentic Truth and love core center, opening new pathways towards your future. At the least, may it create enough curiosity and desire for you to take the next step in that direction. If you do, you will find greater happiness, joy, and love than you could ever have imagined prior. A deeper soul connection and the discovery of your true purpose in life are all available to you as you connect with your *Authentic Truth*.

* * *

Revelations to New Pathways

1) No two people see the world exactly the same way. This is often why disagreements and arguments begin.

2) New perspectives provide solutions previously obscured.

3) Your internal programming residing in your subconscious mind drives you unconsciously.

HOW DID WE ARRIVE HERE?   2

"Some beautiful paths can't be discovered without getting lost."

EROL OZAN

How did a retired Lt. Col. and former F-16 fighter pilot of twenty years come to write a book about discovering Authentic Truth? A book on communication and language from a position of love and compassion? When I first asked Elke, my wife of twenty-five years this question, she didn't hesitate.

"Guy, you are passionate about America. You love what you did for all those years, and you attacked it with an atypical compassion. You are a giving soul and understand the importance of effective communication. You were in a field where lives depended on it every day! Besides, you are a great teacher and leader and have always loved people. You want the best for everyone. Writing a book like this makes absolute sense."

Elke had nailed it. How the mind works has always been an interest of mine. I also spent many years as a flight instructor, teaching the complicated and intricate tactics involved with properly flying, and more importantly, employing a fighter aircraft. Unknowingly, I was living in alignment with myself during that period. Then retirement came, and as the years passed, I began to lose touch with who I was.

Over a fourteen-year period, before and after the military, I had embarked on various business ventures that seemed to have a recurrent theme: I'd get excited, grow, plateau, and then recede back to my usual ways. I became frustrated and couldn't figure out why this repetitive pattern kept happening.

As this continuous loop developed, I became infatuated with personal growth. I became an avid reader of various self-help books, attended countless seminars, and surrounded myself with people who had already achieved what I desired. In all, countless hours and tens of thousands of dollars were invested. It wasn't until eight years after I had left the military that I realized how *stuck* I really was.

I had a great job, wife, daughter, grand kids, but inside I knew I was incomplete, restless, and lost. In seeking out the self-help world, a huge multi-billion dollar industry that *teaches* individuals how to be successful, I couldn't help but feel my power was somehow being taken away internally. This was my first clue of a deeper issue. Even though I followed each instruction perfectly, I continued feeling stuck, and this unwanted pattern remained. So, I kept searching.

Who Am I?

Every year, I read Napoleon Hill's *Think and Grow Rich*, a staple for any entrepreneur. This book is actually an edited version of his more complete work entitled, *Law of Success*. My annual reading in December allows me to perform a conscious review of my previous year's goals and desired direction. From there, I make adjustments and set new goals for the coming year. In December 2013, as I was driving home late one night from work, I pulled up to the gate of our home, reflecting on something I'd read earlier in that book. Out of nowhere, a light bulb went off inside my head! ***I did not know what my definitive purpose in life was***. A major awakening was born.

Reflecting on my twenty years as a fighter pilot, I knew who I was. In fact, when someone would ask me, "What do you do?" I always responded with, "I'm a fighter pilot and it's not what I do—it's who I am." For twenty years, this was my mantra. It encompassed every cell of my body and served me well. That attitude kept me alive in a hazardous occupation where many of my friends from the fighter world were not so fortunate. I'll share more of my story as we move along.

Life is so precious. You are a precious gift for the world to know. Your life matters not only to you but to those you impact as well. This book is about getting in touch with yourself at new levels that allows you to create the life you desire. To enjoy life at greater levels than in the past and in enlightened ways. But where do you begin this journey? Throughout history, one of the most vital questions ever asked is, "Who Am I?"

For instance, Ramana Maharshi (1879-1950) was a great master of internal reflection and Yoga. His unwavering belief, "Who am I?" is the most important question anyone could ever ask.

By raising your level of awareness, you come closer to understanding and discovering your truth—who you are. As your awareness elevates, how you see everything around you changes. You begin to notice subtleties missed before: language patterns, verbal and non-verbal communication, sights, sounds, smells, and visual cues. Implementing some or all of the tools and techniques put forth here will open new pathways, allowing you to discover at a deeper level who you truly are.

Our programming starts with a picture or a download into our mind. Next, we have a conversation with ourselves, and we develop a thought, which gives it meaning and purpose. If the meaning serves us, we incorporate it. If in that moment the meaning is not of value to us, we let go of it "consciously," but it is not lost by the subconscious mind! This process continues on auto-pilot until we become *aware* of it.

If we raise our awareness and understand in practical terms how our mind actually works, things change. We discover ourselves in new ways, which allows us to see how we fit into this collage of humanity, including our purpose. In order to start, we must ask ourselves that all-encompassing question: "Who am I?"

If this question is indeed one of the most important questions we can ask in the process of understanding and discovering ourselves, why is this not explored more deeply in our educational system? I'm not sure. In fact, that's a goal in writing this book; getting this understanding and information into our schools *and beyond*.

Finding Answers

Everything changed after I attended my first Evolved NLP course with Niurka in September 2014, entitled NeoGenesis (New Beginnings). Three months later, while home visiting family outside of Chicago, my sister, Lia, and two nieces joined us for dinner. Afterwards, we sat on the couch, and they began asking questions about my recent NeoGenesis experience. Jenny, the older of the two, had recently completed her Masters in Family Psychology, so she was particularly interested. However, the more I went into my new learnings of communication and Evolved NLP, the more my sister and other niece, Gina, twenty years old, engaged.

I explained how most of our programming happens between the ages of 0-7, and it sets the stage for our behavior and reaction to life for the rest of our lives. Many times, we are not aware of why we do what we do because of this programming.

The power our language has on our programming is fascinating. Our words and actions have far more *lasting* power than we realize. As the conversation evolved, my sister began to cringe, which was directly related to her parenting experiences. It was an honest, heartfelt moment with new awareness to her blind spots while raising her two girls.

We continued talking about the different exercises from the course and belief structures people struggle with. Interestingly, we began to notice Gina shifting, and becoming uneasy as she sat on the couch. Her "physiology" was communicating what she was unable to express in words, a message from the "Neurological" aspect of NLP.

Four years earlier, her struggles with multiple autoimmune diseases and chronic pain led to her dropping out of high school.* Gina literally put her life on hold, leaving all the things she loved behind: her friends, school, and dancing. She no longer had the life she was accustomed to living. Elke and I had felt her illnesses may have been created due to various stressors in her life. My sister had begun recognizing this to be the case as well.

*Happily, Gina has now completed high school and is attending college.

Gina's Release

Now, in my parent's living room, Gina became more and more anxious as she listened to this discussion. Finally, we asked if she had something to share. Being a quiet and deep thinker, Gina surprised us all when she broke down and began to cry. She released so much pain built up inside of her. Years of holding in her inner battles were suddenly released in a magical moment.

After regaining her composure, Gina began sharing. The rest of us were given, for the first time, insight into her "map of the world." In the end, she stated, "This is the best therapy session I've ever had because it was with family! You are what is most important to me." Lia, too, experienced a very real and honest moment with herself.

That evening, my sister and her daughters received a fresh place to start talking and listening to one another. It was absolutely beautiful and may never have happened if Niurka's teachings hadn't entered my life. This is what I like to call *the thin threads of life*—how one soul touches another in ways the originator may never know.

A Very Good Question

What an amazing and *transformational* evening it became. Before it ended, Lia said something that landed in my world in a very significant way. "Why isn't this taught in schools? Why aren't we made aware of the significant and long-term effects that damaging and thoughtless language has? If I had known this then, I could have been more aware of these negative results early on."

She was right. The implications of careless words, actions, and behaviors have far reaching, lasting *affects* and *effects* on others. With children, it is exasperated, for they basically have no filters until around seven years old. During these ages, brainwaves are operating mostly at the Theta level, allowing direct access to the subconscious mind. Piling on to this is the aptitude of the subconscious mind to absorb everything and forget nothing. It is that significant.

Taken further, this is when our Meta-Programs (strategies), how we see the world and begin to develop our maps, takes place. Believe it or not, much of what happens here directs the rest of our lives and is *locked* in place. Relationship issues, financial issues, and self-worth issues are but some examples of where this shows up later in life. The gift of NLP, in general, is the ability to unlock and replace negative programming, which no longer serves us, with something new that in turn creates our desired results.

That night, I made a decision to do my best in supporting Niurka's work and producing this book to explain to the world what my sister wished she'd known years earlier; providing hope to others who are dealing with their own challenges in life.

The Art of Listening

We are given one shot in this body, with this soul, in this life to make it a beautiful, wondrous journey. It sounds so easy to say, "Enjoy life!" or "Life is what you choose it to be!" "Thoughts become things," and, "If you can believe it, you can achieve it!" But for many, this is more rhetoric than substance. We are not formally taught the essential truths of life in the context of communication. Those fortunate enough to be brought up in a family where such concepts are taught have a great advantage over those who either have to live and learn these truths through trial and error, or those who have no understanding at all.

It is almost impossible for us to listen to another person and not learn at least one new thing about them, that is unless you choose not to or unaware of *what* you should be listening for. To be fully present and truly listen to another person, there needs to be an awareness of their words spoken, the delivery of their words, their body language, inflections, complexion, physiology, and the environment you are in. These are valuable insights, that once you are aware of them, provide tremendous insight of the other person's "map." But it doesn't stop there. Not only do you see the other person's map more clearly, you begin to better understand your own.

Oftentimes, the words alone are a fraction of the actual message or internal thoughts of the other person. When listening with all your senses, an entirely new world in the realm of communication begins to open up. You begin listening to yourself differently, which after all, is the most important person you will ever have a conversation with. As a result, you elevate your awareness with yourself and become more connected with your Identity and "I Am," allowing for real change in the direction you desire to take place.

What Are You Conveying?

Let's say Bob has arrived at a place in his life where he is utterly stuck in a problem. If we were meeting for coffee, his story would matter to me. It's important because Bob is important. Every breath he takes, filling his lungs with life creates the conditions for another cycle of his heartbeat. I marvel as his oxygenated blood is fueling his body, while his soul unconsciously emits his energy into the ether that is all around him. I engage with Bob at a deep level, building "rapport."

It is his soul I connect with as we enjoy our coffee, cappuccinos or lattes. But I am also deeply intent on Bob's entire communicative expression. How he crafts his words and expresses them with his eyes, brows, lips, complexion, breaths, gestures, posture, and energy, along with symbolic language, generalizations, and idioms. All is penetratingly important to the grander message he is conveying to me. And I'm listening and observing them all.

Every aspect just explained is vital to understanding the communication model, strategies, and maps of yourself and others. It is the internal map projected outward; the programming, values, beliefs, behaviors, fears, along with the possibilities, potentials, and more.

Now, your personal story absolutely does matter! The circumstances and evolution of your life experiences, the good and bad times, are very important. However, in the context of healing, overcoming, and redirecting your life's path, it is not as important as understanding the programming you've undergone throughout your years of living; the *how* behind why you've arrived here. That's the area of your story (not the *drama*, per se) that is the key to unlocking real and lasting change.

For instance, you arrived at this place right now, exactly where you are supposed to be, reading this book, because of the programming within your subconscious mind. It is what drives your decisions, behaviors, actions, and results far more than your conscious mind ever could.

That is how you arrived here.

It's a Gift to Re-Program

Being attuned to how all of this plays out in our lives can be a matter of life and death. This is true in the loss of many fellow fighter pilot friends and colleagues while flying the F-16, and in Catalaya, a young woman you'll meet later who almost succeeded at suicide. But apart from these extreme examples of poor awareness, communication, language patterns, and programming, many unhappy relationships exist; falling short of their desired achievements of what is possible.

Most often, they realize this consciously but are *unconsciously* aware as to how. What the exercises of Evolved NLP allow is for this unconscious awareness to be brought forward to the conscious mind so re-programming can occur. On the flipside, when this unconscious programming is in alignment with a person's Authentic Self, they live extremely happy, healthy, vibrant lives. Everything just seems to go easy for them, and in a way, they do.

As we continue to delve deeper into how this all fits together and works, you'll receive greater insights on how you can develop new pathways in your life, and uncover what areas of your life are not in alignment. In so doing, the ability to move in your desired direction, to travel where your dreams lie, aligning with your *Authentic Truth*, will become clearer.

* * *

Questions to Ask to New Pathways

1) How do you answer "Who Am I?" Not your occupation or role in your family but on a soul level?

2) Have you asked yourself about your purpose in life? How would you define it?

3) How well do you listen? Do you pay attention to a person's physiology, voice inflection, and words simultaneously?

TAKE FLIGHT 3

> *"Every pilot has a very personal story of how he or she ended up in control of that type of aircraft and in that particular airline's cockpit…every time we pilot a flight, we are bringing with us all of the things we've learned over the thousands of hours and millions of miles we've flown."*
>
> — Captain Sully Sullenberger

Man has been fascinated with flight for centuries. In the past 100 years, flying has morphed into an everyday experience. It is impossible in today's modern world to imagine a life without aviation. All you have to do is look up to see a plane or its contrails in the sky. And we haven't stopped there.

We've gone to the moon and back, landed crafts on Mars, and managed to get Juno to orbit Jupiter after it took five years to get there. And we can't forget Voyager 1 and Voyager 2, launched in 1977 with an expected lifespan of only five years, which are still going strong. Man has done amazing things with flight, and we continue to test the limits all the time.

The Beauty of Flight

I grew up near O'Hare airport in a suburb of Chicago and close to Navy Glenview Air Station (long since closed). Like many others, my amazement with planes began as a kid. The sonic booms heard that rattled our house from the Navy jets rocked my world!* Not only would I watch the planes daily overhead and in the distance, I could hear the commercial airliners throughout the night, especially in winter when the cool, dense air allowed the sound to travel so clearly.

> *Strict regulations prevent sonic booms today over populated areas. Back then they were somewhat common place. But the breaking of windows from the thunderous booms brought that to an end. Think of thunder with a lot more oomph!*

In summer, I'd lie atop a raft in our above ground pool for hours, watching the planes, and creating imaginary figures and shapes out of the clouds overhead. I so wished to touch and float on top of them.

During those moments, I allowed my thoughts to wander, wondering who was inside those planes and where they were coming from or going to. Sometimes, our family vacations required air travel, which was a big deal in the 60's and early 70's. No one looked forward to the flight more than me. I encountered those white puffy clouds up close, with a huge grin on my face, taking in the feeling of my dream coming true.

My dad's work caused him to travel to Asia and Europe a lot. I'd stare out our picture window for hours at night, watching the planes, and thinking about how much I missed him, while awaiting his return. Hard to believe today, but back then, two weeks at a time would pass without any communication. It was tough. Our occasional long distance phone calls were extremely precious, even with that annoying ten second delay due to our voices traveling via wires laid across the Atlantic. Upon his return, I'd eagerly listen to the telling of his adventurous travels. Repetitively, one thing came to my mind: I wanted to be back in the air.

It wasn't until my sophomore year in high school that a friend asked if I would be interested in learning to fly. We looked into it, and the price tag was way out of control for a couple of high school kids. We let the dream remain a dream.

A Dream Comes True

Four years later, my luck changed. I was a sophomore in college, waiting for my dad to return home from another one of his business trips. This time he arrived in a corporate jet—very impressive. Then, the unthinkable happened. He asked if I ever wanted to learn how to fly. Of course I gave him a resounding, "Yes!" Within ten minutes, we were driving to Palwaukee airport, and I received the greatest gift my dad could give me.

On December 4, 1983, I had my first flight lesson. A month later, during my second solo, with only ten hours total flight time, I experienced an in-flight engine failure. This wasn't the only one in my flying career, but at that time, I had no clue and no real training to account for it. With just me alone in that Cessna 150, we (the plane and I) climbed again after a practice landing (called a touch and go). At approximately 75 feet, I was suddenly staring at a *still* propeller.

It was quiet. After the initial gasp (a neurological response to an outside stimulus), I quite literally spoke aloud in a very calm voice, *"This is a joke, right, God?"*

Well, it wasn't. It was real and happening right now. Moments like these force us into *living in the now*. There is no past and quite possibly no future. Gurus tell us this is the ultimate achievement as a way of life, but I wasn't too happy how this was being forced upon me in that moment! I took the little knowledge I had, along with a whole lot of *Zen*, dropped the flaps to 40, and pointed the nose down as much as I could stand it towards the depleting runway below.

Upon touchdown, the propeller spun back up. The throttle was still full, which I quickly pulled back to idle and stomped on the brakes.

Whatever I did worked. The airplane stopped with little runway left before heading onto Wolf road.

There was another challenge with me and flying: airsickness. It was passive and continuously showed up after the thirty minutes of air work when coming back to do touch and gos. I'd push through the lesson, begin driving home, and then pull into the River Trail Nature Center and rest for 30-45 minutes to recover. I knew I could fight my way through this; my *dream* was worth it. It took months of this, but eventually I was able to drive home without having to stop. Finally, the airsickness passed altogether.

Another Life Changing Moment

About a year later, a forever change began to happen. For the first time in my academic career, I was struggling and frustrated. Each new, elevated math and science course sent my hope of becoming an astronomer and/or astrophysicist further away. My real love growing up was the stars. I spent many extra hours at the Chicago Planetarium in courses during and after high school. I built my own telescope there, including grinding the mirror from scratch, all by hand. But I now found myself out of alignment and uncertain of my future.

One winter's night, somewhere around midnight, it all took its toll. I was studying for a major Mechanics exam at the kitchen table of my parent's home. That's when it hit me…the meltdown.

Psychologically, I was totally inside my head, lost, confused, scared, and extremely unhappy. Love and joy were absent. I was holding my breath, thoroughly detached from the world around me and within.* My blood pressure rose as my head seemed to swell. I was oozing out groans of pain as I wept in tears. My body was rocking uncontrollably, quivering, seeking some type of release. It felt as though the release would come by literally exploding from the inside out.

> * Neurologically, as a significant emotional event happens, our first response is to hold our breath. The mechanics of this involuntary action, unconsciously "anchors" in the event. As an example, think back to the discussion on phobias. Just before the phobic programming was anchored in, there would have been a gasp with breath held.

My dad got out of bed to see what was wrong. He consoled me. It was so bad he threatened if I didn't snap out of this disempowered state, he'd take me to the hospital (pattern interrupt). I calmed down and thanked him for caring. Dad never failed me. Truly, he is my hero.

Beyond being the most understanding, caring, and loving Dad a boy could ever ask for, he was also an icon in the world of bicycles. His knowledge and skill was revered as *the* leading engineer throughout the world. He was often called in as an expert witness during litigation cases.

In his hay day, bicycle racing was a national sport. And Dad was one of the best in all of North America. His trophies and awards are in the upper hundreds and include winning the 48 Hour Quebec-Montreal race twice! He was a two-time Olympian (1948 & 1952) and one of the first inductees into the Cycling Hall of Fame. He became the Chief Engineer for Schwinn bicycles and retired as an Executive Vice President. If you ever road a Schwinn growing up, odds are, you road a bike designed in my dad's mind first.

Dad is loved by everyone, and not only my hero, but a hero for many as well. Several days after my meltdown, he asked if I would like to check out ERAU (Embry-Riddle Aeronautical University) in Daytona Beach, FL. Like asking me if I wanted to learn to fly, once again, Dad's timing was perfect.

Sometimes You Need Change

Although three years of college were already under my belt, ERAU would only accept a handful of those credit hours. This meant entering their school as a sophomore and enduring three additional years of education. I decided it was definitely worth it.

Lia joined Dad and I during our travel to Daytona to check out the school. Something was pulling me, like a calling, to explore the ROTC detachment there. No real military background existed in our family, although Dad was drafted and served in WWII. While there, we visited with Lt. Col. John B. Cramlet for about thirty minutes before stepping back outside into the brilliant Florida sunshine.

That's when Dad looked at me curiously with his head tilted to the side and asked, "You don't really want to have anything to do with that, do you?"

"Yeah, Dad, I do," I answered. "The only thing I'm concerned about is cutting my hair." This was silly, but I had really thick, long curly hair that the girls loved! The hair ordeal was fleeting because inside of me, this calling to join the military was unlike anything I had experienced before. It was alive.

I doubled up my first year in ROTC and was on track for my junior and senior years at ERAU. It took a total of six years of college to graduate, but the rewards were beyond my vision. It was one of my first true lessons in understanding that everything happens for a reason.

By the end of my six-year college journey, I had a degree in Aeronautical Science, which is basically a professional pilot degree. But I also excelled in ROTC, becoming the Detachment Cadet Commander of over 500 cadets. This was an incredible honor. Another honor was receiving a Regular Commission of which only a handful are given out nationally each year to ROTC graduates. It was from there that my twenty-plus-year Air Force career was launched.

Planes and People

The fighter planes I would eventually go on to fly put me in the driver's seat of the sonic booms I had experienced as a kid from the ground. As a child, I hadn't considered becoming one of those fighter pilots. For whatever reason, I hadn't given myself the opportunity for that possibility. There's a lesson in there somewhere.

Each plane has a distinct purpose. A commercial airliner's sole mission is to transport passengers from one place to another. A fighter, on the other hand, is designed to be employed as a weapon. They are far more powerful in both pounds of thrust per pound of aircraft weight and dynamics in overall capabilities.

If you've ever been to an air show and seen the Air Force Thunderbirds or Navy Blue Angels in action, you've seen fighter planes show off their speed and dexterity. If you never have, a quick YouTube search will give you an idea. The experience is a rush, something that leaves one awed and amazed.

What's the Point?

Now, at this point you may be wondering, "Why all this talk about planes?" I'm glad you asked! It is two-fold, really. The first step in working with anyone is building *rapport*: the greater the rapport, the greater the success of this work. I wish to bridge that soul connection with you. Second, let's see how we can draw an *analogy* from planes to people and the mind.

Regardless of their designed purpose, all planes have something in common; what you see on the outside are the results of what's happening on the inside. You see, it takes thousands of switches, relays, electrical connections, hydraulics, and mechanical movements within a commercial airliner for something on the outside to be seen (behavior). Without this intricate symphony taking place, a plane would never take flight. And one lapse, one missed step, can change the entire course of the plane's fate.

The same can be said for people.

We all fly differently, depending on what is going on inside of us. Some are erratic, while others are stable. Some drift off course frequently, yet others know exactly where they are headed. No matter what happens in the air, the pilot (your programming), maneuvers the plane (you) through turbulence or smooth rides (the experience).

Changing Your Flight Plans

Throughout our lives, we experience a range of emotions such as happy, sad, joy, despair, courage, doubt, strength, fear, and a host of others. Yet, it is our inner workings that determine how these emotions are dealt with.

The beauty is, you actually *can* have control over it all—the programming, the decisions, and the outcomes. We do not have to operate on *auto-pilot*, waiting for the turbulence to calm. Instead, we can become the Master in Charge. By exploring the concepts within this book, you will realize you have control and the ability to change your flight path and even your destination.

To start, we must understand the how, what, and why behind the results you are receiving on the outside. Your interactions with yourself and others, how you walk, talk, act, and most of all communicate, will help lead to this understanding. Most importantly, if you desire to change the results you have been getting, you have to change your internal flight plan.

That Little Voice

All change starts with a clear direction. This book will help you with that. The greater your vigilance and willingness to take *responsibility*, the quicker and more resounding your results will be. If not, you'll be left wandering aimlessly. Although wandering may seem like a fun idea, this is where crashes take place. In the case of an airplane, a crash can involve running into mountains, trees, and even another aircraft. For a person, a crash can involve suicide, depression, addiction, and a host of other mental challenges. That doesn't have to be the case. Like an airplane, we can create constant corrections within every moment of the day. You may recognize this as the "little voice" inside you.

"Do this, do that! That was a bad idea. Now that was a good idea! You're such an idiot! No, you're amazing. I'm afraid! I'm scared! What would happen if... Am I making the right decision? Who am I really?" The rant sometimes continues on and on, with no end in sight. Everything you think, fear, hope, wish, and feel comes through this system. And it doesn't stop there.

Opposing forces within you use this voice to resist any change in its programming. Similar to an airplane, you must first make an authentic shift *inside* yourself with your internal programming, your thoughts, your habits, and ultimately, your "map of the world" (how you interpret the reality around you), in order to change your direction.

Taking Control

The voice inside you has power and control over your actions and behaviors. How you communicate with this voice (and it with you) is crucial to changing your flight path and ultimate destination. You have to recognize, understand, and honor it and its intention first. There are several ways to accomplish this, one being a Value Elicitation exercise we will get to later. Once that inner voice's purpose is understood, steps can be taken to alter how it behaves, and actual reprogramming can take place. Uplifting this inner voice, changing its vibrational energy, will attract more positivity within your life. Transformation is achieved. Your entire inner dialogue will shift from discouraging and protecting you *from* achieving your dream to encouragement and support of it!

Magically, when you make a positive shift in the direction you desire, the world will respond to you differently. You begin vibrating with a more energetic frequency, allowing the law of attraction to kick into full force in your desired direction. Attracting your desires, visions, and goals into your life becomes a natural way of being, and you experience a far easier, enjoyable way to travel.

This is my experience, along with nearly all the individuals I have personally worked with. You can experience this, too, provided you are ready and willing. The stories discussed throughout Section II of this book are but a small fraction of what can happen within minutes, or at most, hours!

So let's not waste any more time—let's get into it!

* * *

Flying to New Pathways

1) We live in a world of infinite possibilities. Do you believe that to be true?

2) When life challenges you, or a golden opportunity presents itself, it is too late to prepare. Always strive to grow, improve, and be available at all times.

3) If you could record your inner voice for a day, what would you hear upon playback? If I were to listen to your recording, what would I hear?

AWAKENINGS 4

"A kind of light spread out from her. And everything changed color. And the world opened out. And a day was good to awaken to. And there were no limits to anything. And the people of the world were good and handsome. And I was not afraid anymore."

JOHN STEINBECK

My journey towards awakening began some seventeen years ago when I was first introduced to the world of self-help; a continued education outside of school in personal development. There is so much to learn apart from school. Books in this field provide something truly special. They allow a conversation with the author (often long since passed) who poured their heart, soul, and life's wisdom into a few pages for us to learn from. These books provide amazing shortcuts to our own journeys of living life to the fullest.

Yet, my *great* awakening into understanding myself took place during my first NeoGenesis course with Niurka. In order for you to be able to appreciate the significance of this, allow me to provide a quick flashback.

My Anger

As a kid, I had a pretty good temper. Reflecting on this now, I believe there is a trail related to my mother's frequent outbursts of anger. Rarely did she direct these episodes toward Lia or me, but over the years, I began to demonstrate some of her personality traits; most predominantly, her pessimism and anger. Sometimes, I felt as though I literally saw red when that anger surfaced. It occasionally became uncontrollable.

When I was seventeen, I had an accident while working under the hood of my beloved red, 1970 Charger R/T, outside our garage. A heavy wrench had slipped and smashed my hand. The anger exploded in my head. All rational thought left as I uncontrollably spun around and threw that wrench as hard as I could. It traveled at killer speed through the opened garage door, slamming into the back wall.

I stood there, stunned. The anger left immediately and was replaced by an unsettling thought. *"What if someone had been standing in the path of that flying wrench? It may have ended their life."* I vowed at that moment to get my anger under control, forever, and for the most part I did. Outbursts occasionally occurred, but I remained firm in my decision to keep it under control.

Now, fast forward to age 50 and my earlier story of realizing I did not know my definitive purpose in December of 2013. Eight months later, Elke and I attended a 1-Day event with Niurka, who we had first seen some *eight* years prior at a networking event. We found her to be a powerful speaker and purchased her CDs/DVDs then. I was captivated while watching the DVDs, filmed in her home, wishing to be amongst her students. From that moment forward, I wondered what it would be like to learn from someone who was so enlightened.

Niurka is a transformational NLP Master teacher, trainer, and guide. Her depths of study and learnings in the spiritual realms take NLP to a whole new level: Evolved NLP. Her big break came at age nineteen, while working directly for Tony Robbins. She became his top producer and set records she still holds to this day. Working closely by his side for a five-year period, she became the one introducing him on stage. After Tony, Niurka began her own career as an efficiency expert for companies. Eventually, she aligned with her true gift: guiding people beyond their challenges.

NeoGenesis and the Great Awakening

So in August 2014, feeling very stuck in my present state of affairs, Elke and I flew from Phoenix to L.A. to attend Niurka's 1-day seminar. I was critical and guarded. Even though I felt Niurka could reach me, I wasn't quite ready to open up. However, that day I got extremely curious and signed us both up for her NeoGenesis course two weeks later in Sedona, AZ.

NeoGenesis was promised to be a four-day experience that would allow letting go of poor results in any area of life to create real change towards our desired direction in life. It delivered far beyond my expectations!

As NeoGenesis began, I found myself still questioning whether *this* would be any *different* from everything else I'd studied and tried (including hypnotherapy). What I didn't know, but quickly discovered, was that this course was actually designed to create new pathways and evolve my deep core values within, aligning them with my desired direction. This takes changing one's thinking, as I'd been trying to do for years, to an entirely new level!

Niurka quickly built incredible rapport with the 35 students present. Her wisdom and playful manner created a safe and loving environment for all of us to speak directly from our own sacred places. She maintained a level of high energy, regardless of the hour. Niurka exhibited a natural ability to connect with people of varied backgrounds, at different stages of life, facing their own individual challenges. I was extremely impressed.

We soon began diving into some deep-rooted areas. My mind was racing, trying to make sense of the experience. Elke and I talked extensively prior to falling asleep from the exhaustive first day, noticing *something* happening, even though we couldn't define it.

Sunrise Yoga

The following morning, we began with an optional 6 AM Sunrise Yoga session led by Niurka's crew. At its end, I was overwhelmed with incredible emotions. I was suspended in a meditated state, connecting to very deep places within my mind like never before.

I just sat there, my arms wrapped tightly around my bent knees, pulling them into my chest. Tears were flowing from my otherwise motionless body. A few students, including several from Niurka's crew, formed a circle around me in support, allowing this process to unfold. It lasted some twenty minutes, as I was later told.

During that time, I traveled deep within my mind where I'd never been. There, I found myself on a sidewalk with a tall red brick building to my left that extended about 50 feet. There was a grass parkway between this sidewalk and street to my right; no traffic. Along the parkway were some bushes, trees, lampposts, a few parked cars, and a fire hydrant. It was extremely peaceful under the cloudless, sunlit day within my mind's eye.

Then, my inner voice manifested in the form of a young boy. He hid around the back corner to the left of the brick building. I became very curious and called out to him. Eventually, the top of his head peeked out from behind the brick wall. Lost deep in this state, I continued coaxing him in a playful tone, saying, "Hey, c'mon. I really would like to meet you." Slowly, he began to show more and more of himself.

It was a dream-like state where the unreal became very real. I was there on that sidewalk, attempting to communicate with this inner voice which I recognized as my repressed anger. He was my Anger. I had no fear, no anger, no sadness, just a sense of peace. I felt love. I felt oneness. But I could feel *his* uneasiness, his fright, and his young fear. I ended up not meeting the boy at that moment, but something within me was shifting.

As you can imagine, I was a little freaked out, but also at peace. After breakfast, I spoke briefly with Niurka and she calmly assured me to "trust the process" (of the NeoGenesis course) and remain playful. She also reaffirmed my belief that I was exactly where I was supposed to be. I complied, and as the class evolved and the processes unfolded, her guidance proved supreme.*

> *I must clarify that I am explaining my experience. Each person's experience is unique to them. Some are more or less dramatic for others but the end result is the same - release. All of this is done in a very loving and safe environment where the experiences are welcomed and not feared in any way. In taking this work to others, I ensure the same with them throughout the process.*

That evening, Niurka asked me very specific questions in a hypnotic voice to illicit what my subconscious mind was thinking. First we uncovered an answer around my definitive purpose. Then she asked me an important question: "Does any part of you object?" I paused. I later learned that this pause is very significant and represents "secondary gain," coming from the subconscious mind.

Secondary Gain

Secondary gain is the reason why we hold onto old behaviors. Each secondary gain is context specific. No true transformation can happen without first removing the associated secondary gain. To create new patterns in an ecological way, the removal of the secondary gain must be agreed on by the conscious and subconscious mind. After that agreement, the old pattern can be let go.

A prime directive of the subconscious mind is to protect you and keep you safe. This secondary gain became a *required* path when originally programmed in and has guided your results related to its context throughout your life, mostly from your subconscious.

As years pass, this secondary gain of old may no longer be ecological or serving you in the best way. Because it is *hard-wired* into your programming, you cannot escape it until the mind is in fact re-programmed. This can happen naturally, as in the case of a significant "Ah Ha" moment/emotional event, or purposefully through NLP.

In short, this is the **very reason why** a person falls back into old behaviors and patterns. Consciously, the accomplishment of a goal or new direction is desired. They can see it. They begin their journey planning, writing out goals, repeating affirmations, and creating vision boards, etc. Then, months later, they find themselves back in their old pattern; stuck in a frustrating, repetitive behavior. Thus, breaking through this secondary gain is absolutely critical for *real* and *lasting* change.

What Did I Get Myself Into?

This entire NeoGenesis experience was very new to me. Two weeks prior, Elke and I signed up for this course with the hope of making a "surface" change. We had no idea the course entailed going very deep, to the root cause of Anger, Sadness, Fear, Guilt, and Shame.

Everything thus far was a combination of new inputs—the terminology, the atmosphere Niurka created, and the exercises. No one had ever accessed my mind the way Niurka was doing then. And that second night, Niurka kept pushing deeper with more questions, attempting to uncover this secondary gain I was holding so tightly onto subconsciously. The more she pressed, the more I wondered what I had gotten myself into.

I became entranced with her words, as she now drilled me with that question to uncover the secondary gain, "What else does that give you?" I became consciously aware that my answers were now coming from somewhere other than my conscious mind! Several more times she asked, "And what does that give you?" Although she was saying this in a playful tone, I felt *him*, that little angry voice inside, suppressed for so many years, begin to rise and take control.

Her questions continued to aggravate him, provoking him further, as she continued in hopes to penetrate that barrier between the conscious and subconscious mind. Finally, uncontrollably, *he* attacked back. My eyes turned red and my body tensed. I suddenly jerked forward in my seat, and yelled, "Damn you, Niurka!" She backed up slightly, and the room fell silent. I could sense Elke's uneasiness as she sat next to me. All the while, my eyes never wavered from Niurka's.

I couldn't comprehend what had just come out of me. Niurka helped me settle down, which didn't take very long. We didn't break through the secondary gain that night, but that wasn't my primary concern. I left that evening feeling very "confused." Somehow, I knew at that point, I *absolutely* was exactly where I was supposed to be.

Introduction to Timeline Therapy

On day three, I awoke with a new revelation. My mind was racing, and I began writing profusely. The door was opened, and I was ready and willing to fully and completely let go of this anger. After an hour of writing, I again attended the Sunrise Yoga class.

Later that day, Niurka took me through my first Timeline Therapy. It is a consciously aware, dissociated, hypnotic exercise that allows the subconscious mind to travel back in time. Being dissociated prevents the *reliving* of the original (often traumatic) emotions. This is one dramatic difference of NLP from other, more traditional therapies. During this dissociated process, hidden memories are often revealed and new understandings and enlightenment are gained.

The first objective was to release anger at the root cause. My subconscious mind took me back to an experience with Mrs. Fields, an older lady who babysat Lia and me when we were very young. During this Timeline Therapy, I was in a meditated state, "floating," looking down at myself at three years old. There was no doubt this was my root cause of anger. Observing this past event without emotion, and at the age of fifty-one rather than three, I was able to see these past events with new understandings and able to absorb valuable learnings.

For example, one such learning was thanking Mrs. Fields for being there in support of my parents, so they were able to enjoy their private time together. Another example was comprehending Mrs. Fields's lack of communication and understanding that her actions were tethered to her own map. It was that simple. New perspectives allowed the freeing of old emotions originally experienced through the eyes of a three-year-old. The release process began. This is different than merely being consciously "aware" of the event. This is literally reprogramming the hard-wired "subconscious mind."

Letting Go of Anger

I thanked my anger for all the years *he* served me and assured *him* (that boy who created my anger) I no longer needed his protection. I conveyed that my evolution now allowed the handling of any situation in new loving, healthful ways, rather than the anger of the past. Finally, I released *him* from within me, forever.

As I moved forward through my timeline and future paced, imagining specific events in the future where the anger of the past would have showed up, I felt different. When we finished, I was brought back to the moment of now in that classroom. A sense of peace came over me. The anger from the past was gone. It no longer controlled me. I was freed!

Since this release, almost three years later, when an experience of anger presents itself, it flows right through me. The little guy of anger inside of me for so many years is no longer there. I may experience "Anger" but I don't *own* it nor *become* it.

With this transformative event, my inner voice is different, speaking love and compassion rather than protection out of anger and fear. I am in tune with my Authentic Truth more than ever before, and in essence, I fell in love with myself again.

The Gift

This continues to be the gift Niurka guided me to and now I pass onto others. I've completed all of her courses multiple times and travel on the road with her as crew. We've had many traditionally-trained NLP Masters attend her courses and state how enlightening and exclusive hers are.

She *is* very unique. Niurka pours every living cell of her body, connected with her spirit of love, peace, and joy, into those in her class. She is ever-present with passion, knowledge, and wisdom that positively connects with anyone who is ready and willing, regardless of where they are in their life.

Life Renewed

Thus, my new journey began, and not just a *new page* but an entirely *new volume*; my second calling after the military. From this course, I not only reconnected with my inner self, but eventually came away with my definitive purpose in life: to spread this work and to help others fall in love with themselves again.

Niurka's unique approach with Evolved NLP gave me freedom in ways I had never experienced before. I literally broke free from Anger, then Sadness, Fear, Guilt, Shame, Doubt, Hurt, and other similar emotions as well as many limiting beliefs. Over these past three years,

I now clearly understand the answer to the question of "Who Am I?" freed from the garbage of the past.

As a result, I dance again, where I hadn't danced in some thirty years. I feel joy every day. I witness the beauty and love that envelops our lives that often goes unnoticed. I am at peace with myself, and most of all, my relationship with my daughter has been strengthened.

The results are *so* profound in *so* many ways. How many people can benefit from being guided by a true Master in this work? Too many, as highlighted in the opening of our next chapter. This is my mission, and if you are ready, the door is being opened for you.

You Can Use This Now

Can you relate to any of this in your own life? Do you have some hidden anger or just a feeling of disconnection from your authentic self? Have you ever asked yourself, "How can I feel whole and complete? How can I attune myself to my true essence?"

Here's a suggestion; and it is actually quite simple to do and may reveal much. *This is not therapy, nor the Timeline Therapy as mentioned above.* However, this may allow you to connect with your inner self in a new way.

The first step is to be ready, willing, and available for the awakening. This is so important to get beyond the conscious looping you may be experiencing. Once you believe you are ready to take the next step with **curiosity**, I recommend doing the following:

- Set aside an hour of absolute quiet time.
- Have the grounding meditation queued up and ready to go.*
- Read this chapter again with greater awareness of how it relates to your own situation.

*I will cover meditation later, however, you can jump right into it here if you choose. I am sharing Niurka's grounding meditation available on YouTube: https://youtu.be/ZexwyMvAceI

- Clear the screen. This means to remove the current conscious thought. Think about something completely different, even jump up and down, shaking it up.
- Remove all conscious thought and allow your mind to **be still**. Allow your subconscious mind to reveal new perspectives as you enter the grounding meditation.
- Do the grounding meditation. I recommend a dark room with headphones. If you find yourself wandering or challenged to be still, that is okay. Just do it again at another time. Stick with it, and eventually you will find that stillness.
- Write down what you experienced immediately afterwards. Honor whatever comes up. Even if it is pain, say, "Thank You!" and then ask, "What are you wanting to teach me? What are you wishing for me to learn? You have served me well. I appreciate all you have done for me. I just wish to understand you more." It could also be joyful. Honor that as well. **This respectful gratitude is <u>essential!</u>**

* * *

Awakenings to New Pathways

1) Our subconscious mind remembers everything; it forgets nothing.

2) Deep emotional pains from childhood can be profound later in life. Letting go of these old wounds in an ecological manner changes your map of the world. This provides new freedom unlike anything you have previously experienced.

3) There is nothing "wrong" with you. You are perfect and the answers are within you. It's just a matter of accessing them.

THE SECRET TO HAPPINESS (GETTING UNSTUCK) 5

The greatest thing in this world is not so much where we stand as in what direction we are moving."

JOHANN WOLFGANG VON GOETHE

Have you ever felt stuck? I mean whatever you do, no matter where you turn, life just keeps you in a place you can't seem to escape? If so, you are certainly not the first person to experience this! What about feeling lifeless, sad, unhappy, depressed, unloved, anxious, or defeated?

This is actually a chapter of hope for you or anyone you may know who is down on themselves or simply in a bad way. There is plenty of information on all these disempowered emotions and states, but I am about to share with you my own version of what I now am able to "see" as the cause. No one deserves to live life in such a defeated way. We live in a world of infinite possibilities!

Being Stuck

The challenge is we get stuck in a "frame," our "map of reality," and it becomes very difficult to see another perspective. For the person facing a disempowering challenge, like above, they may be unable to see the light at the end of the tunnel. But we've been learning how seeing new perspectives is possible. Although Timeline Therapy, as discussed in the last chapter, is the most *involved* exercise we will cover in this book, the majority of NLP exercises towards gaining these new perspectives are quite simple and fast.

A quick Google search will give you a good impression of just how serious mental health is in our country. Here are a few statistics from the National Alliance for Mental Health:

- One in four adults—approximately 61.5 million Americans—experiences mental illness in a given year. One in 17—about 13.6 million—live with a serious mental illness such as schizophrenia, major depression or bipolar disorder.
- Approximately 20 percent of youth ages 13 to 18 experience severe mental disorders in a given year. For ages 8 to 15, the estimate is 13 percent.
- Approximately 6.7 percent of American adults—about 14.8 million people—live with major depression.
- Approximately 18.1 percent of American adults—about 42 million people—live with anxiety disorders, such as panic disorder, obsessive-compulsive disorder (OCD), posttraumatic stress disorder (PTSD), generalized anxiety disorder and phobias.
- Approximately 60 percent of adults, and almost one-half of youth ages 8 to 15 with a mental illness, received no mental health services in the previous year.

- Serious mental illness costs America $193.2 billion in lost earnings per year.

Mental Dis-Ease

This is a major issue here and around the world. Why? Nossrat Peseschkian, M.D., specialist in psychiatry and neurology, wrote in his book, *Psychotherapy of Everyday Life*, "We too often overlook the fact that the behavior could have the characteristics of an illness. There are definite consequences of our tendency to place value on physical illnesses: if one feels ill, one is inclined to go to a doctor. But one seldom thinks about consulting a therapist, even when it is a clear case of psychic disorder. Some 60%-80% of all illnesses are at least partially determined by psychic causes."

In other words, why is it considered acceptable to go to the doctor for a physical health concern but not necessarily for a mental one? Certainly, the brain is *the* most complex organ in our body. It has to be chemically balanced in its biological world. Yet, we are learning in this book just how significant our overall programming and communication is to our wellbeing. The power of NLP to deal directly with the deep programming (*psychic causes*) of our mind cannot be understated.

I also believe we need to let the populace know that it is perfectly *normal* to have a mental illness, or more euphemistically, *dis-ease*. In fact, freeing yourself of dis-ease is far easier than we've been led to believe. And doing so makes life supremely better for you and *everyone* around you.

The Happiness Journey

Over the course of many years, I, too, have sought outside sources for happiness. My NeoGenesis experience reflected my personal journey to find true happiness. As mentioned, it was the realization of how stuck I was that led me to discovering the secret to making real change happen.

The course allowed my subconscious mind and my conscious mind to align in the knowing that regardless of how successful at business I became, it would never bring genuine happiness. My experience in stuckness and associated unhappiness of the past was coming from a place far deeper than the lack of success in my business ventures.

How do you define success, anyhow? If it is money, you may be surprised by recent studies that prove what The Beatles sang long ago, *Can't Buy Me Love*. Likewise, money alone does not bring happiness. These studies on money highlight that approximately $75,000 is the magic number for comfortable living. They state, that income increases above that level does not bring additional; *genuine* happiness. Many lottery winners are left with broken families, suicides, and destitute. They are stuck in the programming of $50,000 or $150,000 per year income, not tens of millions. The sudden wealth, without the personal growth to handle such wealth, becomes overwhelming.

In this quest of mine to become successful in a business venture, and in turn be happy, I realized after NeoGenesis I'd been going at this all wrong. It wasn't the success or the money that would bring true happiness. So, what was it? Here is what I've discovered.

The Search for Happiness

People are "searching" for happiness in record numbers.* There are now college courses and degrees in Happiness! Books on happiness are being published more than ever before. Why? In my opinion, people are looking to the outside world to make them happy and it's not working. Vanity and selfish behavior abound in this *'me'* society that's evolved due to sociological shifts in America.

> *Norman Vincent Peale in his book, Stay Alive All Your Life, tells a story about the editor of a high school newspaper who asked, "…a question that all of us are interested in; how can you really be happy?" "Let me get this straight," he said. "Are you telling me that one of the great questions to which high school students are seeking an answer is how really to be happy?" "That's right," she said. "Dr. Peale, so many of us are all mixed up. We just don't know how to be happy." The book was published in 1957. If it was a problem back then, what is it today?

One well written and researched book on happiness is, *The Happiness Advantage* by Shawn Achor. He states, "Perhaps the most accurate term for happiness, then, is the one Aristotle used: *Eudaimonia*, which translates not directly to "happiness" but to "human flourishing." This definition really resonates with me because it acknowledges that happiness is not all about yellow smiley faces and rainbows. *For me, happiness is the joy we feel striving after our potential.*"

Here's what I've discovered regarding the definitions of *Happiness* and *Joy* that I've yet to read in any book or hear from any speaker. Even when you look up Happiness and Joy in dictionaries, they tend to equate them; there is little distinction between them. In fact, joy uses happiness, and happiness uses joy in their individual definitions. How odd. Are they truly the same?

My journey concludes otherwise. Happiness is the byproduct of something that has to happen on the inside first. Being at peace with yourself (your body, mind, and spirit) is foundational to true happiness. Chasing happiness outside one's self will only leave you chasing the unattainable. Now that may seem like an old cliché, but allow me to explain further.

Attracting Happiness

Happiness is something you *attract*. It comes to you. That's why you cannot go out in an attempt to *become* happy. Certainly you can change your mood by jumping up and down and yelling, "I'm Happy! I'm Happy!" over and over. It works! Try it right now. Can you feel the shift? That's the happy attitude. What I'm narrowing in on though is a more natural, consistent "state" of happiness.

My personal experiences include my dramatic walk with God and intense study of knowledge. My independent thought on this, I believe, aligns closely with the great sages, gurus, and teachers of the past, including Jesus. Here is my summation:

The pursuit of life, to be happy, is not as important as to be, and feel, worthy. Happiness is the byproduct of living your true Authentic Self. When you are in total and complete alignment with your "I Am," your true inner essence and your identity, happiness will naturally follow. It will flow effortlessly from all around you and little from the outside world can curve it from you.

Life is dynamic; it is not static. When in alignment with your core, you become a radiant being, emitting your soul's energy to the world. You live a life of truth and freedom. As you do, your inner love and joy hold you in a place of unconditional love for yourself. It is as if you deflect the negatives and absorb the positives that surround you.

Thus, not until a person falls into alignment will they experience true happiness. Finding the inner joy and love *must* happen first. Without this alignment, a recent large purchase (for example), quickly loses its luster, and you're off to the next one.

Happiness-Joy-Love

I recently finished an interesting book by Ken Wilber entitled, *Quantum Questions*. From the book's back cover, he writes, "Science and religion are often viewed as antagonists in the quest for truth. It may come as a surprise, then, to find that the leading physicists of the twentieth century were sympathetic to a mystical view." Eight of the greats, including Einstein, Planck, and Heisenberg, share their thoughts of how they viewed their work as scientists and the other —the spiritual side of life. They essentially acknowledge there is more than just science to understanding *life*.

How does this relate to happiness, joy, and love? What is the difference between these three powerful emotions? Earlier, I stated my belief that we are all born in love, in divine love. For me, it is God of the Bible. For you, it may be from another source or simply a natural occurrence of life. Regardless, it is my strong belief that the essence of a human being, our core center, is love, the happy baby.

When I think of these three, Happiness, Joy, and Love, I see them as independent emotions linked to the mind's spirit—our love center. Without this vital connection to our true core center, all sorts of challenges can emerge. ***I have yet to come across a person with severe emotional challenges that wasn't disconnected from this self-love.*** Ultimately, people who are affected by the outside world in various ways are lacking some connection to their inner truth.

Knowing yourself on an entirely new level of understanding and appreciation will bring you into alignment with your core self, bring you constant joy, and in turn, attract more happiness than you can imagine. If you've already experienced this, then you know exactly what I am speaking of.

Challenges We Face

In the nearly three years I've been involved with transformational work, there are four primary issues I've observed people struggling with:

1. Weight
2. Finances
3. Relationships
4. Self-Worth

And in essence, the first three are directly related to the fourth. So, in my opinion, one of the greatest challenges people face is loving themselves enough to fully envelope their true self-worth. When a person falls in love with themselves again (their true, love core center), inner joy naturally follows. The person flows through their day with ease and grace, **without** absorbing the daily cares of the world. They are *unconsciously* supported to deflect the attack on their self-worth from the outside world.

By living in a way that is connected to your essence, happiness naturally is found everywhere you look outside of yourself. Yes, happiness *is* an inside job, but it does not come from within! Happiness, as I am defining it, comes from out there, and is all around you in appreciation and gratitude for being able to experience this life. The value of all that is nature and the material world becomes even more enhanced!

For instance, when in this heightened state of self-worth, no matter what car you drive, you are thankful. This is what allows a mediocre car to bring you happiness. Sure, a luxury car would be nice and enjoyed, but it isn't what makes your life *happier*. This is why so many materialistic type people are so unhappy. They are searching for their fulfillment out there, when it is actually within them all along. They were just disconnected from it; out of alignment.

The Theme to Becoming UnStuck

The overall theme goes like this: We are born in love, then life happens. Our major programming (Meta-Programs) begins without filters from infant to the age of seven years old (approximately). We experience the strong, negative emotions mentioned earlier, and we begin to lose touch with our Authentic Self, our love core center.

Adolescence and adulthood create new experiences, but our initial "programming" of Anger, Sadness, Fear, Guilt, and Shame are deeply rooted. The additional experiences as life unfolds further distance ourselves from our self, creating inner conflicts, and begin tugging at our self-worth. Again, there are blessed people who seemingly and naturally navigate these waters triumphantly. But look again at those statistics on happiness at the beginning of this chapter! Most arrive later in life feeling lost, stuck, or find themselves unable to love who they are at their deepest level.

What we now know is possible is that we can cut through all those layers of life and reconnect a person with their true authentic self, their love core center. When a person is ready and willing and is taken through the steps masterfully, this reconnection can happen in minutes.

What Is Success?

Before closing out this chapter, I'd like to refer back to that search for success I was after. My journey of seventeen years brings this definition of success:

Success is about character.
It is making yourself, others, and this world better
while living your true, Authentic Self.

The secret, therefore, to no longer being stuck is to fall in love with your *self* at your deep core level. We all have that opportunity and deserve to be soulfully connected to our true essence. The closer in alignment with who you are, the easier any struggle, pain, or challenge you face will be.

What's Next?

How do you begin such a seemingly daunting process of falling in love with yourself again or grasping these concepts? Why hasn't this been explained in this way to you before? The answers may reside in the difference from how you've been taught in the past regarding such.

The process is actually simple, but understanding what is happening and why it works (to build your trust in it) requires some developing. This is why there are three more sections to this book.

In Part II, we'll get into the stories of individuals who felt stuck in some way, introducing you to the raw power of this work and what is possible. I picked these because, combined, they cover many of the deeper issues behind the general concerns I've observed people struggle with (finances, relationships, and purpose).

Each person you will meet was on the brink of something terrible or unwanted in their life; stuck inside their problem so deeply, they could not see the answers–*even though the answers were within in them all along!* Through guiding the re-programming of their mind, they achieved breakthroughs that allowed their lives to breathe again. Each transformation was truly amazing to personally witness. They were able to let go of what was holding them back and create a new, extraordinary life from where they were just a short time earlier.

* * *

An Inside Job to New Pathways

1) When the steps are taken in the correct order, the potential to live a happy, joyous, loving life is right there, closer than you could have ever imagined.

2) Happiness begins first by falling in love with your self, leading to the experience of true joy.

3) Honor the spiritual side of life.

SECTION II
TRUE STORIES

FROM TRAGEDY TO TRIUMPH

CATALAYA WAS SHACKLED - PART 1   6

"Sometimes even to live is an act of courage."

SENECA

Catalaya arrived at a small coffee shop outside of Phoenix as a beautiful sixteen-year-old girl who felt she could no longer trust herself. Disappointing others became her mantra. She was shackled in a self-imposed prison cell which included years of cutting (a practice amongst many teens of self-inflicted razor cuts to the body). But you wouldn't know this during the first ten minutes of our initial meeting. She laughed, joked, and smiled with her sister and Mom as we sat around a coffee table getting to know one another. Overall, I was impressed with Catalaya's candor.

Yet, Elke and I almost didn't get to meet this beautiful young girl. Three weeks prior, she attempted to end her life in an extremely deliberate manner.

Life Challenges Us Daily

It was at that time, while perusing Facebook one evening, a post caught my attention from someone I wasn't that familiar with. Claudia was crying out for support. She was in a state of real fright over her daughter. This post began as if Catalaya had indeed taken her life, but finished by stating she barely survived. A mother and her daughter; two people I didn't know whose lives were nearly destroyed. My heart sank, wondering how this could have happened.

Claudia and Catalaya are not alone. Here are some sobering statistics from the Jason Foundation. Keep in mind our previous chapter on Happiness as you read through these:

- Suicide is the **second** leading cause of death for ages 10-24. (2014 CDC WISQARS)
- Suicide is the **second** leading cause of death for college-age youth. (2014 CDC WISQARS)
- More teenagers and young adults die from suicide than from cancer, heart disease, AIDS, birth defects, stroke, pneumonia, influenza, and chronic lung disease, **combined**.
- Each day in our nation, there are an average of over 5,240 attempts by young people grades 7-12.
- **Four** out of Five teens who attempt suicide have given clear warning signs. [http://jasonfoundation.com/prp/facts/youth-suicide-statistics/]

Claudia was lost as to what to do. Spiritually, I felt her pain and reached out with a comforting initial contact:

"Claudia, if you need to talk I'm here for you. Sometimes a stranger - but one who understands love and human behavior - can be a place to help find solace. I will be awake for a while. 623-XXX-XXXX. You read my posts; you know my deep sincerity. Blessings"

Claudia came back with a very cordial response, and we messaged a couple times that night but that was it. This was not surprising since we didn't know each other personally (lack of rapport). It was at least a good first step, but I let it go for the time being. I continued checking back on her wall for updates, while keeping them both in my prayers.

Three days past when Claudia posted they had found a facility for Catalaya, but it would cost $50,000. "Help!" was her cry as a single Mom without such resources. I reached out again with another message, explaining that answers exist and asked what Catalaya's *central issue* was? She responded with, "severe depression."

Introduction to Language Patterns

What is "severe depression?" Can you see the *generalization* in that statement? It means different things to different people. This is called "surface structure" filled with deletions, distortions, and generalizations. In order to get to the *central issue*, the "deep structure," the specifics would need to be clarified. In simpler terms, **how can you fix something if you don't know what's broke?**

This vital information was not making its way to Claudia's conscious mind. Richard Bandler and John Grinder (the creators of NLP) first developed their Meta-Model which allows the therapist to dig into this deep structure. By asking very simple but poignant questions, the conscious mind is forced to access areas within the subconscious mind it normally does not. This in turn uncovers that which is being deleted, distorted, and generalized.

So, I responded with, *"Deep depression is very serious. Do you know what her central issue is, though?"* Claudia could not understand the question and the communication soon ended.

From what I could perceive from her Facebook posts, she and Catalaya were struggling with extreme communication issues. Time was passing, and I felt strongly that Catalaya was not getting the *real* assistance she wanted and needed.

Over two weeks later, another one of Claudia's posts caught my attention. This time it was in regards to her ex-husband creating more havoc for her and the two girls. I shifted my approach to being more assertive, explaining that most likely things may not improve without an intervention that penetrated into the *central issue*.

Seeking Help

Deep within me, I knew Catalaya was a ticking time bomb. Many factors drove Catalaya to this breaking point, and based upon the language patterns I'd been seeing on Claudia's posts, my gut zeroed in on the *mother/daughter* relationship. My immediate concern, however, was Catalaya's survival; giving her new air to see the world in new ways. Although I instinctively believed in the tools I'd learned, I also realized that this was well outside any work I'd been exposed to or was specifically trained in. I questioned if taking that kind of responsibility with another soul was wise. After all, *I'm just a pilot!*

My goal was getting Catalaya to a psychotherapist trained in NLP who could truly break her free from her pain. But Claudia held the cards. It was first about breaking through that barrier. In my gut, I felt throwing out some Authentic Truth about the situation might arouse Claudia's curiosity enough to want to know more. Here is the actual message I sent to Claudia:

> *"The greatest benefit for you right now is reframing. For your daughter unearthing what is driving her behavior, not the behavior itself. This deals with getting to her core values - those deep within her subconscious mind that drive her life and primarily the big five negative emotions - Anger, Sadness, Fear, Guilt, and Shame. The effect these have on our lives is profound. Repetitive behavior, even when a person doesn't want to do it, is driven by core values. I pray the place she is going to for help works on these from a dissociated state (not reliving the experience which is dangerous). Anyhow, I'm here anytime you'd like to talk and off all day tomorrow as well."*

And it worked. Claudia got curious and responded with, "Wow... I literally read and re-read that several times. Thank you!" We messaged several more times the next day, and finally, Claudia agreed for us to meet; I would bring Elke, and she would bring Catalaya.

Meeting Catalaya

The following afternoon, 22 days after Catalaya's attempted suicide, we met at a coffee shop. Elke and I waited for their arrival. At twenty minutes past the appointed time, we discussed the possibility that they had gotten cold feet and whether or not we should leave. We decided to wait another ten minutes. Just short of that *drop-dead* time, Claudia arrived with Catalaya and her younger daughter, Ruby, fifteen. Being the first time any of us had met, we spent time getting to know each other. Having Elke there was so beneficial. Eventually, Catalaya and I broke into our own conversation, allowing us to figure each other out and begin building that ever important rapport. In listening to her speak (her body language, tone of voice, gestures, etc.), I was looking to discover the depth of sincerity of her being truly *willing*, *ready*, and *desiring* the change being offered. Without doubt, she was.

Scratching the Record

Catalaya wanted to be free of this heavy weight she lived with every day. I explained the process of "scratching the record," an analogy from Niurka.

Think of the record albums of old where the record player's needle could only follow one specific groove (the programming). What happens if you scratch up that record? The needle can no longer play that "old" groove again for it no longer exists.

I went on to explain this programming of her subconscious mind as the "how" behind her every action that led to her disconnecting from her love center. Tears formed in her eyes.

Rapport was being created. I explained that her life's story absolutely mattered but the specifics of what happened didn't.

I was looking for insight into that groove in the record she was playing. As we talked, her tears were flowing more and more, especially when I explained we could absolutely scratch that old record, never to be played again. She was shifting in her comfy chair as her physiology opened up; signs of curiosity and deepening rapport. This rapport is so important in getting past the defensive ego and allowing the subconscious mind to faithfully engage.

After about twenty minutes of this, Catalaya began to brighten. She explained how my approach was *so* different from the therapists she'd been seeing. Additionally, she explained what they *had* been trying with her wasn't working, which acknowledged my suspicions. It also gave me wonder if maybe I *could* help her when she said, "I'd like to work with you." With a leap of faith on my part and Claudia's approval, we set a date to begin that following Monday.*

> *It wasn't until months later, when fully ready, she voluntarily shared with me her entire story of the suicide attempt. It simply was **not** important at **this** time. This concept is so significant to effective healing. The curiosity was there, but this was about Catalaya, not me. I only desired a little understanding of her past. Reliving past trauma is counterproductive. At this coffee shop, I ensured her our work together would come from a safe and loving environment; without her **reliving** the trauma of the past. Catalaya then shared her relief because reliving the trauma is what the professional therapists she was forced to see **kept creating**, essentially, deepening an already horrific situation.

Developing a Plan of Action

While awaiting Monday's arrival, Claudia and I communicated via texts regarding positive changes observed with Catalaya just from the little time spent at that coffee shop. Claudia was hopeful. Then, Sunday night, I received word that there was a huge blow-up the night prior. Claudia was at her wits end with Catalaya.

I asked Claudia if she was willing to address *her* concerns when I came by to work with Catalaya. She responded with a passionate, "Yes!" This was exciting news. With Claudia's full cooperation, we could now begin to uncover and access what that *central issue* truly was.

During those six days prior to this gathering, I spent much time meditating and asking God for His wisdom and guidance. Although I was about to enter uncharted waters, I was confident in the wisdom and power of this work. I absolutely knew creating new pathways for Catalaya's mind was possible as well as breaking through this communication barrier within this household.

When Claudia shared this latest blow-up, I had a flash of insight. My plan was to have Claudia and her two daughters take a simple five question test individually *without any* explanation. It is a simplified NLP Representational Systems test Niurka uses in one of her courses.

The presumption was that their results would provide supreme insight into how the three of them communicate with each other. More importantly, my gut told me the results would reveal the answer to the *central issue* that Claudia couldn't provide a month prior. I felt strongly that the family would, for the *first time, see* on paper the *central issue* themselves. The objective was to generate curiosity and confusion, getting them to step outside their current "frame" and "map of the world." Ultimately, to **create the necessary shift for them to see the problem from a new perspective!**

Introduction to Modalities

Representational Systems, or Modalities, include Visual, Auditory, Kinesthetic (feeling), Auditory Digital (process), Olfactory (smell), and Gustatory (taste). The primary modalities we're concerned with here are the first four. Each of us has a *primary* and usually *secondary* way of seeing and describing the world. For instance, one person may *see* a performance and another *hear* it. Still, another may *feel* the performance and a fourth, describe the *steps* (process) of the performance.

How do you know what a person's representational system is? Listen to their language. They will tell you. In the case of this family, I believed it was of utmost importance they comprehend each other's primary modality. This test would be the doorway to begin, unlocking the communication challenges gleamed thus far.

Discovering the Central Issue

That Monday, arriving at their house, we said our hellos, and Catalaya handed me a glass of water. We sat down in their living room and I said, "I'd like each of you to complete this simple test. I'll explain it afterwards." Ten minutes later, the results proved *astounding!*

A chart on the last page of the test represents numerically the emphasis put on each of the four modalities. Ruby, the youngest, was also the most balanced with fairly even numbers across. Catalaya was extremely Kinesthetic and Mom, guess what she was? Claudia was off the chart Auditory Digital (AD), 19 of a possible 20 points!

Bingo! Instantly, we uncovered the most likely, *central issue* behind Catalaya's attempted suicide: a communication challenge between her and Mom. I explained to them it would be like a flower and computer attempting to communicate. Because Catalaya was all about touchy/feely, she spoke with that type of language and needed that type of attention. Claudia, on the other hand, was polar opposite in the way she communicated.

Claudia was looking for process-oriented communication from Catalaya. But Catalaya's score was near zero in the AD column; she just didn't think that way. Meanwhile, Catalaya would express herself Kinesthetically, but that language simply did not register with Claudia. Thus, little to no communication at the deep subconscious level was happening between the two in a way the other could effectively comprehend.

In typical, traditional personality tests, how a person is evaluated often comes down to their behavior. For example, are they extroverted or introverted?* Where NLP differs is in getting below the surface of behavior to the individual's programming, their modalities, *and* language patterns.

> *If interested, there is a great book on personalities entitled, Personality Plus, by Florence Littauer

You see, Claudia was as fun loving and outgoing as anyone I've ever met. This would classify her as a sanguine, the opposite of someone who you'd typically think of as process-oriented like a scientist. But her underlying language patterns were not that of a typical sanguine. Understanding this distinction is essential to getting to the root of an issue and creating *real* change.

Understanding Modalities

Let's say I'm extreme AD and you are extreme Kinesthetic but each of us is "unaware" of such. I go to the County Fair, and afterwards, *attempt* to explain to you my experience. I say something like, "Wow, there were a total of 13 rides, 52 different game booths, and 25 food vendors! I bought a book of ten ride tickets, which gave me a bonus of five more. I went on this ride then this...." and continue to give you a detailed play by play of my day's experience.

And you're falling asleep! Nothing I'm saying is getting you excited. You eventually interrupt me and ask, "Yeah, but *how was it?*" I continue, "I'm telling you! The game I liked the best was where you were given 3 baseballs to knock down a pyramid of 10 stuffed clowns..." You interrupt again asking, "Yeah, I got it, but how was it?" This goes on and on with each becoming more frustrated with the other.

Going Deeper With Modalities

What's happening here? What words are *you* looking for? "It was an amazing experience! I could feel the excitement from each ride as I was tossed around. When I touched that baseball, and felt the woven threads, I just knew I'd throw that strike and win that soft, fluffy stuffed animal. And here you go; I won it just for you!"

All along I *was* sharing with you *my* excitement from my "map of the world" of my day with enthusiasm, but to you it seemed boring. Unless I'm speaking your language, it can be difficult for you to *hear* what I am saying.

How does this apply to relationships? It's huge! What about the teacher/student interface? Without this knowledge, is it surprising so many kids get wrongfully *labeled*, and *struggle* with learning?

Referring back to Claudia and Catalaya, magnify this by a factor of ten, and hopefully you can begin to imagine this *Ah-Ha* moment now in their living room. We talked about communication within the household for over two hours! A lot came out, but to summarize, Catalaya did in fact feel as though she was not being heard. Claudia was upset because Catalaya didn't follow the *rules* she insisted were for Catalaya's own good. Catalaya felt like she could never do anything right, and Claudia felt she was failing as a parent.

Prepare For Part 2

The love for each other was there – that was obvious! But no matter how much they tried, they just couldn't see each other in a way that worked. Each of their communication maps, and thus maps of the world, were starkly different.

In Part 2 of Catalaya's story, we'll move into how quickly her transformation happened. Years of cutting and depression magically ended in under ten minutes' time. I'll also briefly explain what she told me a couple months later about that night of personal tragedy. I have only one answer why she did not die: God wasn't finished with her being on earth just yet.

* * *

The Process to New Pathways

1) Rapport is essential in creating an environment for change. A person has to be ready and willing to scratch the record and let go of the past. The deeper the rapport, the greater the release.

2) Identify what part of the story is relevant to the programming and navigate around drama.

3) Identify a person's primary modality in their communication by listening to their language and adjust yours to speak into their language.

CATALAYA WAS SHACKLED - PART 2   7

"Life, in all its uniqueness, would not be life without the negatives and the positives. That is why it is important to be a serious student of both."

Jim Rohn

As we just read in Part 1 of Catalaya's story, a cannon had been loaded and finally went off as a genuine cry for help in the form of an attempted suicide. The impact was significant, and thankfully, Claudia was awakened. She knew something had to change.

Breaking Through the Communication Barrier

The love between all three, Claudia, Catalaya, and Ruby was deep and authentic, but because of the communication barriers, frustration reigned. Each arrived at this juncture with their own individual maps of how they saw themselves, each other, the environment, and all the interpretations of such. Remember, no two people see or interpret the world (situation) exactly the same.

By completing the Representational Systems test, the doorway to new pathways had been opened for changes in the family's overall communication dynamics. Each was now stepping *outside* their old "frame" of the past with essential curiosity. For the first time, genuine hope emerged in their eyes, language, and physiology. It was *felt* spiritually by all within the room.

With the family's attention, we began to work together towards creating new pathways and new understandings of each other's map of reality. During those two hours of discussion around their communication and language patterns, much pain and aggravation was unearthed—all in a loving and honoring way. Ensuring they stayed focused and respected each other throughout, keeping them *out* of the drama was crucial during this time. We talked about "reframing" the challenges in a way they could relate to. The sigh of relief was captivating as they arrived in agreement. It was a huge step in the right direction.

There is one other vital piece to this family's puzzle which surfaced. In short, Claudia's ever present "Anger," combined with a pattern of deep financial strain, ominously added to the overall stressors within the household. This exasperated the communication challenges between her and Catalaya. Because of her extreme Kinesthetic modality, Catalaya could "feel" this pain and anger and internalized it. Conversely, Claudia was **unable** to *see* or understand this absorption in Catalaya. We'll cover Claudia's transformation in the next chapter.

Since the two of them were unable to communicate on a deep, heartfelt level, Catalaya, *the flower*, wilted and finally crumbled. Unable to cope, I believe all coalesced into her inescapable nightmare with suicide becoming the exodus. But now, new hope abounded!

The Preparation is Complete

In just over two hours, already unbelievable breakthroughs had occurred for them. The entire mood had shifted in the living room, and it was a good place to stop. "Timing" in this work is crucial. Intuitively,

Claudia and Ruby left the house to run an errand. Now the real work of breaking Catalaya out of her prison cell, deep within her own dungeon, began.

With the house to ourselves, Catalaya was in an extremely disempowered body position, all curled up in a ball on the couch. She was cuddling a pillow as if it was her lifeline. Everything I'd been taught would say, "Get her up and shift her state into a more energetic one." But my gut told me to just let her be. There was already *so much* "processing" happening within her mind. Although her physiology was closed up, Catalaya had a new easiness about her. She explained that the family discussion we just had was already a huge relief and would make things better.

With enormous rapport achieved, the stage was now properly prepared to start eliciting her subconscious mind to discover her "strategies" that led to her attempted suicide. *Most* of this was a new experience for me, as I'd never dealt with something as serious as suicide before. Yet, there was a sense of almost unexplainable but absolute confidence within me. There was no specific "script" I'd learned to handle where I now found myself with Catalaya. I tapped into every bit of knowledge, wisdom, and intuition possible. After one last silent prayer, asking for supreme guidance to give this girl her freedom along with my gratitude for the opportunity, we began.

Discovering the Cause

Remaining extremely flexible with my approach, I asked, "Catalaya, what is troubling you most?" Similar to the week prior at the coffee shop, she explained her constant disappointment to others. Her mom, her friends, and now Ruby, negatively affected by what Catalaya had done (Ruby was the first to discover the *lifeless* Catalaya). Catalaya felt she couldn't do anything right. As I dug deeper with questions like, "How so?" and "Specifically, what do you mean by…" (Meta-Model), the real truth emerged. Finally, Catalaya spoke authentic truth from deep within her subconscious mind: "I don't trust myself," she said in a whimper.

I asked her how long this had been the case and she responded with, "I cannot remember a time when I did."* Under tears, she stated, "I don't remember much of my childhood." I assured her it was perfectly okay she did not remember and it may be for very good ecological reasons. Catalaya was greatly relieved when I explained that we would not bring to light something her subconscious mind was not ready to do. Yet, there also seemed to be a certain curiosity around her wanting to know. We agreed to allow her subconscious mind to decide.

> *This is a perfect example of how we delete, distort, and generalize: "Never?" "Really?" "Not even once in your entire life?"

Catalaya was Ready

Catalaya was sixteen years old with sixteen years worth of experiencing the world in a specific way; one that almost took her life. How long do you believe it would take to change her view of the world and years of self-doubt, cutting, and also eliminating thoughts of suicide?

We've all heard stories of people in therapy for months or years. I am not discounting such, but what if relief could happen much quicker in certain situations? This is the gift Virginia Satir left with us. She was the initial therapist Bandler had studied intensely. He identified seven different strategies she utilized (she was only aware of five!) that quickly provided amazing results with her clients. It was her work that first inspired he and Grinder to create NLP.

So, what I am about to explain may seem impossible from what we know or have been taught, but it is exactly what happened. Catalaya's *old* record was *scratched* in a most remarkable way. In fact, I'd say she broke it completely and inserted a new one. The strategic plan I'd been working with all week on how to proceed with Catalaya was now out the window. I was in full *Master mode*, flowing with the ever-changing dynamics of the situation.*

> *It is important to clarify that this is not about what "I" did, but, as the guide, allowed Catalaya the entry to unlock her own shackles. By "Master mode" I'm referring to adjusting, adapting, and overcoming a situation appropriately (remaining flexible) in order to attain the greatest positive outcome.

All the work accomplished up to now, from the coffee shop forward, prepared Catalaya's subconscious mind to the brink of bursting for the change to happen. This is why building rapport is *so* important. She was absolutely ready to *let go*.

The Transformation

Here's what happened next. Still curled up in a ball, holding tightly onto that pillow, I felt guided to walk her through a hybrid of a NLP exercise called the New Behavior Generator (NBG). Going with "not trusting herself" as a significant cause of her shackles, I asked her to think of someone she knew that absolutely, off the charts, trusted themselves. She chose her sister, Ruby. She couldn't have chosen a greater "model of possibility" because they were extremely close, allowing for optimal integration to occur. We did a quick test of her willingness to be guided under a slight hypnotic trance and to follow instructions. She passed easily.

Next, with Catalaya still curled up on the couch, I sat by her side in a chair. I asked her to close her eyes and imagine walking into her favorite movie theater, which was empty, and sit down in her favorite seat. Once she was there in her mind, I asked her to go into this old behavior of not trusting herself one last time. She knew this behavior well, but I wanted her to fully absorb it and encouraged her to fully "associate" with her senses (modalities), that awful feeling she'd been living with, *one last time*. Recognizing she was fully there, I asked her to *throw* this image of herself up on the imaginary movie screen in front of her.

CATALAYA WAS SHACKLED - PART 2

Instantly, her physiology shifted. Her tears stopped, she straightened a bit, and her physiology opened a little. These were all positive signs she was now "dissociated," meaning she was detached from the "I don't trust myself" *emotion*.

Sitting on the couch with her eyes closed, Catalaya was now imagining herself in a movie theater, looking at an imaginary image of herself, doing that old behavior on the imaginary movie screen in front of her. This is similar to a dream-like state where the more a person *allows* it to happen, the greater the experience and result becomes.

Assured she truly was watching herself doing that old behavior on the movie screen, I had her imagine her model of possibility. Ruby walked onto the movie screen from the right doing the "New Behavior" of *trusting herself* fully. I instructed Catalaya to see exactly how

Ruby *is* standing, breathing, talking, looking. Going further, I helped her create a full-color, bright, panoramic picture of Ruby doing *this* behavior perfectly, and then *doubled it*.

From Catalaya's closed eyes, I could see tears begin to flow again, but they were different. This was unfolding unlike any NBG I'd seen—just like about everything else in this entire Catalaya experience. It was all new, but I could *feel* we were on the verge of something major and kept pressing forward.

Catalaya was now ready for the next step. I asked her to double the details of Ruby a second time, seeing Ruby on the screen behaving and acting with all the strength and power Catalaya desired.

With the image of Ruby trusting herself solidly established, it was time for the Catalaya image on the screen to begin mimicking (model) exactly what Ruby was doing. The more Catalaya allowed herself to fully enrapture the moment, the greater the scratching of that old record would be. My instructions continued, "See yourself on the screen, breathing the way Ruby is breathing, standing the way Ruby is standing. See how she moves her body, arms, and hands. Look into her eyes; see what she is seeing. Feel what she is feeling. Hear what she is saying. Feel her energy, her power…"

Catalaya, on the couch, was now filled with tears and emotion in ways I wouldn't know how to eloquently explain. But here is what I saw: a transformation happening right in front of me. I was literally watching Catalaya scratch the misery, suffering, and pain of that old record with resolve; dissolving her old neural pathways (programming), and creating new ones. Her complexion began to flush while her energy was increasing and body strengthened. I kept building and building this modeling until I unequivocally knew she had it.

What Catalaya was now experiencing was seeing her old self behaving in the exact manner, with absolute congruence and alignment of how she wished to be. I continued to build this image of the *new* Catalaya, making the visualization bigger, brighter, crisper, and clearer. The Catalaya on the couch came *alive*! The tears subsided, and she even broke a smile across her face. I had her double what she saw on the screen, building it up *even more*.

Finally, I said to Catalaya, "Now, just as quick as you allow, I'd like you to merge with the new you on the screen. Ready? 1, 2, 3, *merge!*" It was quiet. I let her sit there for a few seconds and then asked her to open her eyes and tell me what was different. Without hesitation, she, at only sixteen years of age, calmly and peacefully uttered these words I will *never* forget: *"It is as if the entire gravitational force of the world has been lifted from my shoulders. I feel free."*

Unshackled

Less than ten minutes had passed from the moment we began this exercise through its completion, to include the future pacing (testing specific future events). Catalaya hasn't cut nor contemplated taking her own life since. She can't. **That previous groove in the record, that pathway, can no longer be played because it no longer exists within her mind!** She erased the "strategy" that led to her suicide and replaced it with a new one. That is the power of this work.

We did one more exercise to provide her with greater inner strength to overcome future challenges, especially with her mom and friends, called "The Circle of Excellence." Niurka has elevated it to "The Circle of Power." I'll cover this in more detail later.

Amazingly, as if on cue, Claudia and Ruby returned home right after. Ruby went straight upstairs, but Claudia sat down in the same chair she had earlier. She was kind of in a state of shock seeing this dramatic shift in Catalaya, not knowing what had just happened. The two of them attempted to talk, but Catalaya kept responding with, "I don't know, Mom, I just *feel* completely different."

Claudia, the ever "AD," was using language such as "that's great" and "What do you mean? Tell me what happened," attempting to illicit the "process" of the experience. Frustration was building. Finally, I interrupted and said, "Claudia, **she** is Kinesthetic! **Hug** her!" Claudia leaped out of the chair and piled on top of Catalaya, giving her the biggest bear hug you could imagine—further *anchoring* in this entire positive experience for Catalaya. Their tears of joy flowed effortlessly as they held their embrace; a love connection of *Authentic Truth*, with Catalaya experiencing a true connection to her love core center.

So, What Had Happened?

Two months later, I took Catalaya to a church where a good friend of mine is the lead pastor. This was a special day for he had a guest speaker who came from living on the streets. She was involved with drugs and prostitution, been stabbed, and lost her sister from being shot, to name a few of her troubles from the past. I'd seen her speak before and thought the timing was good for Catalaya.

It was a very moving service, and Catalaya was deeply touched. She went up and hugged the speaker in a warm embrace afterwards. The lady said to her, "We have a lot of work to do," which I assumed was a suggestion for Catalaya to help others get out of their dark chambers.

As we drove away, for the first time, Catalaya began talking about *that night*, and she didn't stop for almost an hour. Tears flowed as she just let it out from deep within. This time, the *story did matter*, for now it was coming from a different place.

She decided she wasn't worth the trouble to anyone anymore; that she was nothing but a screw up and didn't matter. She began by cutting herself on her arm—21 times near her wrist and then moving up her arm, cutting 21 more times. Then up again another 21 times. Four times up each arm. I asked her why 21, to which she stated, "That's when the pain stopped." In other words, she needed to *feel*.

This alone could have been enough, but she didn't stop there. Her mom had a surgery earlier, and Catalaya took all of the left over *heavy* narcotics—nearly 50 pills. That alone was enough to kill her.

But she wasn't done yet. At an earlier time, she had looked up how many Ibuprofens was needed to overdose. That number was 16, so, she took the rest in the bottle, nearly 150!

She passed out and later awoke in her blood and vomit. Her first thought was, "Oh, my gosh, I puked out the pills and am going to live." So, wanting to ensure that didn't happen, she grabbed a jug of bleach and drank it down.

Catalaya had looked death straight in the face, and she survived, miraculously, becoming a beacon of hope for others in her situation. As I said, how she lived through this ordeal was an act of God's grace.

* * *

Strength Within

Catalaya's story brought up my own memory of the person who led my heart to Christ at twenty-seven. With zero contact in twenty years, I finally found Janna in 2007, destitute and consumed by drugs and alcohol. My heart ached for her. I threw myself into an environment I knew nothing of and without any sort of "tools" as I have now. For over a year, I did my best to make a difference. But my friend never recovered. Armed with what I know today, I believe Janna could have been saved.

The frustration was intense during that time. One morning, I awoke, and wrote out this poem for Janna. Today, its message lives on for me in Catalaya, someone whom the difference *was* made.

<u>**My Oak Tree**</u>
So tall, so strong, that which started as a seed
Reaching towards the heavens
Marvelous it is, this life of the gallant Oak Tree

Decades of experience, enormous in size
Reaching out with its years of life
A spectacle to see and oh so extremely wise

Full grown she stands, a pillar in the crowd
Her trunk straight upward, her limbs stretch outward
Strength beyond measure she is so proud

She boasts beauty, courage, and valor to see
She wears nothing in Winter, Green leaves in summer
How amazing her Fall colors, all change for free

She's alive for sure, with passion inside
Rings of weathered storms of years gone by

Again and again it is from within she revives

So where is her power, what makes her so strong
To stand up to sun and the torture of storms?
It is that which you cannot see, and without she would be gone

Her roots, my friend, is where it all began
Reaching downward at first gripping hold of the earth
Then spreading aimlessly without direction in hand

Further and faster they grow
Seeking all that is life from the soil below
A mission, no restriction they flow

Nothing of much is seen above
A sliver of hope, a wisp of new
Oh what grander, this patience of love

They are her foundation of all that she is
They formed her beginning and carry her to end
They never falter, leave, or betray as she lives

She rests solidly upon her vast origin's foundation
Building, intensifying, bolstering a little at a time
Giving a soul to behold, a beautiful creation

So grow strong, reach out, grab life, no fear
And if a limb or branch breaks along the way,
It is only a slight redirection not an ending career

The fragiles of life come from our commencement
Happiness, pain, joy, sorrow; endless feelings of life
They are the substance of formation that creates our enhancement

The Art to New Pathways

1) No true communication can occur without listening. Too often we wish to speak from our map which is skewed from the other person's. Understanding each other's maps is essential to true, effective communication.

2) What a person initially conveys is rarely from deep within. Meta-Modeling gets beyond the drama, deletions, distortions, and generalizations to uncover *Authentic Truth*.

3) Play "full-out!" Give yourself permission to experience *all* of life.

MOM'S TURN　　　　　　　8

"For each of us is reborn each day, Our life renews again, And with the help of God we will find a cause That makes us want to win."

WILLIAM E. BAILEY

As you have just read, transformation can happen very quickly. Catalaya was given a new pathway in which to view and live life. You may also recall a couple struggles her mom, Claudia, was dealing with: anger and finances. Being a single parent is complex. You most likely know of someone who is a single parent or you are one yourself. The challenges are many and such was the case with this family. However, this is not a book about *them*, but a book on language, communication, transformation, and ultimately, *Authentic Truth*. Therefore, let's focus on those aspects as we continue with Claudia's story.

What's Next?

With Catalaya's transformation, Claudia now had a daughter who saw herself and the world around her in new ways. Yet, Claudia was mostly unchanged, still operating from her previous "map." Catalaya was fragile and would be processing all that happened for a while to come. If Claudia continued in her current behavior, she could easily set off a trigger within Catalaya, creating *new* patterns of the old behavior. Deeper resolution for Catalaya would be completing a "Value Elicitation" (VE) and "Timeline Therapy" exercises, but her safety was the immediate concern and we'd accomplished that. Now, permanently changing the *language and behavioral* patterns within the house was paramount. That had to begin with Claudia, the *leader*.

Like so many I've encountered in this work, Claudia came from a troubled past. It was from that place her explosive anger was created. Unlike Catalaya, she was aware of her early childhood years. The most effective method to release such deep-rooted anger is via Timeline Therapy. You are already familiar with this from Chapter 4 and my personal experience. With first-hand knowledge of its power, this seemed like a logical way to proceed.

Conflict Continued

Although I had left Claudia and Catalaya together (and individually) with constructs of improved communication, all was not going so well. Then, I received a frantic call from a hysterical Catalaya. "My mom just kicked me out of the car and left me. I'm standing here all alone." A bit dumbfounded, it took me a moment to collect my own thoughts.

Catalaya began *going into the story*, which I quickly interrupted. I asked her, "Are you sure you didn't do anything to provoke this from your mom?" "No!" was her immediate reply (ego). Certainly, Claudia would not have reacted without provocation, so I probed, asking if she could explain what *would* cause her mom to react in such a way (Meta-Model).

The challenge most of us face is the desire *to be right* which is driven by our all-powerful ego. It's not that the ego is "bad." Much the opposite, for we would not be able to survive without it. However, not understanding it can lead to all sorts of problems. The ego is quick to defend and often masks deeper processes within the mind.

Being Authentic

Claudia's anger was taking its toll on all three. Because she was still operating under *her* "map," she refused to believe Catalaya had created a *new* "map" herself.

So, there now was Catalaya standing alone on the side of the street, genuinely confused and scared in this frantic phone call.

We so easily allow ourselves to go *into* the story. But that is the ego. Taking "responsibility" is raising the bar. That is being *authentic* with yourself, regardless of the circumstances. Even for the most horrific past experiences like rape, molestations, abuse, etc, ultimately, it is **you** who has to deal with the repercussions (at cause). At some point, the blaming and self-pity, if present (in effect), needs to end by being dealt with in a healthy way.

When you recognize only you have the power to create the "meaning" of the story within you, you realize it is only you who can *change* the meaning. Irrespective of what someone else may have done *to* you, they are not dealing with the ramifications as you are, possibly even on a daily basis. After all, it is *your* map. Any energy expended on *them* is wasted from that which could be serving you. This is taking responsibility, and when learned, you'll create more personal power than imaginable.

This strategy was working with Catalaya as she settled down during this call and became more forthcoming in what triggered her mom. Claudia did return, and Catalaya ended the call as she got back in the car.

I was quite concerned and decided enough was enough. The next day, I called Claudia with a plan to eradicate her anger for good, or at least minimize these occurrences. I explained that if she was willing to play full-out, she would be freed from it. She was eager to get started. I commended Claudia for her courage. After all, she'd be bearing her soul in front of her kids for the very first time.

Understanding the Release of Anger

It may be desirable to infer that Claudia is not a good Mom. Nothing could be further from the truth! She is a fantastic Mom, and these girls gelled in a beautiful way when the stress was low and communication was good. The Anger created within Claudia is not directly her *fault*. Read that again! *It isn't Claudia's fault she had her Anger.* However, this is different from taking *responsibility* for it. Let's recap and delve a little more into what we've already learned.

Remember Niurka's words, "You are exactly where you are *supposed* to be." It's a play on words as she loves to do. Claudia's behavior was due to deep-rooted programming from childhood that was no longer serving her or those around her. At some point, this anger was inserted as a coping mechanism to keep her safe and make her feel loved. As we age, years of wisdom allows for new ways to handle situations differently from the past. But, the programming is *stuck* in the past.

As mentioned at the beginning of this book, your results in life are because of your core values and established programming that runs your behaviors and your actions. You may not like the results you are getting, but this is why they happen as they do.

Quite possibly, the secret to achieving that which you desire most, along with everlasting freedom and happiness, is a different avenue than you've heard before. Here's what I've come to realize: Releasing the powerful, primary negative emotions of Anger, Sadness, Fear, Guilt, Shame at their root, (the very first time they occurred and are stored in your subconscious mind) allows you to fall in love with yourself again at your love core center. In so doing, you come into alignment with your *self* as your entire persona vibrates at a new, higher level and attracts happiness all around you.

Picture yourself holding a string of pearls from one end, while the other end hangs down. What happens if you cut the string right above the very last pearl at the bottom? The remaining pearls can no longer stay in place. After that bottom pearl falls (root), the rest race down the string. Lost forever is the *string of pearls*.

For this discussion, let's say the string itself represents the "timeline" of your life, and the individual pearls represent significant moments of Anger you've experienced.* Utilizing Timeline Therapy in this way, we are given the opportunity to remove the "root" pearl (root cause of Anger) and magically, *all* the other occurrences of past Anger dissolve. Your entire "timeline" is instantly re-contextualized in the context of Anger to the extent that *the emotions centered around the Angers of the past are no longer present.* They can't be for the *pearls* are no longer there! Even more remarkable, how anger is experienced in the *future* is also quite different. If it *never was* then you are not recalling previous programming to *interpret* and give "meaning" to *new* occurrences in the same way.

> *My wife loves pearls and asked if she could imagine a string of marbles instead. Of course, I replied

My experience since releasing that root pearl of Anger is astonishing. Sure, I still get upset, but it is not the Anger of the past. Rather, the emotion flows through me. I don't harbor it or become it. I am able to give it a meaning which **serves** from a place of *responsibility* rather than being the victim of it. This is the incredible freedom I continue to experience today.

The Plan for Claudia

The plan I suggested to Claudia was for her to come over with her girls and do a Value Elicitation (VE) exercise. The VE dives deep into the subconscious mind and prepares it perfectly for the Timeline Therapy, which we would do afterwards, releasing not only Anger, but Sadness and Fear as well. Because this is such a tight family, I wished to engage the girls with their mom's release of anger. Even though I wasn't exactly sure this was the smartest approach, I felt it would be enlightening for all. A few days later, the three were at our home, ready to begin.

Elke and I took them for a tour of our home, to include seeing our four horses out back. It was Elke who had the idea of hanging with the horses inside their paddock to see how the interaction went with the three of them. Horses that are still free in their mind (not broken of their will), are extremely spiritual and *see* right into a person's soul. Not everyone is comfortable around horses either, so we were curious to see what would transpire. They all got along great which told us a lot about the love within this family.

Unearthing the Deep Stuff

The VE exercise is a series of specific questions and is quite extensive. Its purpose is to unearth "core values" around a specific area of your life. These core values tell a story of your value's "motivation" towards or away from your desired outcome.

As a general overview of the VE, you are asked a specific question about yourself, or area of your life that's not working, and you provide a one or two-word response that is written down. This continues until you begin to "loop," repeating words already spoken. Once this is exhausted, there are several follow-on questions that reveal even deeper motivations. I've seen this exercise takes anywhere from one to over two hours.

In Claudia's case, she chose the area of personal finances, one of the major stressors in the household. Claudia stated she has "never been good with money" (generalization). I agreed this was an excellent choice. Catalaya and Ruby wrote down her answers on a huge white board as they flowed out of her. It took roughly 90 minutes and Claudia was amazed. She could now *see* why her results were showing up as they were. This was powerful insight, especially the motivations *away* from her desired results, creating her inner conflicts around finances.

Unearthing all we did was a lot for her to take in; honest truth from deep within her subconscious mind exposed. This was also very refreshing in generating necessary curiosity and confusion opening the door to new pathways.

Claudia's Timeline Therapy

A challenge I'd been having with Claudia throughout was her resistance. Resistance is a sign of secondary gain as discussed earlier in Chapter 4. Additionally, Claudia's strong mindedness and being process orientated (AD), tend to make Timeline a tad more challenging. After a break, I decided it would be best for Claudia and me to work alone. Elke and the girls got to know one another a bit more outside while Claudia and I headed for my office.

By this time, I had attended NeoGenesis twice as a student and twice as a crew member for Niurka. In all, up to this point I had approximately 560 hours of exposure to Niurka's teachings as student or crew. This also includes earning my Evolved NLP Masters certificate with her. Although I knew I hadn't completely broken through Claudia's secondary gain of holding onto Anger, I elected to give the Timeline Therapy a go. There is no risk involved in doing so. The only concern was not getting the full release desired.

The process proved to be very emotional, and yet, freeing. Claudia received new insights from her subconscious mind that came as a complete shock—she was holding onto a lot of resentment towards her mother. During the therapy, she actually *experienced* the memory of being delivered and lack of love from her mom. It was her dad and grandmother, in the delivery room, that provided her with love.

New ways of understanding that resentment towards her mom allowed the release of it. We went on to release Sadness and Fear with positive results, but I felt Claudia was still holding onto some resistance. I had doubts that we truly broke her free of Anger. As we finished, I gave her some tools and suggestions on how to continue processing on her own. For several days, I debriefed my own strategy and execution of the process.

The Anger was Still There

During the subsequent week, Claudia noticed many positive shifts including catching herself before blowing up. New "awareness" was prevalent, but the "Anger" was still there. Breaking Claudia free of her anger was every bit as important for her as it was for Catalaya's wellbeing. After much thought, I decided to try another NLP exercise called Quantum Linguistic (QL) questions.

Within NLP there are different types of QL questions. Their common goal is to force the conscious mind into accessing the deeper structure of the problem stored in the subconscious mind. It is one of my favorite exercises for its easy and it works!

Niurka utilizes the Cartesian Coordinate method in her courses, which uses four questions. The first two can be answered from the person's current frame of the problem. The second two force the person to search outside their "problem frame" for the answer. I offered this approach to Claudia, and she agreed to give it a try. We'll cover the specifics of the exercise in more detail later.

Starbucks

We met at Starbucks a few days later and began what would turn into an almost three-hour session. We had already done so much work towards releasing her anger. I felt if we just worked at deepening our rapport, there was a good chance of her breaking free of it. After some two hours, we had pages of answers from the QL exercise and she mentioned *feeling* different. This was a positive sign, but we still hadn't broken through her secondary gain of Anger. The release just wasn't there.

She left for a cup of water, and before sitting back down, she paused with a strange look that brushed across her face. It was one of unmistakable, deep internal processing. She then spoke, asking about relationships, and how she keeps being taken advantage of.

I asked, "How so, specifically?" (Meta-Model). At that moment, I saw her eyes swell and tears form. Her breathing became rapid and shallow. Her heart was beating faster as her face flushed. Last, her hands began to clinch into tight fist balls (Neural response)—her exact strategy when getting angry.

Finally, she calmly asked, "Guy, can I ask you a question?" "*Of course, Claudia.*" "If I don't have Anger anymore, how do I *defend* myself in relationships?"

Bingo! That was the secondary gain! This is why she was holding on so tightly to her anger, unwilling to let it go. And we weren't done yet. Now the "transformation" could begin!

I looked at her and said, "*Claudia, you just broke through your ego! Do you realize that? That is your highest intent of holding onto Anger, and now you are ready to release it!*" This was a hypnotic induction, but it was also very true. We capitalized on the moment.

I grabbed her hands and said an invocation and prayer. We honored her Anger, thanked her Anger for serving her all these years, but, that now, her Anger of old was no longer serving her in a healthy way. I pointed to her the list of answers already present to replace her Anger. Everything she needed was already within her. Now, her conscious mind also could see this, too.

I continued, "*Your strength is renewed with new positive learnings where you no longer need your Anger. It's time to let it go.*" She agreed and elation was her new expression. After honoring, respecting, and thanking her Anger one last time, she released it for good.

"Everything you need is within you, Claudia," I fortified. "It always has been and will always be so. Now that you have released Anger fully and completely, you can begin living in alignment with your Authentic Truth as a *loving, caring Mom and human being. And you have your faith in God, and God is with you always, there with you, inside you. This is the source of your true strength."* We ended with a prayer of gratitude and love.

As Claudia opened her eyes, she *looked* completely different. Most everything about her physiology changed. Her complexion softened, her tenseness was absent, her eyes filled with love, and her heart beat calmly. We stood and hugged for a long time in the center of Starbucks. Onlookers had been watching this entire experience and seemed as though they wanted to clap. In hindsight, I wish I'd encouraged them to honor and celebrate this sacred moment, this pivotal freeing in Claudia's life to anchor it even more.

We sat back down and future paced. Nothing. Anger was nonexistent, even when specific with Catalaya. It was another miracle that happened right in front of my eyes. Almost forty years of living with this uncontrollable anger was re-contextualized.

Two days later, Claudia took her two girls hiking up in Sedona. She texted how amazing this new peace feels in their lives, particularly for Catalaya: smiling, laughing, and enjoying nature. It was a dramatic and welcomed change for all.

Following just one session with Catalaya, and two with Claudia, the entire dynamics within their household flipped. Challenges still exist but more effective communication is now the norm. Catalaya is safe and challenges are met with soundness rather than emotional flares. What a blessing for this family. With so much pain in our world, there are solutions without medications or long-term therapies, if people only knew. That's why I wrote this book—to awaken that awareness.

* * *

Persistence to New Pathways

1) "There is no failure, only feedback," as Niurka makes so clear. If your first approach does not work, be flexible and try something else.

2) Understanding the deep rooted issues that hinder your desires is possible. Taking the time to prepare the mind is essential.

3) Love is very powerful in many ways and it is who you are

A PLANE RIDE TO FREEDOM 9

> *"Hope is the foundational quality of all change, and encouragement is the fuel on which hope runs."*
>
> Zig Ziglar

I truly love people. Although some theologians may differ with my philosophy that we are born in love and are *good* at our core center, I emphatically believe this to be true. Most of the ugliness that exists in this world is a disconnect from Authentic Truth. We are a collective, and yet, each soul adds uniqueness to this earth. Every day we are presented with opportunities to learn from others regardless of their joys or inner battles.

It has become a blessing to witness a person as they peel back their layers and reconnect with their inner truth. And each time their breakthroughs occur, I am grateful to be linked in some way with their journey. When you consider the complexities affecting our years of living, it's a gift to discover that you have always been whole and complete. It was just the clutters of life that obscured this truth.

I'm Not a Life Coach

Kelley reached out on Facebook, asking if I was a life coach. This was my *first* introduction to her. We did not know each other, and her question came from a reply I had left on a friend's post. In a private message, I explained to her that life coaching is not what I did. Instead, I guide people into thinking in new ways in a short period of time. A person, regardless of their unique situation, can be led through a transformation and arrive on the other side with new enlightenment, changing negative meanings of their past as experienced.

She became intrigued and informed me that her previous life coach was no longer coaching. After speaking over the phone, we set up our first meeting to take place at my home several days later. This was a welcomed change from driving long distances from the desert and across Phoenix to meet with others, as I often do.

Meeting Kelley

Kelley arrived at 10 AM after an hour-long trip. She emerged from her car, dressed beautifully in a dress and high heels. The first order of business was to have her lose the heels and step into a pair of my flip flops for a tour of our dusty grounds. Since this was our first meeting, we began with introductions and building rapport with one another. As we walked, I paid special attention to her "physiology," which would tell me more about her in ways words never could.

As for the horses, there didn't appear to be any great attraction. She enjoyed being around them but that was about it. Watching her physiology and listening to her language, it was evident she had a *busy* mind and was dealing with a lot emotionally.

Kelley was stunning and extremely healthy in her vitality. Yet, emotionally, she seemed detached. And it quickly became apparent why. She, like so many women I've spoken with, was currently married to a verbally abusive man. Her attitude was absent of love in describing the relationship. My immediate inclination said this was not the first time she'd been in a relationship with someone like this, and it wasn't. So, the direction of my questions was to uncover the pattern behind her story—her results.

What's a Normal Relationship?

Abuse tracked back to Kelley's early childhood and made perfect sense for where she was today. For her, being with an angry man or in an abusive relationship fit the pattern of a ***normal*** relationship learned from her mom and dad.

Deep down, her *subconscious* mind saw this as the *safe* place to be. Consequently, regardless of her attempts to escape the abuse, she couldn't break free of the chains and prison cell she was trapped in by her programming.

Kelley had two young kids from her previous twelve-year, broken marriage that was laced with similar patterns. Her kids began questioning her dating pattern and actually asked, "Why do you always pick angry men?"

The life coach she'd been working with had some interesting approaches that I didn't agree with. For instance, whenever her husband screamed and yelled at her, this life coach instructed Kelley to just walk away and come back after he cooled down. On the surface, this may sound like a reasonable suggestion. To me, I wondered how this behavior would *resolve* anything.

Kelley's response acknowledged my concern. When she'd return after walking away to attempt a rational discussion, he would not talk to her. His position was, "You've ignored me for the past two hours, so I'm going to ignore you for the next two."

How childish and immature, I thought. He apparently had some deep issues as well to be processed in order for their marriage to work. According to Kelley, however, he had no interest in counseling or therapy. As you may recall, we cannot control what is outside of us, but we can take responsibility for ourselves. Her husband was not the one sitting in front of me, it was Kelley. And I understood the goal was raising this awareness in her enough to allow the release from her abusive dungeon.

Rather than walking away as her coach suggested, we thought of alternatives. One solution was for Kelley to put her hand on her heart and lovingly convey how much the relationship meant to her. From there, she'd mention her vision of the marriage and ask if that was what he also desired.

If real communication opened, I encouraged her to again place her hand on her heart and ask him, "What is your highest intention of your anger?" It was possible that anger was the only way he knew how to communicate his feelings or maybe a way for him to exude a false sense of control. Or maybe his strategy was for Kelley to reciprocate such angry emotion back.

The goal was for her to better understand his map of the world. Regardless, asking him the question directly would create a pattern interruption because it would be different from Kelley's *usual* pattern, and possibly reveal insights into his programming.

Pattern Interruptions

If you have toddlers or have been around them, you are absolutely aware of pattern interruptions! You know how diverting their attention by introducing something completely different is highly effective at redirecting their behavior. This is similar to purposefully utilizing pattern interrupts in NLP.

Pattern interruptions are out-of-character responses that create a pause or question mark in the other person's normal behavior. This is useful in snapping someone out of a disempowered state or getting them out of their "problem frame" within their *story*. Examples include, saying something funny or something that makes no sense at all. Even simply asking them what they had for lunch two days ago will often work. The concept is to get them to *stop* with the "looping" in their head. Whatever that person says next will access a different place of their mind rather than where they'd just been. Listening closely to all the cues, verbal and non-verbal, can provide incredible insight.

Pattern interrupts can also include shifting a person's physiology. Have them stand if sitting, go for a walk side by side, or do jumping jacks if you are talking over the phone. It's about being creative doing anything that changes the dynamics of the current state, just like with a toddler.

New Tools

By this point in the book, maybe you've begun to pick-up on the pattern I typically use with a new person. Maybe you are catching onto how this book itself is laid out?

The first step is getting to know the person and the relevant aspect of what brought us together. Second is building rapport and maintaining it throughout. It is the most crucial of all the steps. Third is to provide some background on what NLP is, and how powerful it can be, while stressing the importance of creating "confusion" and "curiosity." Fourth is to introduce language and physiology patterns along with an exercise. This is where I was now with Kelley. The other steps include testing the work, providing more detailed explanations, additional exercises, and following through.

I began filling Kelley's toolbox with more techniques. Our first exercise was a New Behavior Generator similar to Catalaya's dramatic, atypical experience. Kelley wished to be more secure and had an excellent model of possibility.

Following her NBG, Kelley could feel a difference. A warm smile widened across her face, but Kelley wanted to anchor in a state of absolute confidence. We had time for one more exercise and chose *The Circle of Power*, as Niurka calls it in Evolved NLP. I briefly mentioned this exercise in Catalaya's story but let's cover it now.

The Circle of Power

Niurka's evolved NLP exercise, the Circle of Power, is a unique hybrid of the Circle of Excellence in traditional NLP. Her style enhances the "anchoring" of emotional states.

Suppose you are about to enter an extremely important meeting and wish to be able to call forth the feeling of being totally unstoppable and full of confidence. All you'd do is *throw down* your imaginary circle and step into it. Immediately, your entire body would summon unstoppable confidence at a "neurological" level. You become that state, and your mind engages your behaviors and actions to achieve your desired outcome. You were a rock star in that meeting and everyone took notice!

To achieve something like this, you would be guided to recall three very distinct life experiences from your past where you felt unstoppable and/or full of confidence. With eyes closed, I'd begin to have you recall the first past event and help you build the experience to a peak until you are bursting with enthusiasm over it. At that moment, I'd have you step into your imaginary ring, about three feet in diameter on the floor, in front of you. This is your circle of power. By stepping into the ring, with the full embodiment of the heightened emotion, a neurological association is created (anchor).

This anchor *locks in* this heightened neurological and psychological state. Thus, when desired in a future occurrence, this empowering state can be recalled on a moment's notice. How? You simply step back into the ring, firing off that anchor (locked-in emotional state).

This process is repeated for each of the other two past experiences. Thus, you now have three very powerful states "stacked" on top of one another. In this example, whenever you were to *step into* your Circle of Power, you'd become unstoppable and full of confidence. It is very effective and can be used for just about any empowering state you'd wish to be able to invoke in an instant.

For instance, before doing this exercise with Catalaya, I demonstrated mine. She was shocked at seeing my dramatic shift in physiology. I instantly stood taller, smiled bigger, and she could feel the intensified energy I was emitting. It was so powerful that even I was a bit surprised! But I have anchored this so many times in different ways that it absolutely provokes an unstoppable state within me today.

Kelley responded well to the exercise and was excited about it. I was glad she had this additional tool to better cope with her situation at home. She left that day after about three hours, not fully understanding all that had happened. It was a wealth of *new* information along with two exercises. Yet, she could see a brighter future ahead.

The Marriage Battle Continued

Kelley's troubles at home continued and actually seemed to be getting worse. It was clear that her husband was demonstrating all the classic signs of extreme narcissistic behavior. One night it got so bad, she secretly began recording it on her phone. She sent it to me so I could *hear* what she'd been describing to me. I sat silently, *completely* **dismayed** at how anyone could treat another person in such a way, much less in a marriage, and especially someone as sweet as Kelley. She didn't drink, smoke, or fool around. She was driven and professionally successful.

Beyond Kelley's safety, my other real concern was the damage being done to her kids in this environment. Although different circumstances this is similar to the discussion of my sister, Lia; you can't take such negative exposures back. In those situations, the kids are being programmed. You can only hope that guidance exists to help them make sense of it all.

Kelley was making strides, but this home battle really was playing havoc with her overall wellbeing. As time passed, we covered other exercises including Niurka's signature *Empowering Questions*. Later on, you'll read in detail about these, as I've devoted an entire chapter to their magic. They are sort of like affirmations, but very different. Instead of affirming ideas, they form questions which bridge the gap between the conscious and subconscious mind.

On a Plane to Chicago

A few weeks later, we travelled to Chicago together. Kelley had a conference to attend, and I was headed home to visit family. During that plane ride, we chatted for about twenty minutes to catch up and then ventured into Quantum Linguistic (QL) questions. These are what led to Claudia's breakthrough inside Starbucks.

QL questions are so powerful, it is not uncommon that by the end of the exercise the person does not even *remember their original problem!* I've seen it happen more than once. Even Kelley was initially searching for her original problem at the end. The four Cartesian Coordinate NLP questions are:

1) What would happen if you did have this problem?
2) What would happen if you didn't have this problem?
3) What wouldn't happen if you did have this problem?
4) What wouldn't happen if you didn't have this problem?

There are two follow-on questions that Niurka teaches as well to test the work, which are proprietary. The art of this exercise is in the delivery and persistency of asking the question, while constantly monitoring the physiology as well as the verbal responses of the person.

Kelley wanted to explore her insecurity around intimate relationships. In her forty years, she'd been involved in only one healthy relationship!

There was a decisive, repetitive pattern signaling something *within her*, not the men, to create this.

Her challenge with insecurity stemmed from early-on and from steady abuse during her childhood. Subsequently, it was as if she *needed* this from her intimate relationships to feel *normal*. As strange as that may sound, it actually makes perfect sense.

Although the Value Elicitation is a deeper exercise, I chose QL questions because they were simple, and we were sitting on an airplane at 41,000 feet. We ended up with *over twenty columns* of responses, which absolutely amazed her. In fact, Kelley thought she was complete after her first ***eight*** answers! This is typical because those first answers come from *within* the "frame of the problem" (conscious mind). It's reflective of "looping" and being stuck within the problem, limiting the available choices that do exist. And this is why there is an *art* to guiding this exercise effectively to unearth what the subconscious mind knows.

QL questions revealed to her conscious mind what had been going on deep within her to produce her results in intimate relationships. She realized, for the first time, why she was attracting such men and why the relationships ended the way they did. It was a real eye-opener for her.

Only Thirty Minutes Remaining

This revelation was also discomforting to her. We only had about thirty minutes left in our flight, and I didn't want to leave Kelley in this state. I paused and sat quietly for a moment, listening to my intuitive wisdom, remaining flexible to the situation. Although we were far from the ideal environment, I decided to do Timeline Therapy.

As we prepared for descent, I asked Kelley if she was willing to give it a go. Her answer was an emphatic, "Yes!" without any objection from her subconscious mind. I first tested to see if she would allow herself to go into a semi-hypnotic trance state, allowing free communication with her subconscious mind. She responded extremely positive and so we began.

Doing this on an airplane gave us the sensation of "floating" (disassociation) but was also impossible to control the numerous distractions: various announcements, cleaning up, chatter from in front and behind us, turbulence, chimes, etc. But Kelley was ready and willing to experience the release from years of abuse, and I felt she had earned this chance.

Instead of releasing the root cause of her insecurity, I elected to go straight to her anger, believing it was directly linked to the entire entanglement of her insecurity issue. We completed her Timeline Therapy in about twenty minutes.

Immediately afterwards, Kelley just sat motionless with this solemn gaze across her face. After a few moments, she stated in an extremely calm and soft tone, *"Now I know what peace feels like."* She sat absolutely still for what seemed like an eternity. To her recollection, it was the first time in her adult life she felt that kind of stillness and quietness within her. It was so amazing to witness.

Kelley *allowed* this journey to the full release of her anger to happen. Her insecurity, it turned out, had to do with not knowing she could make it through life on her own. The Timeline Therapy, combined with the QL questions, allowed her to see that she absolutely could do this easily, time and time again. Sounds so simple, doesn't it? It is, once the *resistance* is removed.

We met up again two weeks later at our home. Both Elke and I were blown away by her transformation. **Her doubt had been completely removed**. She had switched her vocabulary from words of needs to words of desires: from being "in effect" to taking responsibility and living "at cause." Like powerful bursts of the sun's energy, she was blossoming on all levels. Kelley had left her abusive husband, took her two kids, and moved into a lovely, brand new townhouse.*

DISCOVERING YOUR AUTHENTIC TRUTH

> *At no time during our working together did I ever suggest she leave her marriage. This was not my decision to make or even offer advice on. In the work I do, it's about the person's deep-decision process to ensure it is Authentic Truth.

Before she left, I remembered to pass her the saved pages of answers to the QL questions we had accomplished during the plane ride. She held them and began trembling. I watched her become queasy before tensing up. Kelley tossed them back at me, saying, **"That is not me!"** She was right!

That paper represented the Kelley of the past. The new Kelley had emerged more powerful than ever and experienced life in a whole new way. She was now more in touch with her love core center and living her *Authentic Truth!*

* * *

Plane Rides to New Pathways

1) Kelley wanted change – she reached out on a wing and a prayer. How many do not?

2) Get authentic and know you did not get to choose the negatives of your childhood. But, only you have the power to take responsibility for the programming that resulted from it.

3) If in a bad situation, especially with kids involved, ask yourself if a new flight path may not be best. Seek guidance from a professional.

AN INNER BATTLE 10

"Cherish your visions and your dreams as they are the children of your soul."

NAPOLEON HILL

Each day I post an inspirational message to Facebook. One day, it referenced *personal power*. The meme I created had this message inside the sketched outline of a heart symbol:

Since Love is Power,
and Love is all around us
and within us, You are Power

The accompanying thought was:

I often write how we are born of love, God's love. In Breaking the Habit of Being Yourself by Dr. Joe Dispenza, he explains much of the science behind transformational work. In one paragraph, he deduces, "How can a consciousness that has created all of life be anything but love?"

God's love is all around us, and its enemy, too. Be aware, put on the armor of God every day, and shine your love to others. Yep. It amazes me how many "scientists" always come down to design and love, but refuse the existence of God. Fascinating.

AN INNER BATTLE

The post received a resounding response overall. Then, in my inbox sat a simple seven-word private message from Monika, a person I did not know. The message stopped me in my tracks: "**I wish I could get it back.**"

Lost Power

Let's break down the underlying structure and presuppositions behind this insightful statement: *I wish* is disempowering language reflective of being "in effect" (reasons) rather than "at cause" (responsibility). *I could* is similar. For instance, *I desire, I will, I am*, would be words of "at cause." ***Get it back***, presumes she once had it, but it is now lost.

Awareness of our language, especially when spoken from a place of *unawareness* (subconscious mind), reveals much of a person's programming. Several questions raced across my mind while staring at Monika's message:

What happened to this person? What pain is she suffering from? How much trauma has she experienced in her life? Why does she feel so disempowered? Does she believe in God? How did she lose her power?

I thought purposefully about so many people suffering this inner battle of disconnect from authentic love and joy from their world, keeping happiness ever elusive. But this was about *power*, and I recalled feeling stuck without my power before my first NeoGenesis.

After much deliberation, I went with something potently simple, *"Your Power?"*

"Yes," she replied.

I responded with one of the most powerful Meta-Model questions of all: *"How so?"*

Discovering Monika

The strategy worked perfectly. Only two questions, four words total, resulted in Monika letting loose in a long message with details that provided great insight into understanding her map. Beyond the *story*, I'd learned she was twice divorced with a pattern of physical and verbal abuse from several narcissistic men. The other repetitive pattern was self-sabotage. Whenever her life seemed on track, something would invariably derail it.*

> *Later, when we finally did speak, Monika's voice trembled saying it was the Devil himself constantly stealing her joy. I explained to her, whether it is the Devil or not, you believe it is. We talked about her strong faith and how the Bible addresses such issues – consciously. Of course, this would have little to no impact on her internal programming from her subconscious keeping her stuck in this vicious cycle of abusive men and self-sabotage.

I thought we were making real progress over the next couple of weeks with our messaging. Then, without notice, her messages stopped. I thought about her now and then, wondering how she was doing, knowing it wasn't up to me to compel her to seek help. That had to come from within her. So, I waited for her to reach out once more.

That reaching out finally happened about a month later. Monika messaged saying, "You know, what you wrote back then has really helped me." Of course, I had no idea what she was referring to specifically, or of knowing what had actually happened. I was so surprised and elated to hear this news!

The dialogue opened once more to include, at last, verbal contact over the phone. Monika *lightened* as our first conversation evolved. I heard real hope in her voice and knew she could find her power again, if she had the courage and will to explore.

By the end of our conversation, Monika agreed to meet for lunch.

And then the morning of she cancelled.

And then she cancelled again.

Each time she cancelled, she had a valid *reason*, (in effect) yet a pattern was certainly developing.

Shifts Begin

Finally, our lunch did happen. We did not cover an exercise but talked extensively about language (building rapport). I provided her with the outline to Empowering Questions. I also gave her some homework of a grounding meditation and a question to which she would need to answer during our next scheduled meeting a month later. She left excited.

The next day, Monika expressed tremendous shifts as a result of our conversation. Each week following, I received multiple texts about other new and exciting things happening with her work and personal life. However, as time neared to this next meeting, her messages were less frequent and then ceased.

Resistance Continues

On the morning of our scheduled meeting, she cancelled.

It was very disappointing because I knew the planned VE and Timeline Therapy exercises could free her. We rescheduled for the next time I'd be available which was three weeks out.

Message traffic in the meantime was minimal. The night before our meeting, I texted her to ensure it was a go. She seemed gleeful and excited to meet.

The next morning, I set off for the hour and a half drive to her home. Ten minutes later, my gut told me something was off. I reached out and she responded, having to cancel. This time I immediately called her back, and to my surprise, she answered. Monika began going on with a *story* that she had somehow double booked herself (in effect).

I turned around to return home, but we continued to talk. Monika volunteered that she had not yet done the grounding meditation; assigned homework from two months prior!* There are times to be soft and there are times to be direct. Monika was self-sabotaging herself again and intuition said it was "Fear" controlling her.

> *Over the course of these two months, this conversation surfaced several times, ending with, "I will do it." Something quite simple, specifically targeted to help her in her situation, yet her resistance to it was stronger than her will. Interesting.

I chose to be direct and asked a pivotal question, "How much longer do you wish to go on like this?" I knew Monika *wished* to be different, so I continued, "Monika, what is your resistance? What is holding you back from doing the homework two months later? Don't you want to know?"

She responded with a hesitant "yes," a step in the direction of courage that came from deep within her mind. "Turn around," Monika said. "I'll cancel my other appointment." I flipped another U-turn and arrived at her house, excited with anticipation for Monika's breakthrough.

The Work Begins

As she opened the door, there was an uneasiness felt with the greeting. We were out of rapport. She was also in a disempowered state with her shoulders drooped, eyes swollen, looking down, and many other physiological signals of being "in effect."

It had been two months since we last met, and we had little communication in between our meetings. Regaining rapport, along with rebuilding her self-esteem, became my first priorities. It was not easy—her resistance was so strong.

After about fifteen minutes of awkward conversation, we moved into a New Behavior Generator exercise with an interesting result; her breathing deepened and became much calmer after the modeling. In fact, her entire physiology relaxed, yet, I still felt in a tug-of-war with her resilient resistance.

We learned with Claudia's story the importance of taking the time to properly prepare as much as needed. I'd now relearn this lesson with Monika.

The original objective of this meeting was to release Monika's Anger, Sadness, and Fear at the root level. But I found myself rushing the process. So much time was spent on just attempting to build rapport that I began feeling pressured, wanting to accomplish Monika's release. I suppose in the back of my mind, based on her previous pattern, I doubted if or when I'd get another chance, especially if this session didn't go well.

Physiology Speaks

So, reluctantly, I suggested we begin the VE exercise, and it was the first time I had one go so wrong. Monika's resistance became even stronger, like when my Angry voice rose against Niurka. I could see and feel it within her, yet my tenacity kept pressing forward. As her resistance continued to strengthen, she began complaining of this pain in her back, chest, and neck. I observed it in her physiology: her facial cues, complexion, breathing, and body language. It also became apparent in her tonality.

Two months prior, during our first meeting, Monika experienced these symptoms of pain, albeit far milder. She had described the pain like a *dagger* in her back. I literally went through the motions of *pulling* the dagger from her back area and throwing it away. It helped her then.

But this experience now was much worse. Monika was cringing in pain. I asked her to describe it, beginning with its shape and color, and she responded, "It's big—a black cylinder going right through me," she pointed to her chest. I asked how big it was, and she made a circle with her hands of about six inches in diameter. I tried to remove it without success. I had her try pulling it out and it got worse! *Uh-oh*, was my thought.

The Power of the Pause

At that point, I had my own realization (pattern interrupt): *Stop making this about you, Guy, and start asking yourself questions of possibilities that will help Monika!* I had lost focus on "the process" and became limited in choices with self-induced pressure to complete the mission (the fighter pilot in me). Without properly preparing Monika, I had begun forcing to make resolve happen. True transformation does not occur that way.

We did stop, and a *pause* was created. I could see her relax, but she was still in pain. Remember, NLP is as much about physiology as language, for they are directly linked. The fact that her pain was increasing, while we were sitting *comfortably* in her kitchen, signaled it was a manifestation of her ongoing resistance. This pain was acting as a defense mechanism from the subconscious mind, as if saying, "I am protecting you. Stop going here with your thoughts, or you will experience that trauma again." Her resistance was doing all it could to protect her. But can you now conceptualize **it is precisely this resistance that keeps the "root" pain anchored in?** The resistance (secondary gain) was no longer serving her ecologically.

The question was how to break through it. While I was attempting to tap into *Mastery*, she began telling a *story* of abuse of the past *from her own eyes*.

Perceptual Positions

In NLP, there are three ways of experiencing things around you called "perceptual positions."

"**1st position**" is looking out through your own eyes. You see/read/interpret the pages of this book. This is where we live most of the time and includes all emotions.

"**2nd position**" is through the eyes of the other. This is seeing the world through that person's map. When fully in 2nd position, you actually experience what the other person is seeing/thinking/feeling. You experience this book from *my eyes, my thoughts, my emotions*, as I wrote the words.

The final is "**3rd position**," the "observer." You see *yourself on the screen* as the object and thus the *emotions are absent*. You see *yourself* reading this book from a position *outside of yourself*.

This is why Catalaya's physiology immediately shifted when she threw herself up on the movie screen, doing that *not trusting herself* behavior. She immediately dissociated into 3rd position and became the "observer," separating herself from the emotional experience. She was looking from her seat in the theater (through her eyes) at the projection of her, doing that old behavior on the screen.

Much of the work in NLP is a combination of these positions, with 3rd position used exclusively whenever we desire to "dissociate" the emotions, especially in dealing with trauma.

For example, in Catalaya's NBG, she began in 1st position, doing that old behavior, and then went into 3rd position, sitting in the movie theater, observing herself doing that old behavior up on the screen. She utilized 1st, 2nd and 3rd positions as she witnessed and modeled Ruby doing the new desired behavior perfectly. Finally, she merged with the new her on the screen fully, returning to 1st position.

I'm Losing Monika

As Monika went *into* this abusive story from her past, she was *fully* "associated" in 1st position. She literally began to **relive** the *story's* trauma! She was vulnerable to this in part because we had begun to remove filters between her conscious and subconscious mind with the NBG and VE exercises.

Monika began trembling, then shaking. Her voice quivered, tears were flowing. It deepened as she went more and more into it.

Instinctively, I had her stand up and shake it off (pattern interrupt). With tremendous animation, I immediately had her throw herself onto the "movie screen." Thankfully, she stepped out of the experience into 3rd position and began to calm down.

What happened next was unexpected. In hindsight, this entire sequence since arriving at Monika's home played out perfectly.

My gut told me to move right into Timeline Therapy, even though the VE was far from complete. With what had just happened, it came down to "timing," for I sensed she was on the brink of something major. I couldn't leave her in this state anyhow, and by this point, there was little to lose and much to gain. I tested her willingness to proceed, and she passed with flying colors.

Here We Go

Her first memory of Anger was initially at sixteen years of age. I was looking for something between the ages of 0-7, so we delved deeper, and she revealed her dad at the age of four.

This was the perfect place to begin. In Timeline Therapy, we do several *trips* back in time and return to the moment of now to "check-in." This allows the person to internalize the learnings both consciously and subconsciously. It also allows an opportunity for the guide to make adjustments as necessary.

At four years old, Monika's view and understanding of the world was quite limited compared to the Monika of today. At four years old, that initial (root) Anger event took her from the place of safety she had known to trauma in an instant. That shock created an imprint around Anger.

Monika was quite relaxed during her first check-in. Her significant learning was that the person she had been angry at all these years consciously, was the *wrong* person. Her Anger actually was at her mother who did nothing to *prevent* her father's abuse from the onset.

Her mother chose not to believe Monika and ignored the abusive behavior all together. Amazing insight for the first time in her life! Most remarkably, as she shared this story, the black cylinder and pain began disappearing. Monika was in awe with new hope.

Then came another significant breakthrough during her next check-in: Monika realized that her dad abused her siblings as well. She actually began feeling sympathy towards her dad for the Anger that he was harboring (forgiveness and Love replacing Anger).

Monika was doing wonderful. There were tears which was perfectly okay because she was in 3rd position, even stating, "No girl should ever have to endure what she did." The process was working because she had bypassed her resistance (secondary gain) and was allowing the decades of this deep-rooted pain from her Anger to transform. By now, the pain in her chest and neck were almost completely gone.

Releasing Monika's Anger

Finally, Monika was properly prepared to fully release her Anger. Having witnessed how dramatic her physiological reaction was fifteen minutes earlier when she had gone *into the abusive story*, I knew one thing: **this was going to be a *real* test of the work!**

I had Monika travel back to the "release point" prior to her first occurrence of abuse. She then moved forward in time to the event and then traveled *into* the event. I had her test other past moments of anger in her life and we future paced as well.

Monika's release was a phenomenal success. She immediately felt calmer and more at peace. *All* her pain, she believed to be from decades worth of physical abuse from her husbands, had *vanished*!

Hours after our session, Monika sent me several text messages, exclaiming how she was so surprised that she was finally pain free.

Two days later, another blessing arrived. I was out of state and something gnawed at me to check-in with her. I'll never forget the call:

"Guy! You won't believe what just happened!" she exclaimed.

"Hi, Monika, what's up?"

"I just got off the phone with my sister; the one I told you hates me. We had a wonderful conversation! She even invited me and the kids to visit and stay with her. I had *just* hung up with her when you called. Isn't that strange?"

Monika had reconnected with her estranged sister! The strife Monika believed had no chance of being salvaged now had newfound hope.

Monika's gift of transformation was a blessing. Her Anger release left her both mentally and physically healed. She truly connected with her Authentic Truth in new ways, reconnecting with her true love core center.

* * *

Freeing Yourself to New Pathways

1) Physiology provides great insight into the subconscious mind.

2) Remain flexible, for often the greatest breakthroughs happen right after you think to quit.

3) When Anger is released, the body vibrates at a higher level, attracting what it previously resisted.

THE POWER OF A "REFRAME" 11

"Being able to think about things in a variety of ways builds a spectrum of understanding."

RICHARD BANDLER & JOHN GRINDER

I'd like to begin this chapter with some philosophy to set-up our last two stories.

We do not get to choose the situation in which we are born into. Each of the circumstances leading to our creation involves a unique sequence of events of two people (with their own unique lineages, experiences, and programming) merging to create a third.

Whether born in America or a remote part of the world, you had no choice. You may have been born into extreme wealth or extreme poverty or anywhere in between. You may have been born in a loving environment or an abusive one.

Each above is outside of your control. What changes as you become an adult is the ability to take responsibility for who you are and your direction in life. The challenge is, I don't believe we are adequately taught how to do this.

THE POWER OF A "REFRAME"

We are told *how* we should be, *what* we should be, *who* we should be, but very little is formally taught on how to *create* the life we desire and discover our essential truth, our Identity and "I Am." In America, as well as many other parts of the world, ample opportunity exists to create magic for ourselves, if we understand who we are first.

Understanding Your Uniqueness

You are a unique being of life's creation. No one else ever has or ever will possess the behaviors, skills, talents, love, and view of the world exactly like you. You are such a gift to this world with *something* no one else can give back to it. Yet, in the mass of humanity, it is easy to lose sight of your importance, the individual.

Like the tree within the forest, what would one less tree really matter? But to the ecosystem, that one tree provides much. From the birds and squirrels who nest there, to the insects who live and feed there, the shade it provides and oxygen it produces, that individual tree has importance all its own.

The tree is also born without choice, but the tree must accept her fate to only live in the moment of every second. She is forced to handle whatever nature throws at her without contemplation, decisions to be made, worry, anxiety, or depression. The tree just does.

You, of course, are far more complex, and unlike the tree, your mind has the ability to contemplate life. Unlike any other living creature on the planet, you have been given the ability to determine your future. We do not choose how we entered the world, but we have personal power and choice over the direction of our lives.

Your experiences up to this moment of *now* created your individual "map of the world." Unlike any other creature, let's say a monkey, you get to ask the questions of, "What if…, How so…, Why is…" playing out different scenarios of your life's direction. You get to choose where you go from *here* at any moment in time. The monkey's fate is largely at the hands of the environment he is in. The monkey will always be a monkey. You are in control of who you become.

The Power is Within You

In a world of infinite possibilities, you can create yourself in the manner of your choosing. You can tap into your hidden treasures and become the artist, the sculptor of your life. Even though you did not create the circumstances of your birth, early programming, or environment you grew up in, within you is everything you need to create the life you've always wanted.

This is why I hope, by now, you are grasping the importance of this information—this book. As we've already seen with just a few examples, past traumas or horrors can be released for good, allowing for a brighter, freer future. Your power can redirect your life in a moment with even greater communication.

You can also take all your positive qualities and greatly enhance them! Once aware, you now know tools actually do exist to assist you in creating your own breakthroughs with ease and grace.

Many who've gone before us, born in tragic circumstances, have left us with incredible hope of what is possible. Often called an *awakening*, when you discover your *Authentic Truth*, how you view the world is forever changed. Once this paradigm shift happens, it is impossible to see the world again in the previous way. You have a *new* map of the world.

A Troubled Soul

I'd been following Lexi's public posts on Facebook for over a year and could see that she had obvious challenges in her home life. We had never communicated prior, but things began sounding even more troubling for her, so I reached out.

THE POWER OF A "REFRAME"

She didn't respond to my attempts, but her complaints regarding her miserable life continued. Weeks later, I replied with, "People have offered to help." I had seen an outpouring of love from her friends, and I, too, was also ready to help. This time, she did respond in the form of four video messages sent to my inbox. No words, just the video messages.

As I watched the horrific display of verbal abuse from her grandmother, it was apparent this was not a golden-spoon environment. Lexi was a young woman in a world of challenges and hurting, and I wondered if she was ready for an authentic change.

Awakening Lexi was possible, but years of being subjected to an abusive environment would take mastery. Knowing she was looking for cries of sympathy in sending those videos, my response was, "Thank you, but I already knew that."

Soon after, we began messaging for forty-five minutes, building rapport as she wrote her story. Lexi was twenty-four. Her mom dropped her off with grandma soon after she was born and *left*. The grandparents raised her with little to no communication from her mom. According to Lexi, she'd been beaten and abused her entire life. In turn, this was her pattern in her personal relationships as well. After years of abuse, her mind was undoubtedly scarred and programmed in ways that were not serving her.

She also faced dialysis twice daily. As a result, she was adamant stating she cherishes her health and does not do drugs or abuse alcohol.

Her challenges were daunting, yet she seemed honest in saying, "I love people, and I have so much love for life and others." I really felt for her and believed in her vision of making something of herself and helping others. Anyone raised in an abusive household deserves a better chance at life.

Let's Work Together

I decided to work with Lexi, provided she agreed to some strict guidelines, for I knew beneath the surface there was much more to her story. One of the ground rules was trust and honesty; if she lied to me, I was gone. I expressed clearly I would always honor her and would never intentionally violate her trust and asked for the same in return.

Another was her willingness to play full-out and not hold back. I explained that for this to work, she needed to be ready and willing without resistance. The last precept was that after her healing, she would pass along what she learned onto another troubled soul.

She was very agreeable to the *rules*, and finally, we talked.

In our first ten-minute conversation, I did most of the talking to ensure our roles were established. Normally, it would be the other way around, where I'm doing most of the listening and learning. However, my gut was telling me she was looking for a leader, true leadership which she never had. Clearly defining the leadership role, therefore, was essential.

I've glossed over her years worth of very disturbing, dark, and at the time, downright ugly Facebook posts. Let's just say she had a lot of *sass*; more than likely a part of her survival strategy. I could not let her feel in any way she was in control of me or take advantage of this opportunity. Of course, this was all done with loving care and compassion. Ultimately, it did earn her respect.

Lexi was stuck in a loop of blaming others for her situation. Who could argue with her? But, as long as she remained "in effect" (reasons), she could not dig herself out of her frame of misery. That can only be accomplished by switching her current frame of thinking to the frame of being "at cause" (taking responsibility). ***No problem can ever be solved while "in effect"!***

What is Reframing?

One of the great challenges we all face is being *stuck* in our own problem. For when we are *in there*, we cannot *see* another perspective from *outside* ourselves. As Albert Einstein cleverly stated, "We cannot solve our problems with the same level of thinking that created them."

An NLP process called "reframing" does allow one to step out of their current frame and into a new frame very quickly. An effective "reframe" creates new neuro-pathways so powerfully that *the mind cannot see the old situation the same way ever again.* (Refer to the pathway through the forest analogy in Chapter 1, and scratching the record in Catalaya's story)

In their book, *Reframing*, Bandler and Grinder tell the story of a woman who was driving her family out of their minds with her constant nagging around keeping the house absolutely clean and orderly. Anything out of place or worse, especially a mark on her beloved carpet, and she'd lose it. Her behavior was so extreme the rest of the family was ready to leave.

The therapist asked if this happened only in the house or did it occur outside of the house as well. The husband responded that they could go anywhere and all would be normal, including eating out at restaurants. It was only inside the house that this outlandish behavior happened. Notice, the therapist did not dive into all the particulars of the *story*. She only needed to understand this woman's strategy.

Inside the house, all agreed the carpet was the worst trigger, to the point she was vacuuming it seven times per day! The therapist decided a reframe would solve this quickly.

Putting the woman in a slight hypnotic state with her eyes closed, the therapist asked her to imagine her beautiful plush white carpet without a mark on it. The therapist really built up the "Sub-modalities" such as the color, the feel, cleanliness and absence of footprints. The woman's physiology reflected total bliss.

At that heightened point, the therapist then suggested to the woman, "That means you are all alone. None of your loved ones are anywhere near." The woman's physiology changed instantly, now slumping in her chair. Her gleeful smile drooped suddenly into a saddened frown.

From this disempowered state, the therapist next suggested for the woman to imagine a single footprint on the carpet that symbolized, "Your loved ones are near-by, and you are surrounded in love."

In an instant, with this powerful reframe, what had been troubling this family for years, nearly ending in divorce, was wiped out. How? New neural pathways were instantly established in how she perceived cleanliness in her home, erasing her decision strategy of the past.

Lexi's Turn

While collecting important information to better understand Lexi's current frame, she had shared her deep passion in photography and proficiency with Photoshop (photo-editing software). Again, from the book, *Reframing*, *"You can't reframe anything to anything else. It has to be something which fits that person's experience."* This eventually led to the perfect "reframe" opportunity with Lexi now.

I began with, "Let's say a girlfriend of yours took your photo and just posted it to Facebook (3rd position). Later, as you are perusing Facebook, you see that post. You look at that photo and say, 'Wow! If only I had the chance to touch that photo up in Photoshop *before* she posted it. I'd look so much better (1st position).'"

"***Exactly***!" was Lexi's response.

I asked, "How does seeing that photo just showing up on Facebook make you feel?" (Meta-Model).

She responded with, *"Disempowered."*

Continuing to set-up the reframe, I suggested, "What if you had control over that image from the beginning rather than it being in someone else's hands? You could then create it into the masterpiece you

THE POWER OF A "REFRAME"

knew it could be. You could alter the colors, change the background, smooth out the lines before posting the final image, a real masterpiece, on Facebook. What would that be like?" (Hypnotic suggestion while enhancing "Sub-modalities")

Naturally, she loved that idea, and responded with strength in her voice, *"That would be Empowering."*

Here Comes the Reframe

"So, what is more empowering," I asked, "giving up control of the direction of your life to others by making it about them, or taking control of your own life, creating it the way you desire it to be? Having complete control over the image you create, your thoughts, how others treat you, your actions and behaviors?"

There was a very long pause from her end. She seemed to get it and the call ended soon afterwards.

The Result

With no further communication, two days later, I received a text from her saying, "I don't know what you said or did, but whatever it was, it clicked!"

That's the power of reframing at work! One short session over the phone changed this girl's life forever.

Later that same day, Lexi posted words of empowerment onto Facebook: "You are in control! Nobody will ever love you better than yourself. You are capable of embracing yourself. There is no better person to validate *you* than *you*, the truest owner and credit holder. Your path belongs to *you*, not somebody else. No other opinions matter. A new beginning…it's time to love yourself."

A full *reversal* of a life-long pattern of playing the victim happened in an instant, and all of it came ***from her! Those statements of action, being at cause (responsibility), were within her all the time! They were***

just hidden out of view from her conscious mind, disconnected from her Authentic Truth. Once those new pathways were established, they unleashed who Lexi was at her love core center. The pathway through the forest was shortened, the old record was scratched.

But Wait, There's More

Of course, I wish a simple reframe is all that would be needed for Lexi, but her programming was deep. We moved our attention to the challenges she was having with her grandma. Lexi had to be out of the house and on her own within two months.

Lexi had just graduated as a technician in the medical field and was job hunting. She was also attending night school to further her professional education and broaden her opportunities. Having enough money to live on her own became the main problem she desired to overcome.

With these challenges, she wasn't sure how to arrange her schedule to accommodate submitting resumes and applications, job hunting, her dialysis, and school.

On top of all this, her grandma refused to help in any way. That led to a huge fight Lexi lost. I explained to Lexi that until rapport was established between them, no real negotiations or compromise could take place.

Since this was another example of Lexi getting caught within her frame, I elected to try another approach. I explained that it was possible that her grandma's resentment toward her was a projection from the unwanted situation that was created when Lexi's mom abandoned her. Lexi even commented how her grandma was nice to others in the family but just mean toward her.

Shifting Positions

Lexi had not believed that her mom had anything to do with this current situation. Helping her see things through her grandma's perspective (2nd position) brought forth the family dynamics in a new light.

This allowed me to ask if there was ever a time when her grandma expressed even a hint of decency toward her. Lexi paused for an extended time, and eventually said, "A couple of times." This broke Lexi free of the generalization her conscious mind tells her of grandma *always* being mean to her. Creating even just this one doubt causes confusion, which as stated earlier, is necessary for change to occur.

Love Languages

Remember how Catalaya and Claudia communicated differently? Claudia was Audio Digital (process oriented) and Catalaya was Kinesthetic (touchy feely). Their modalities are polar opposites. Misunderstandings often surface when people of different modalities attempt to communicate love.

There is a terrific book entitled, *The 5 Love Languages*, that explains how people register love communication differently. For instance, in a relationship, a person may feel most loved by acts of service from their partner, while another person feels loved through words of affirmations.

The result is two people may truly love one another, yet the messages are not conveyed or received in a way the other comprehends. Let's say a son loves to hear words of affirmations from his mom, his love language, and his mom's love language is acts of service. How does this play out?

Mom can't understand what a lazy boy she has because he never does the tasks he is given. And the boy is sad because his mom doesn't understand his desire to be praised. She is thinking, "How can I praise him when he is not doing what he is supposed to be doing?" It's a vicious cycle that creates all kinds of miscommunication between them both.

In Lexi's situation, what I hoped to decipher were communication patterns, love languages that actually *worked* between Lexi and her grandma. It appeared a pattern of acts of service and words of affirmation had the greatest positive response from her grandma. After relaying this to Lexi, she said something that really touched my heart.

"Guy, you really know how to handle me, and that is not easy. You don't allow me to go on and on with my drama like the psychiatrists and psychologists did in the past. You cut right to the point. And how and what you say really registers with me in a special way. You are really good at what you do." I was extremely grateful to hear those words of her being "at cause."

A Second Reframe – Gratitude

I suggested to Lexi that she try something different. Because there was so much angst between them, I proposed that she write a letter to her grandparents, expressing her gratitude for them. Then she could decide what action she wished to take regarding it: throw it away, hand it to them, save it, or actually speak to them about it.

"There is this barrier between you guys," I explained, "and what you resist will persist—it is a universal law we cannot change. To break that, and open the door to the possibility of real communication, you'll need to take a different approach.

"Over the years, your grandparents have sacrificed a lot for you, and it hasn't always been easy. Start by thinking grateful thoughts and having gratitude for all that they have done. Write it all out.

"Of course there is a lot of anger within you towards them too, Lexi, but you have told me that you are inherently a good person and love people (a reframe). So, let's express that.

"You see, there is a tremendous division in your psyche right now between the programmed anger you've dealt with your entire life and that innate goodness that is within you (a double-bind / parts). We both know that you are a good person, Lexi. Your goodness has been smothered under all that hate. It is why you have your mood swings."

I closed the conversation off by saying, "There is nothing wrong with you, Lexi, other than trying to figure out this internal battle of survival versus living your authentic truth. You are out of alignment with yourself, and that is the only issue we need to address right now. In writing this letter of gratitude, you can begin to break through that barrier between your ego and your true self.

"Allow your goodness, your love, to emerge fully with pen and paper. Allow your words to flow from deep within you, bypassing all the hate and anger. Do this in a quiet place alone with your thoughts. Stay with it. And if anger surfaces, breathe deeply, and reconnect with your inner being."

Monumental Shift

This was the last conversation we had up until asking for her story for the Afterward section of this book. I followed her through Facebook, and she experienced more continuous joy than in any recent memory. Looking at her problems in a new way, and creating new neural pathways changed everything. And for that, I am extremely happy for her.

She moved out on her own within those two months, got a job she loved in her field, and continued her education. At Christmas, she proudly displayed pictures of her Christmas tree and decorations in her own home. Incredible, life-altering change.

* * *

Reframing to New Pathways

1) You are a unique creation with gifts and talents no one who has ever walked this planet has. Honor and explore all that makes you who you are.

2) A powerful reframe is the quickest way to create new pathways.

3) A reframe has to be meaningful to the person – be flexible in your approach.

CONNIE WAS ADDICTED 12

"Show me the most damaged parts of your soul, and I will show you how it still shines like gold."

NIKITA GILL

Connie was a recovering alcoholic and meth user, three months sober, when she decided to reach out to me through Facebook in a desperate plea for help. Although we were Facebook friends, I didn't recognize her picture or name. When we first talked, she was extremely unhappy and filled with incredibly disempowered language.

Eagerness Wins My Heart

This work is almost always best done in person, but it can be done telephonically, as with Lexi. Even better is through a video media system such as Skype or Facetime. The reason for this is, although you can interpret voice inflections over the phone, you cannot see their physiology. And as you now know, physiology is a big key to the entire process.

Connie, like Lexi, also lived in a different state than I. After getting to know one another, the first exercise we did was a NBG to address her issue of constantly being late to work. We did a Facetime session where the NBG took less than five minutes. She wasn't again late to work. Connie's rooted changes had begun.

Over the period of several such sessions, we did Empowering Questions, QL questions, and several other exercises. We also did a lot of just talking with one another. What I loved about Connie was her willingness to learn and improve. The tragedy of her abuses had taken their toll, but Connie was seeking *real* change. She genuinely wanted something better for her life and was striving to achieve such.

Don't Blame the Addiction – It's the Strategy

You may recall Catalaya's attempted suicide, as well as Claudia's Anger. Neither *chose* these paths as a way to a better life. But circumstances and choices they made prevented each from seeing *other* possible pathways.

Similarly, Connie, like most addicts, was stuck in a proverbial spiral of self-defeating motivations away from pain. Wires get 'crossed' and an unhealthy "strategy" is inserted to protect them from the emotional pain that drove them to their addiction.

We have decision "strategies" for everything we do, eating, driving, work, play, relationships, finances or consuming alcohol or recreational drugs. You name it, there is a strategy behind it.

For instance, someone who is obese and wishes to be of normal weight, has a decision strategy that does not serve them. By recoding the strategy, achieving their normal weight is effortless, without any fancy dieting or frustration. It becomes a normal course of action. This is the same philosophy that is taken in changing an addict's thought process (decision strategy) to continue or *discontinue* their destructive path.

The irony of it all is that the addiction brings *far greater* pain. Worse, it almost eliminates viable alternatives/solutions to the addict for they are *blinded to them*. They are deeply stuck in 1st position—their "problem frame." Like the severely depressed individual living in the past, they just cannot step out of being "in effect" and into "at cause."

As I made the claim that Claudia's Anger was not her *fault*, I'd similarly argue that point in regards to the addict. The specific strategies leading to their addictions developed subconsciously without awareness. My friend Janna's story satisfies this same pattern as well as anyone else I've known suffering from addiction.

Think of it this way:

Most unrecovered addicts lose their job, family, friends, and even their life. If you had the opportunity to ask them if that was their highest intention for living, their vision for their life, their dream growing up, the legacy they envisioned leaving behind to their family and friends, before they became the addict, how many would have said, "Yes!"

The Cost of Her Addiction

As a result of her addictions, Connie was no longer permitted to practice as a nurse. She lost her true love, her sons, most of her family, and only had a handful of friends left.

When I worked with Janna, I learned more about the disease of alcoholism than I ever cared to know—of which I knew very little when I first stepped into her world. I attended many Alcoholics Anonymous (AA) meetings and more rehab facilities with her than you would believe.

I rescued her from meth houses in the nastiest of neighborhoods and deplorable living conditions with families she did not know. One time, she told me over the phone, "You'll recognize the house when you get here because it's the one with garbage bags over the windows." She wasn't kidding; every window around all four sides of the house was covered.

Authentic Desire

I believed Connie had hit her rock bottom during her last binge. The fact that she was three months sober was significant. To do this work effectively, it is best a person has already demonstrated their commitment by detoxing and staying sober for a period of time. Three months was ideal for that also provided the biological brain healing time.

And Connie was proving to be an excellent student! However, as our work together continued, she began feeling unsettled and out of place with herself. She felt different and didn't understand it. I saw this as a sign that the transformation was truly happening but with an added twist I hadn't seen before.

She had been living and identified herself as an "alcoholic druggy." She was neither of these things anymore! For decades, she knew herself and what was *normal* in an abnormal way. Now, with new programming and rediscovery, almost everything felt different. But, if you remove one thing and not replace it with another, a void will form. This, I believed was happening to Connie.

I wanted to see her get into *action* to begin filling this void. We talked of several ways to do this, including my urging her to volunteer. Nothing heals the soul better than giving of yourself for another. I offered plenty of suggestions, including animal shelters, as these furry friends are naturally very therapeutic.

Connie's Powerful Reframe

Our work continued and Connie reached the point where I was comfortable in accomplishing a VE exercise over Facetime. When we did, something unexpectedly and magically unfolded.

We were going through the unearthing process around her self-esteem when it happened. About an hour into the exercise, from her subconscious mind came a very calm, almost child-like statement that on the surface didn't seem like much. But, when I heard it, I jumped on it!

She started getting lost in some thought and then out came, "I don't know who I am. I can't see the future."

Bravo! *"Connie!"* I exclaimed, *"Do you realize how wonderful that is?"* Of course, the look of confusion that ensued was priceless.

She repeated, "But I don't know who I am."

Why did I recognize this as a *wonderful* breakthrough?

In the past, who was she? She was an *alcoholic*. She was a *meth user*. She was a *loser*.

She was *unhappy*. She was *miserable*. All of these are *her* words.

And now, less than two months later, she *didn't know* who she was.

Connie no longer identified herself as *the alcoholic*. She was speaking from a completely different place within her mind. The words themselves were spoken with an entirely different tone and state.

In the past, such words would have been from "in effect" with a victim's mindset *(woe is me, the world is against me)* frame of mind. That was mostly absent now. This was her subconscious mind, asking a very curious, driven question. Remember, for true transformation to take place, there must be confusion and curiosity. That is exactly what was present now!

Here is how I "reframed" it for her:

"Connie, do you realize how wonderful this is? We have broken through your ego, dissolving old pathways within your subconscious mind that felt were protecting you with alcoholism; old pathways that in actuality were hindering you! You now have a clean slate! You have been given an amazing gift.

"You had no family, no friends, and no career. **Now you have a whole new life ahead of you that you can design and create any way you wish to.** *You now have control of allowing which family members you desire in your life. You get to choose what friends you allow into your life. And you get to decide a career path that fits this new you.* **Nothing any longer holds you back from discovering who you are at your core center."**

I continued, *"You have no distractions from the outside world. Everything you need is within you now, and your subconscious mind is letting you know that it's time to discover your true essence. For years, you have identified yourself in a way that was not your authentic truth. You were grossly out of alignment with yourself. Now, that diversion is gone, and you have this amazing gift to be able to move on and be who you truly are deep inside. And that is what you are going to discover and will unfold as we continue."**

> *To be clear, this is not to say she was cured of her alcoholism. What it is saying is that the strategy behind what drove her in the past was being altered. The old pathway through the forest was becoming overgrown and a new path was being created (confusion). My intention was to assist in creating the new path, new neural connections with strong suggestive language while having this current access to her subconscious mind.

Watching Connie on my computer through our Facetime link, she began to come alive like a kid at Christmas. The innocence of her inner child emerged. I encouraged her to enter into a "grounding meditation" later that evening with these thoughts of a new life unfolding and to embrace this feeling of letting go of the old behavior that no longer served her.

Life Moves Forward

Over the next several months, much did change for the better for Connie, but not all was grandiose. She began reconnecting with her family albeit a slow process. Anyone who has ever been associated with an alcoholic in the family understands the difficulty in regaining trust. For them, from their map, it's more sarcastically like, *"Sure, Connie, we believe you this time that things will be different."* But she truly was closer to full abstinence and reconnecting with her family than in many, many years.

Yet, her past did come back to haunt her. She was fired from her job (she was unhappy in) due to a meth charge a year prior. She had not told her employer of it, hoping they would never find out. Another valuable lesson in this new, *growing up,* Connie was undergoing with vast courage.

When we lose something, often it's to allow something better to take its place. This is a reframe in itself and what I encouraged Connie to focus on. She soon landed a new job in a different career field as she continued searching for something better.

She began dating again but was still going through her ups and downs. Our communication dwindled as there wasn't much more I could do for her from afar. We accomplished a Timeline Therapy session via Facetime, but it wasn't as impactful as I had hoped.

Breakfast

Finally, after some six months from our first contact, we met face to face. I had an overnight with my airline job in her home city. Timing couldn't have been more perfect.

We met in the morning and had the most splendid breakfast as we were both excited for actually getting to sit face to face. She presented me a token, a gesture of her thanks and faith. It was a small rock with a cross on it. By how it was worn, I assumed it had very special meaning to her. She confirmed my belief.

She handed it to me, saying, "I hope this doesn't bring you bad luck."

Oh, boy, what was that? I thought.

Dumbfounded, I placed the stone on the table as we continued to talk. I think she picked up on *my* physiological reaction for she then began telling me about the awful sequence of events from the day prior. To be honest, it was a calamity of misfortunes that would have driven me to a Scotch at the end of the day! And for Connie, she nearly did break her sobriety.

I immediately began reframing the day in a positive light, especially driving home the fact that she did not have that drink! This proved to her (and me) that her strategy had indeed been shifted.

Guiding Back to "At Cause"

I then had her take that token back and said, "Connie, why don't you present this to me again, this time with empowering language of what this rock truly means to you and why you wish me to have it." She did so beautifully, with entire "at cause" language, and I placed the rock on my person.

Why is this little story important? It's about "awareness." It's about catching disempowering language. Connie allowed herself to fall back into victim mode, deep in 1st position. It's about recognizing it and immediately correcting it.

So often we miss such golden opportunities to connect with the subconscious mind. If I had let this go, it would have validated her thought. I simply could not allow that to happen. This type of "pattern interrupt" is so important, and I am hoping it raises your awareness too regarding self-talk and in your conversations with others. We will cover much more on this in the remaining sections of this book.

Freedom at Last

As we continued talking, her inner pain was still quite evident. I asked her if she'd be willing to do more with the Timeline Therapy. She leaped at the opportunity.

We found a nice quiet place and Connie found her key. By the end, she had released her anger for good. The root was an interesting story around her brothers making fun of her when she was four years old. *Sticks and stones may break my bones, but words will never hurt me.* Nothing could be further from the truth. We will cover this in great detail under *Language*.

By the end, she recognized what it was with a new perspective from that of a four-year-old. We successfully released her Sadness and Fear, as well. As we walked to the exit of the hotel, she was acting *like* a four-year-old! She was all giddy, happy, smiley, joyful, and playful. It was amazing!

Her story is ongoing, but I wanted to highlight a couple things. Connie's transformation was longer and more involved than the previous stories with most of her process done telephonically or via video conference. That alone demonstrates how powerful Evolved NLP is.

It's unknown if our work may have been shortened if all was accomplished in person. But, all the preparation leading up to our meeting had readied Connie for her freedom with total ease and grace and without surprise.

Connie reached out on a whim and a prayer. She was ready. She had enough awareness to recognize an opportunity and with tremendous courage reached out. As a result, she now has an entirely new toolbox of tools from which to pull from to keep her life's journey on track. Connie has overcome major hurdles but challenges remain. There is still much her and I can accomplish at freeing her completely, but she is now in a better place than in decades.

Final Thoughts

Alcoholism and addictions are a far greater issue in this world than often recognized by society. During that year and a half I worked with Janna it consumed me. As a pilot in the commercial airline industry, I averaged 18 days on the road per month back then. That equates to meeting about 50 new crew members monthly or approximately 900 during that period of time.

Because I was so thoroughly involved, the subject of alcoholism constantly came up. And each time it did, (which was almost every day I flew) inevitably one or more of the other four crew members had an association with alcoholism. They, themselves, were either a recovered alcoholic, or had a spouse, family member or friend that was one or had been through it. It blew me away.

Many of these personal stories I learned were similar to my experiences with Janna while attempting to make a difference with her. There are obviously varying degrees of alcoholism, and from what I could uncover from the web, the statistics seem a bit skewed from reality, at least in the airline industry. My argument here is regarding the type who goes into rehab, (equally true for drug addictions) and either doesn't finish or is drunk on the drive home afterwards.

Worse, the chances of this type of full blown alcoholic ever completely recovering are very small. Most end up passing on from this life, buried in the pain of their wounds from some tragedy/trauma that occurred in their life. One familiar theme I kept hearing from the various AA meetings I attended with Janna was "1 in 50 die sober." From what I personally witnessed, I'd agree.

> *"If people return to alcohol or drug abuse, there is no guarantee that they will ever be able to stop again. This means that their relapse may turn out to be a death sentence."* http://alcoholrehab.com/addiction-recovery/beating-the-relapse-statistics/

But There is Hope – Real Hope!

What possibilities exist with this work? They are immense. Richard Bandler tells the story that his way of testing his work with an alcoholic was to take them to a bar and have them order a drink. According to him, they were able to have just the one and enjoy it like as if the person had never had the issue to begin with. Although Richard is the ultimate Master in NLP, it certainly opens doors to possibilities. Why isn't this science of NLP more recognized? A *million (s) dollar question*, isn't it?

This work is so powerful that I believe, under the guidance of a true Master, most behavioral issues, most emotional despondence, most addictions could be wiped out, *provided* the person suffering is truly ready and willing to escape their misery.

* * *

Forging Ahead to New Pathways

1) Drugs and/or alcohol compound addictive behavior for now the brain is chemically affected. This may require more than a simple exercise. However, for behaviors such as smoking, cutting, workaholic, etc., new pathways can absolutely happen in one exercise.

2) Desire is key and that is difficult to teach. Appropriately targeted Meta-Model or QL type questions have the potential to move a person out of 1st position and uncover the deep structure of their strategy. Stay flexible.

3) As the Bible says, *love the sinner, but hate the sin*. Keep perspective in **understanding their "map."** Know the person did not *choose* to go an ugly path; their map was already skewed.

SECTION III
DEEPER UNDERSTANDING

Awarness & Language

TUNING UP 13

"If you can grow in Love, you can grow in awareness. If you can grow in awareness, you can grow in love."

Osho

How are you enjoying our travels thus far? Let's see where we are…

You've been introduced to some basic concepts and terminology. We've also seen this work in action producing amazing results. Hopefully, your horizons are broadening with each unfolding chapter, slowly increasing your overall knowledge base.

Later, as we move even further into Section IV, I'll introduce how to put all this into practicality in real life situations. Your overall consciousness will continue to rise as you read on, creating new possibilities and pathways, while also leading you towards an even greater connection with your *Authentic Truth*.

As your journey continues onward, you'll learn more of what is actually happening with the mind. You will begin to see yourself in new ways and that of the world around you. In fact, as time moves along, you will find yourself incorporating these new learnings naturally into your daily life.

Importance of Responsibility

As profound as this work is, there is something else I wish to share before moving on. Life is not stagnant. By its nature, life is either growing or decaying. Whether it is the tree in the forest, the flower, or any other living creature, first is its birth, then its growth. Eventually, the living peaks, and finally recedes.

Life cycles vary, of course. For instance, Mayflies live a total of 24 hours, while some sponges in the sea are still going strong today, well after 4,500 years! Humans, on a global scale, currently average about six decades on this planet.

In this light, new challenges surface constantly. Who we are today is not the same person we were yesterday. In fact, if you really want to get technical, it is virtually impossible to actually live truly in the moment of now! For as soon as the thought is even contemplated, that moment has already passed. Eckhart Tolle addresses this beautifully in his beloved book, *The Power of Now*. But, philosophical point aside, yesterday (not to mention last year, last decade) gave you new challenges, new learnings, new wisdom. As a result, who you are today is not the same as who you *were*. In essence, your map of the world is not stagnant either.

Because of this, regardless of the transformational outcome, if one is not attuned (aware) to the daily challenges of life, new unwanted issues can easily surface. Therefore, this is an *ongoing* process because *life* is an ongoing process. Without awareness, old behaviors can even creep back in as new, disempowering events and emotions actually create new neural pathways that do not serve our Identity ecologically. The more enlightened a person's ***awareness*** and personal ***responsibility*** is taken on a daily basis, the greater their overall life-long results and benefits will be.

What is Awareness?

I love the opening quote by Osho. It so eloquently describes the core of this entire book. The roots of your *Authentic Truth* are in living with **awareness**. Without that, we live unguarded, allowing something from *out there* to inadvertently cause our wires to go out of tune. Over time, this can result in a problem and can eventually lead to being stuck within our own frame, unable to see the grander picture of the *world's reality*.

Following my argument from earlier that we are born in love and then life happens, we become trapped as it becomes more and more difficult to step outside that frame. Unless *awoken*, the clutters of life begin to limit our awareness to the possibilities that surround us. The end result is that our ability to truly love ourselves authentically gets obscured.

So, Osho has it exactly right, except I'd say the *process* is reversed! By becoming aware, we open the door to greater love, and the greater the love, the greater the gratitude we have for all that is around us. This actually further increases awareness and results in raising our *overall* consciousness.

We are going to delve more intensely into this concept of awareness later. For now, let's begin exploring what's going on inside the mind a little deeper, building the understanding behind why those transformations occurred in Section II. To properly set this up, allow me to explain a little more about NLP.

More Background on NLP

The creators of NLP, Bandler and Grinder, explicitly repeat that their techniques are guidelines, and therapists should exercise creativity with them. This has been proven true as NLP has evolved over the past several decades. New exercises continue to emerge as therapists experiment and alter techniques finding their own niche in effectively helping others to overcome their challenges.

And it is not just in techniques. The level of understanding also has strengthened. For instance, there were originally 23 NLP "Meta-Programs." Now, some 51 have been added over time and are growing. Your "Meta-Programs" are basically the operating manual for your mind. Bandler and Grinder state in their book, *the Structure of Magic*:

> *"...the arena of tension, conflict, or difference involves our very thinking patterns. How we are thinking, rather than what we are thinking, is the problem...The form or structure of our thinking, as our thinking style, exists at a level above or meta to our thinking itself. We designate these thinking styles as Meta-Programs...They represent the "programs" we use as we sort for things, pay attention, and process information."*

Why NLP is a *science* and differs from other traditional therapies is in its search for the "How" (programming) a behavior arose and not so much the "What" (behavior itself). In respect to effecting change, therefore, NLP is not concerned about the specific circumstances that *happened* (the story), but in how the person's decisions were made that got them there (their strategies).

Therefore, NLP is focused on the structure beneath the behavior. When the structure and strategies behind how a person does what they do is understood, then their future decision processes can be changed to align with their authentic truth and desired outcomes, satisfying their truest intent in the most ecological and loving way.

Understanding this thoroughly will alone begin changing how you view communication. It solidifies that no two people see the world exactly the same, and that we each operate within our own individual map of reality.

Analogy of the Black Piano

For even greater understanding (and keeping with *flexibility*), this analogy came to me while vacationing in Hawaii last summer. May it drive home the implications of all we've covered thus far.

Think of a beautiful, black lacquered grand piano all tuned up and ready to play under majestic concert hall lighting. You are in the audience, dressed in elegance, ready to embrace the artistry, as five award-winning pianists sequentially play personally selected masterpieces. The stage is set, the house lights come down, the spotlight centers, and the piano keys, so elegantly touched by our first pianist, begin moving, leaving their neutral position. Through the mechanical design of the piano, the keys move their respective hammers that in turn strike the piano wires. Thus, the unique vibrations we recognize as the sound of a piano are created.

The tonality of these vibrations is represented as notes that are carefully crafted and linked together. And then the true magic happens. They reach your ears and you begin sinking into its blessed creation. Note after note, piano wire after piano wire combine in vibrational flow that moves your entire bodily sensations while listening to a piece written by Mozart centuries ago.

She finishes, and the next pianist takes his seat behind the same "grand" and delivers another beautiful sequence of notes; Beethoven this time. And on it goes as the next three pianists take their turn creating harmonic bliss.

Yet, *mechanically speaking*, regardless of who wrote the piece or is playing it, the *structure* of the piano has no choice but to give back what is was designed to give. Over and over, any individual can sit down and play on that piano, and the piano will continue to produce tones based on its structure; push on a key and a wire vibrates at a preset frequency.

Whether a child is just pounding away or a grand master plays with grace, a piano is a piano. It is in the technique of *how* the keys are struck that creates its "behavior" that makes the difference.

A piano thus is simply an instrument allowing the music to be made. It is very structured in its specific design. A grand piano could never sound like a violin. What type of music (if music at all) emerges is based on the pianist's skill and discernment of a piece.

How Does This Relate?

Although there are different styles of pianos, they generally work the same, and you recognize the sound of a piano when being played.

Similarly, we know in general what a human being looks like and the expected, associated behavior. Like different styles of pianos, there are human variances of course: personalities, temperaments, sexes, ailments, disabilities, etc., but we in general know what a human looks like. In this analogy, imagine under the hood of the piano, out of view from the audience, are the wires and mechanical linkages that produce the vibrations. Allow these to be the deep structure of the subconscious mind.

Now, let's go back to that first master pianist who was playing Mozart moments ago. She finishes and the crowd roars with joyful enthusiasm as the final notes diminish. She bows, and the curtain closes.

Minutes later, the curtain reopens, but this time rather than bringing out the next pianist, to your surprise, it is her again sitting behind the piano. She begins to play the *same* Mozart piece played just moments before, only this time it sounds horrific!

The piano looks identical to the one just played, and in fact it *is* the same piano! What you didn't see behind the closed curtain was a quarter of the wires at random were put grossly out of tune. Consequently, no matter how good the pianist is, the music coming out of that *same* piano will not be the same. More than likely, you will not be moved with deep resonance, but rather shrieking as the obnoxious *missed* notes are played over and over again. It's the same piano, isn't it? But something on the *inside* has changed the piano's behavior.

In fact, not one of those five pianists will be able to make that ill-tuned piano sound as beautiful as the original because its **internal wiring is different**. Could this second, out-of-tune piano be brought back to its harmonious *Authentic Truth*? Certainly. The piano tuner simply goes inside and adjusts the strings, realigning the piano's deep structure to its true designed nature.

There is Nothing *Wrong* With You

There is nothing wrong with any of us. Our wires get crossed, or maybe better said, out of tune. You are exactly where you are today because of how your mind is wired and tuned. This is extremely freeing!

When not in alignment, when we feel a dis-ease, a life rooted in despair, stuck, trapped, or not producing consistent effective results, it is a signal that something within you is out of tune. Once *aware* there is nothing *wrong* with you, that you are a beautiful grand piano capable of emanating the most beautiful creations from within you, should a tune-up be needed or desired, it can begin. *Even the piano requires frequent attention to keep it perfectly in tune.*

That Pesky Secondary Gain

Yet, there is often a real obstacle to true change **even when the desire to change is there**. Often that hindrance is rooted in some sort of resistance (secondary gain). If the hood of the piano cannot be opened, how can the wires be tuned? Without bringing full awareness to, and removing that secondary gain, no lasting change can take place.

This is because you are not getting beneath the behavior, to your programming as mentioned in Section I. At best, you may make an adjustment to your behavior but it will be with work and effort.

Changing the programming at the deeper level of the subconscious mind eliminates that! It just becomes your natural resonance, your way of being.

And, if that retuning of the piano is not completed, it can never echo the masterpiece as Mozart intended. Rather, it will continue getting the same obnoxious results over and over.

A person trapped within a problem frame must first be moved out of 1st position and into 3rd position, outside the looping of their problem in their conscious mind, in order to *hear* or see just how out of tune they are.* From there, the *hood can be opened* and the secondary gain removed. The piano is now available, ready and willing to return to its beautiful creation as intended.

> *As in several of the stories from Section II, what people often feel as normal is living with an out of tune piano. When looping, one cannot understand why their 'normal' is abnormal (out of tune) at the deeper subconscious level.*

Back to You

Now, get this: Each of us *is* a Mozart! **Each of us, when in alignment with our core, plays our own beautiful music from love, through our own grand piano, in our own unique way.**

NLP allows us to quickly bring our piano wires back in tune as a professional tuner would. Each piano may be slightly different, but the professional, the master tuner, sees the full potential of the beautiful music that black lacquered grand piano is capable of producing. The master understands that the piano was created to *sing* at its highest potential.

How that piano behaves is set before anyone touches a single key. The tuning of that piano will determine whether the Mozart masterpiece will move you to Xanadu or have you scrambling for the emergency exit!

When we get stuck in a behavioral, repetitive problem, or seeing a repetitive pattern developing that is unwanted, it is not as important in NLP as to what the problem or pattern is but that it exists (the wires just happen to be out of tune).

The "Reasons"

Some may say that, "Yeah, but you don't understand *my* life," or, "You don't know me. You don't understand what I've been through. If you only knew what this person did to me," etc.

Do such thought processes aid in any way to bringing the wires back in tune? No! Life is not always fair, and yes, some have been dealt a raw deal. There simply is no getting around that fact.

Yet, what is the end goal? What is *really* desired? To live a life of reasons, or to return to your Authentic Truth? Thus, in the story of our piano playing poorly, it is the necessary "awareness" to know something is not right that must occur first. Once this is recognized, what becomes most important to the *healing* is the *underlying structure* creating the misery (the out of tuned wires themselves).

In the person, it is something in their decision strategies, their core values, their programming, this deep structure that is out of tune. Their suffering is a direct result of the *associated* wires (root) and not the behaviors being out of tune. This, then, must be the focus; not so much the story of *why* the wires went out of tune, but that they *are* indeed out of tune. *Which wires* and then simply help the person to re-tune them.

Those Imprinting Years

Hence, what happened very early in childhood during those imprinting years is often the root of cause of when the wires began detuning. We are born in love, then life happens.

Diving into the deeper structure thus allows the Master NLP guide to identify the piano wires in need of tuning, adjusting and even sometimes, replacing them all together. This analogy only goes so far, but the point is your mind is structured in a very unique way. This structure is the key to changing the unwanted, undesired, behavior and results, and begins with the hope, the knowing, that change is possible.

The Answers Are Within You

Once this is fully recognized and understood with awareness, the re-tuning can begin by uncovering exactly which wires need to be tuned. This is where the *how* (rather than the why) of the person's strategy enters the picture. ***For, it is ultimately changing this strategy we are after.***

Again, this is just an analogy to help build a picture, and to help you grasp what is going on behind the scenes of your mind. In reality, **you** are the piano, the player, and the tuner! The Master conducting the NLP work is simply a guide. But it is you, in the end, that corrects yourself. How? The answers are already inside you. The Master simply unlocks them for you, allowing you to tune yourself back in alignment, reconnecting with your *Authentic Self*.

Computer Analogy

There is one more analogy that may help to clarify and solidify these thoughts. In the world of personal computers, like this laptop I'm writing with now, there are basically four parts:

1. The physical housing – *our body*
2. The CPU – *our brain*
3. The hard drive – *our programming*
4. Software – *our behaviors*

The physical structure lets us know it is a computer.
The CPU, as it relates to our physical brain, is fixed from the factory.

The hard drive is the programming aspect of our minds. Science has proven that our minds have the ability to be re-programmed (Neuroplasticity). When a computer's hard drive gets cluttered and out of tune, the user notices a different behavior. It locks up, slows down, or crashes all together. Defragging, cleaning up an old hard drive or replacing it all together is similar to reprogramming of the mind. This greatly improves the efficiency of the CPU, aligning it with its authentic truth.

Finally, there is the software. *Microsoft* and *Apple*, for example, often come out with new operating software for your CPU to operate from. It is the *interface* between the CPU and the *real world* (you and the external world). This can relate to the surface structure and outward behaviors that others witness.

* * *

Now that you have this basic concept, we'll build upon it, going into greater detail of how our core values, awareness, and language combine to create the results we have in life. Understanding this allows for changes to begin in our daily lives as well as at the deeper behavioral and meta-programming levels.

* * *

TUNING UP

A Tune-Up to New Pathways

1) We are either growing or decaying; constant awareness keeps us in better tune.

2) With even slight adjustments, we can sing even more beautifully. All the answers are within you.

3) We do what we do because of our programming – and this is elastic, not static.

INTRODUCTION TO CORE VALUES 14

"Tell me what you pay attention to and I will tell you who you are."

JOSÉ ORTEGA Y GASSET

Building upon this theme of our mind's foundation, the constructs of our programming formulate our "Core Values." Core values define who we are and what is important to our lives. Each aspect of our lives has its own set of core values. When we are enjoying life, truly joyful and full of love, we are in congruence with our core values. When frustrated, depressed, lost, easily upset, we are out of alignment with the related core values. In relationships, when things gel naturally, there is congruence with the *other person's* core values; when arguments arise, they are out of alignment.

Core values are so powerful that it is why there is truth in jesting that politics or religion should be avoided at family gatherings. It's a perfect example of the deep-rooted values people associate in those areas. When a core value comes under attack, the defensive ego gets revved up into high gear, and *emotions* often take over. Once this happens, all true communication ceases.

Core values determine how we spend our time, energy, and resources and establish our belief systems; they even drive our attitudes. Douglas Pride puts it this way, "Values are stable constructs from which belief systems are generated. The rule of thumb is values can be expressed in 1 to 3 words. Beliefs need a full sentence. Attitudes tend to need a paragraph."

Values vs. Behaviors

As I began researching on the internet how values and behaviors are studied, I was perplexed by what I found. Page after page of Google results, from research studies, professors, and Psychology said that values are our behaviors. I thought to myself, *"That is absolutely* not *true. No wonder there are so many challenges out there if this is how the traditional therapeutic world views the two."*

Our behaviors are *linked* to our values, but **they are not our values**. Behaviors stem *from* our values. The piano wires are deep within the piano, hidden from you as its music reaches the audience's ears. The plane flies through the air, an object kept in flight and on track by its internal structure. Likewise, the observer witnesses the *results* of behavior coming from a person's inner structure, their core values.

In our analogy, the piano wire represents a core value, while the tonality represents the behavior. **If your piano wire is itself out of tune, no matter what you do, you will not be playing Mozart as intended!** You will not get the desired results you are so desperately searching for.

Therefore, in our ongoing discussion of working with others, to *effect real, lasting change* to their patterns or behaviors, the focus is on the core values coded deeply within the subconscious mind, often hidden from view by the conscious mind.

Values and Beliefs

Where do our values and beliefs come from? Everywhere! Our environment, our parents, friends, acquaintances, news, culture, religion, school, internet, books, sports, entertainment (TV, movies, plays, theater, music, concerts, etc.), and social media to name a few. The list is endless. And since most of us are *not* living in a state of **awareness**, we are open to being "programmed" and influenced by anything out there – especially during those imprinting years, but, true throughout our lives as well. Keep in mind neuroplasticity and our constantly adjusting map of the world throughout this discussion.

The other day, I was with a mother of three teenagers. We were on this topic when she pointed out the lyrics in some current songs that are programming our youth to feel worthless, lost, and that basically, they suck. She showed me the actual lyrics via her phone and I was floored!

The more you raise your level of awareness, the greater your filtering of what you allow your mind to be affected by becomes. Opposingly, without awareness, your mind is being programmed by whatever it is exposed to, and the subconscious mind is aware of everything! Thus, you sing along with a song that has a good beat but is programming you to believe you are worthless. Nice.

This is why it's dangerous to watch TV late at night as your brain waves slow and your guard is down. If there was one simple change to make in your life it would be to not watch TV at night, especially just before going to bed.

Worse is falling asleep with the TV on! That is programming going straight into your mind without filters, like that of a child. Rather, read a good book, spend quality time playing games or discussion with the family and/or your partner. And just before going to bed, the best is simply meditating alone, setting an intention in preparation for the day to come.

Belief System Development

In essence, a belief system is a grouping of beliefs around a core value. To the surface structure of the mind, these values are often abstract. Famous sociologist, Morris Massey, stated core beliefs form during three distinct time periods:

- Age 0-7: Imprinting years
- Age 8-14: Modeling period
- Age 15-21: Socialization period

Additionally, William James, philosopher and psychologist added a fourth period:

- Age 22-35: Business persona

Here is what Abby Eagle, NLP Personal Coach, Hypnotherapist says about values:

> *"Values exert a powerful effect upon your life. They determine how you relate to your family and your partner; what products you buy; how you perform your job and who you vote for. Values dictate your leisure time activities, your interests, what you learn, your religious convictions and so on. The 'generation gap' is a statement about values"*

A person's personality emerges when their core values, beliefs, and behaviors are taken together. What they are willing to fight for, die for, their definitions around success, status, family, God, material possessions, humanitarian needs, etc. You can see why this can quickly evolve into an immense subject area of life! However, in this book, we are primarily focused on the core values, the root of the programming.

Fix Me

Too often, we are looking for someone or something outside of us to *fix* us on a daily basis. We're looking for that new partner, a new job, more money, a new house, a new car, etc. But if already unhappy or dissatisfied, no matter how hard, or the number of times tried, if we don't adjust what's on the inside first, nothing out there will bring that inner peace searched for. **This is why I earlier devoted an entire chapter just to happiness.** Maybe this now helps bring that argument full circle for you.

In my own journey, years of reading self-help books, attending seminars, and engaging in enlightening conversations by successful people, I did begin to shift my thinking but not so much my results. It wasn't until NeoGensis did I begin to understand why.

And what happened? I retuned my piano wires to play Mozart again. How? My core values regarding my *definitive purpose* and reason for being, my Identity, were brought back in tune with my "I Am," my *Authentic Truth*.

The actualization of a person seeing their situation from a new perspective is the key to unlocking that feeling of being trapped or stuck within a problem. In the concept of core values, the VE exercise helps to do that. This is where the "guide" begins the process of someone to *fix* themselves.

Exploring Core Values

Our core values run our lives, yet up until now, have you ever thought about them in that way? Have you sat around the dinner table discussing them in detail and helping each other discover them? For a concept so vital to every aspect of our lives, it amazes me I had to wait until fifty-one years of age to be awakened to this awareness!

Why does one person turn towards addiction, molestation, rape, murder, become narcissistic, over bearing, lost, depressed, and another turns to love, self-improvement, curiosity, wonder, amazement, and sees possibilities – with more or less *similar circumstances*? For the purpose of this discussion it comes down to their core values beneath the behavior itself.*

> *As previously discussed, the environment during ages 0-7 has significant impact on the formation of these values and Meta-Programs. Additionally, epigenetic states that our genetic coding is altered as we go through life. Even more fascinating, The Genome Project has proposed evidence that genetic coding is passed on to offspring. The importance of this is extraordinary. For instance, let's say a person suffers a severe, tragic occurrence around anger. Their genetic code is altered and Anger is inserted from this environmental impact. According to studies with mice, they proved this to be passed down two generations! This could explain why a person is born "Angry; it's in their genes." This is a fascinating area of study but outside the context of this book. I bring it up as an awareness tool. During Timeline Therapy, the subconscious mind will often take the person back to previous generations. Some will also travel back to past lives. Whether true or not, what is important regarding the therapy is how this information is stored (coded) in the subconscious mind. Since it is coded it can be re-coded allowing epigenetics to then take over. This elasticity is why ongoing awareness and responsibility are crucial to lasting change.*

Empowering vs. Disempowering

Why core values are so important is that they inherently determine whether you are moving towards pleasure or away from pain. As discussed earlier, these are expressed in our physiology and language as *empowering* or *disempowering*.

Let's say you are genuinely enthusiastic and inspired by something. Here are some words that will naturally flow from this **empowered** state: *will, desire, choose, inspired, determined*. These are representative of being "at cause" and taking responsibility.

Conversely, words such as, *have to, must, should, want, wish, need*, are **disempowering** and have you moving away from what you *don't want*. These are examples of being "in effect" and providing reasons and excuses. Often, there will be the word "but" inserted within their sentence: "I should be doing this *but*…"

In natural conversation, words of action almost never have "but" inserted in the sentence. Try it!

"I'm determined to make this happen, *but*..." Such a statement just doesn't flow and would normally be stated, "I'm determined and will find a way."

Contrary, words moving away will often have this "but" ('reason' to follow) inserted after the desired wish: "I'd like to make this happen *but*..." This is far more likely and an "in effect" statement.

Listen closely the next time your child, spouse or friend discusses something of interest to them. You can quickly decipher their internal representation, their map of the world in the context of the subject being discussed (which represents their inner, often hidden, ***core value***).

When "at cause," taking responsibility for their situation, moving towards a desired result, they will use empowering language. When moving away from pain, they are in effect and will give reasons using disempowering language. Such language keeps a person stuck within their problem frame.

So, to keep it very basic in the beginning, you can simply begin to listen for the word "but." Allow the word "but" to be a signal to the rest of their language, alerting you to listen more carefully to the other words and patterns being used. You can not only catch others using it, ***but*** yourself as well (pun intended ☺).

One of my dear friends and mentors, Susan Walsh, use to tell me long ago, "Guy, get your 'but(t)' out of the way!" Pretty funny, but it worked in building my awareness as to how disempowering my language actually was at that time. The more you recognize this in others, the more quickly you can begin applying it to yourself.

The essence of this is that simply by raising your awareness, you can already gain insight into why *you* are receiving the results you are. ***Your language tells the story.*** This can become quite fun! Make a game of it to see how often you can catch yourself and others utilizing empowering and disempowering language.

INTRODUCTION TO CORE VALUES

Word of caution, this is first for your awareness. Make sure to receive another's permission, while in rapport, before pointing it out to them: *"Hey, Tim, would you mind a little feedback on something I've noticed?"*

Breaking Free

All of this is linked to our core values. Understanding these begins an entirely new way of seeing who you are and that you have within you the power to break free:

- To break free of unwanted behaviors
- To break free of unwanted emotions
- To break free of those beliefs that no longer serve you
- To break free from undesired results
- To break free from pain
- To break free from feeling stuck or trapped

Breaking free of your repetitive, unwanted results begins by understanding these core values around work, relationships, money, life, love, school, church, race, cultures, God, etc. The list covers every aspect of your life. But, it is how these values are actually coded in our Meta-Programs that ***drive*** all these areas of our lives. Many of the exercises in NLP are addressing these Meta-Programs, strategies, coding and deep structures, while others only go to behavioral issues as with the New Behavior Generator.

The VE exercise is specifically designed to uncover how the subconscious mind is storing these core values. The exercise brings to paper the internal representation deep within your subconscious mind.

By replacing, rewriting this coding in a way that serves your desired direction, your results begin to change, not at a behavioral level but at a deeper level of your Identity. And all of this can be accomplished, easily, effortlessly, and most importantly, naturally, without any medications or need of long term treatment for most people. It only requires seeking the knowledge to learn NLP with a Master, or, simply seeking out a Master NLP practitioner.

On a personal note, there are many uses of NLP and not all are empowering. If you decide to search further into this understanding, may I suggest vetting who you choose to learn from. As you can imagine, NLP is extremely powerful and can be utilized in unethical ways as well. I am blessed to have learned under Niurka who evolved NLP to an even higher state. There are other credible Masters out there as well, including Richard Bandler himself who is still teaching at the time of this writing. Just a note of awareness.

It's Not a Secret

The secret is not a secret—it is just a lack of knowledge—knowledge that does exist, even if not promoted by mainstream therapies of today. Your results in life come from your actions, driven by your behaviors, which are ultimately rooted in your core values. If your results up until now are not that which is most desired, wouldn't it make sense to go to the ***root*** and replace those values that no longer serve you?

Why not, for if you take that leap, you will experience a freedom in that area of your life, allowing it to flow naturally in new unexpected ways. You truly can be freed and live your *Authentic Truth*.

Discovering Your Core Values

We talked about the VE process in Claudia's story. Why most of these exercises are better performed by a guide rather than going it alone is because of the trance state induced by someone else doing the questioning. Without first being put through the process by a guide, you most likely will be too much in your conscious mind with your ego blocking access to your subconscious mind where the answers live.

Once you've been through the process several times, you absolutely can do these on your own. This is true for most of the exercises. I have

INTRODUCTION TO CORE VALUES

in fact released much in doing Timeline Therapy on myself. But this has come with the experience of working with others and the ability to allow my conscious mind to *take a break*.

However, with all that being said, I encourage you to begin. It won't hurt and if you can allow yourself to go into a trance state, such as during meditation, you can access those deeper aspects of your mind and find release. It is why meditation is so therapeutic.

How to Begin

In uncovering a core value, you want to be as specific as possible penetrating the mind to *that* core *value* behind the meta-programming, driving the results in that area of your life. *Personal finances* is more specific than just finances; *success in business* is more specific than simply success; *how I discipline my kids* is more specific than parenting.

The simple question to begin with is, "What's most important to me in the context of _____?" and insert your specific undesired result that is showing up, the area you seek to change. To help determine what that specific area is, you can start first by asking, "What's one area of my life, that if the results were to change in that area, it would create the biggest change in every other area of my life?"

Once you've identified an area, you can start asking yourself, "Where have I been investing my time, energy, and resources in that area up until now?" Notice, this is not where you know you should be investing but where you *actually* have been! If you know what is required, and you were doing it, you wouldn't be stuck. So, something in your thinking is keeping you from doing that which is necessary in order to get the results you seek. And more than likely, it is subconscious, beyond your conscious awareness.

For example, let's say I want to get in better physical shape (a true goal of mine). By doing so, I would experience more energy, vitality, and be able to go hiking or skiing at will, knowing my body was properly prepared. I'd simply feel younger, while also protecting my future health.

Yet, time and time again, I find reasons to avoid the gym, cycling, Yoga, etc. Each would improve my overall physical conditioning, but for whatever reason, I am investing that time, energy and resources with something else. Why? This is what the VE will uncover.

Examples from a VE may include playing guitar, reading, writing, or playing backgammon with Elke. These events exercise my mental shape but not my physical. As this inquiry continues, deeper values would surface as to what is occupying my time from exercising (moving away).

This question, "What's most important to me in the context of_____?" should be asked over and over again, for as long as it takes to dig deep enough that answers begin emerging that you didn't know were in there. Eventually, say in an hour's time, you will begin looping with no new information surfacing.

You may be able to recognize why this can be challenging to do by yourself. It's easy to quickly come up with the "reasons" that have already been looping in your conscious mind rather than the truth as coded in your subconscious mind. But if you stick with it, you will uncover much more.

What is it for you? What is that one area in your life you wish to change? I'd love to hear from you and your thoughts from this chapter and book. Feel free to reach out to me via, www.guybrilando.com. Additionally, great references and videos exist online to learn more from in this area if it interests you further. It could be a book all unto itself.

Wrapping it Up

To summarize, core values are the deep-rooted structure behind everything we do behaviorally. It is the core essence of our identity. They define us and by the age of seven, most of this coding has taken place in the form of Meta-Programs. Life's dramatic imprints are interpreted

INTRODUCTION TO CORE VALUES

and unconsciously programmed in with the knowledge, wisdom, and understanding *at the age they occurred*. As we move forward in this reading, we are going to begin discovering just how the actual structure of language impacts all of this as well.

When our core values align, you begin vibrating in tune with your entire being. Rather than being split into "parts," as in one part wants this (moving towards) and another wants that (moving away), all work together in the direction of the desire.

This leads to greater inner peace, greater self-worth, and greater self-love. The Law of Attraction naturally begins to flow in your direction without resistance, creating the world you always dreamed of. It leads to discovering your *Authentic Truth*.

* * *

The Core to New Pathways

1) Core Values drive our behaviors, which drive our actions, which drive our results.

2) Once uncovered, undesirable, moving away core values can be re-written, allowing for real, lasting change of our desired outcome.

3) Core values are hard wired into our subconscious and related to our meta-programming from childhood. Changing them is like swapping out the hard drive of a computer.

A PERSONAL STORY 15

> *"I promise you that if you dedicate yourself to the process of finding out who you are, it will be the most exciting trip you've ever taken in your life."*
>
> LEO BUSCAGLIA

Is all we've covered thus far making sense? Are you building a framework in which to be able to contextualize the essence of what we are discussing? I truly hope you are, for now comes the really good stuff!

You've been introduced to the awareness and language aspects, but now it's time to delve even further. When we become more aware of our surroundings, including language, we allow greater perspective. Awareness of our language is so powerful, it actually changes our individual maps!

Here's an interesting past experience that contains a little drama and excitement from many years ago. I've shared this story often over the years, but here I am sharing it with you in the context and importance of awareness and language.

Life's challenges come from all directions, attempting to throw you off balance. Many times they hit us unexpectedly. When prepared mentally with increased awareness, handling storms calmly as they

A PERSONAL STORY

arise, allows life to move along far more gracefully. Hence, this story also emphasizes the importance in being prepared for the unexpected.

The more vigilant you are on a daily basis, striving to become just a little better each day, the greater your ability will be to weather the storms. As you read through this, I encourage you to reflect back on a life event of your own. Ask yourself how well you handled it, or, if there were ways in which you could have had yourself better prepared.

A Dangerous Environment

When you reflect back on your life thus far, do you remember a moment where the world stopped, if even for just a little bit, in the face of danger? Do you remember the emotions, thoughts, feelings, and actions that took place?

In my two decades of flying the F-16, I can assure you I had many. Near mid-airs in simulated aerial combat, being shot at for real by Anti-Aircraft-Artillery in Iraq, and having my "electric" jet experience serious electrical malfunctions over the Mediterranean Sea hundreds of miles from shore, just to name a few. All were exciting events in my world of flying fighters.

The Viper was an extension of who I was; an expressive part of me. We spent thousands of hours together through thousands of sorties (takeoff to landing). The intense training fighter pilots undergo has two primary goals – to be prepared and to keep cool under pressure.

The Viper is the most versatile and widely utilized jet fighter in the history of aviation. Its capabilities allow it to shoot missiles at an aerial target some twenty plus miles away and deliver ordnance ranging from 500lbs bombs all the way to a single nuke ten times more powerful than that of Hiroshima.

Therefore, the single Viper pilot has immense responsibility. Unlike most fighters that employ air to ground weapons that have two pilots, there is no check and balance in the human decision tree in this cockpit.

No matter the situation, if a fighter pilot loses the ability to think clearly and mis-prioritizes tasks when things go wrong, tragedy can strike. From bombing the wrong target, running out of gas, colliding with another aircraft, or making the wrong decision jeopardizing an entire package of airplanes, it's not just one pilot's life at stake. Others in the air and on the ground entrust the fighter pilot to make the right decision, every time.

There I Was

It was October 23rd, 1990, a day that brought all new meaning to my life and life in general. I was nearing the end of my first operational assignment in the F-16 at Kunsan, Air Base (AB), Korea.

I was still a young pup with about 200 hours in the Viper, a far cry from the 3,600 I'd retire with. It was a day that called forth all my training, allowing for peace and calmness amongst imminent danger. It was proof positive in the value of being prepared and ready with unexpected fate. As my mentor and friend Brad Hager says, "When opportunity arises, it is too late to prepare."

You may never fly an F-16, but we are all put into unexpected life-challenging situations, both positive and negative, which require us to be at our very best. When opportunity knocks are you ready to capitalize on it? Are you prepared to be aware in recognizing it when it does? How about the unexpected?

How do you prepare for the unknown? How do you strengthen your resolve to plow through life's challenges without losing your authentic self in the process, maintaining your awareness, and aligned with your supreme self?

We are often blinded from our authentic truth as we have seen. But every once in a while, we get a chance to prove what we are truly capable of and to know we can stay ahead of this game of life.

The Mission

This story begins with a mission in South Korea during their week long, *Fall Eagle* exercise held annually. It involves the armies, navies, marines, and air forces of the US and South Korean militaries.

Our mission that morning was to fight our way in against aerial adversaries and ground-based defenses to deliver BDU-33s (practice bombs) on target in one of the northern ranges of South Korea. We stepped to our jets with loaded 38 revolvers, full combat gear, and classified smart packs. It was incredibly exciting.

I can remember stepping to my jet that early Tuesday morning when this unusual, surreal thought surfaced, reflecting on how I'd arrived at this point in my life. My female crew chief climbed the ladder, assisting in the strapping of the jet to my person in customary fashion.

Uncharacteristically, I watched her hands guide the metal connector of each riser from the parachute packed in the seat behind me into the fasteners of the harness I was wearing. I still see her fingers from that action in my memory today. She then looked me over, ensuring all the different 'connections' were secured: lap belt, shoulder harnesses, G-Suit hose. She also cross-checked that the canopy and ejection seat safety pins were removed and stored.

After she climbed back down the ladder, we awoke aircraft tail number AF86354 for what would be its final time. Twenty minutes later, our eight-ship Viper package was airborne, each loaded with external fuel tanks and bombs for the two-hour mission that lay ahead.

Typically, we would employ as four-ships, four F-16s flying in visual formation similar to the four corners of a playing card, two by two. The forward two aircraft were flying 1.5 miles apart, side by side. The back two would be about 2-4 miles in trail. For this mission, we were two such 4-ship formations in trail of one another, eight Vipers in our mini package, and I was at the tail end. For this discussion, we'll focus just on the second four-ship where I was Viper 4.

Ingressing to the Target

Being simulated combat, there were lots of other fighters also airborne, some on our side and others fighting against us, orchestrated with strict Rules of Engagement to ensure all returned home safely. The Navies and Armies of the two countries were exercising their war games as well during the 24-hour-a-day operations of the exercise. In other words, there was a *lot* going on at once.

Our plan was to ingress at a low altitude (500'), traveling over varied terrain of mountains, valleys, and hills at over 550 M.P.H. for approximately forty minutes. We would do our best to avoid being detected and targeted by any air or surface threats, drop our bombs on preplanned targets, and then fight our way out, back to Kunsan AB. The mission proved to be very dynamic and fluid with many moving parts, a culmination of intensive mission planning, briefing, and execution.

The Unexpected

Everything was moving according to plan as we ingressed at low level. Our air cover was protecting us well. We were about 60 miles to the Northwest of Taegu when our low level route required us to make an almost 90 degree turn from the North to the West. My rolling into this turn was timed visually off of Viper 3. On this day, Viper 3 happened to be the Wing Commander, the big guy in command of everything at Kunsan. We had flown quite a bit together and gelled well in the air.

As I rolled out of the nearly knife-edged turn, I was thrown violently forward into my harness—like being a passenger in a car when the driver suddenly hits the brakes hard. I was like, *"What the heck was that?"* Immediately, I gazed down the engine instrument panel to interpret what was going on.

My engine was still running but at reduced power. My next thought was the engine had transferred for an unknown reason to its secondary mode and my suspicion was soon confirmed. The engine was now

A PERSONAL STORY

running in its backup, *get me home* mode. I began an easy climb away from the ground and made a quick radio call to our four-ship. This single radio call would eventually create massive confusion and cloud clarity for all four of us!

Communication is Vital

I blurted out, "Terminate, I've got a problem." Missing from that very important radio call was my position number and reason for the Terminate call. It should have been, "Viper 4, terminate. I've got an engine problem."

Can you see the simple deletions, distortions and generalizations between the two? Now, the other three had to interpret what they heard and make sense of it while hurling along the ground at 550 M.P.H., fighting their way to the target area. By not identifying who I was, needless confusion was injected into an already non-normal situation. How often does this occur on a daily basis in normal life? A lot.

Under the heightened stress of the event, I made a poor radio call. Making matters worse, Viper 2's radio failed and never heard the transmission or subsequent ones on that frequency. He had no idea of my issue or what continued to unfold.

The result was Viper 3 thought it was Viper 2 with the problem, never once thinking it was his wingman (me). Viper 1, busy flying visual off the four-ship in front of us, recognized my voice so assumed Viper 3 was supporting me. Viper 2 was oblivious and happily flying off of Viper 1. All this left me alone, miles behind them, as they continued on the planned route.

Several human factors were evolving at this point. There's confusion in Viper 3's mind as to why Viper 2 is not climbing away from the ground. Viper 1 believes Viper 3 is supporting me. Of course, I'm busy taking care of my emergency and just assuming Viper 3 is with me. In Viper 3's mind, he has convinced himself Viper 2 has the problem.

Reduced awareness, a "mind-read," "projection," and additional stress all because of one poor radio call.

Dealing With the Problem

Inside my jet, the engine instruments began dancing like the Jitter Bug and my immediate thought was, "Oh, this is not good." But, unlike my first engine failure in that Cesena, this time I was prepared.

I followed the memorized checklist procedures and the engine instruments stabilized —all the way down to zeros. One big event I had trained for and hoped would never happen was happening! I was in the middle of nowhere over rugged mountains. My mind began to race as I made the next radio call on the VHF radio: "Knock it Off, KIO, KIO. I've got engine failure." Still no call sign!

I began zooming my Viper, attempting to trade as much energy for altitude as possible. I punched off the external wing tanks and bombs and glided upward to about 4,000 feet above the terrain.

"Confirm this is an exercise input?" Viper 3 belts out. He is convinced this is not real, but role play, because the guy he *thinks* has the problem is not maneuvering his jet accordingly.

"Negative, negative!!" I exclaimed. "This is for real!"

Viper 3, solely focused on Viper 2 instructs the immediate action items over the VHF radio, "Zoom, Stores Jett."

"I've already done that," I responded while cresting the top of my climb. Now, I'm wondering silently, *"What the heck is he talking about? Can't he see me?"*

Viper 3 is wildly confused and now so am I! He cannot force himself out of his "narrowed frame" which convinced him that it is Viper 2 with the emergency, even though he was still flying peacefully along off of Viper 1.

By now, I'm about eight miles behind them, in a glider not meant to be one, believing Viper 3 was right there with me. It never dawned on

A PERSONAL STORY

me that I hadn't used my call sign and that Viper 3 wasn't there. All of this because of one simple omission!

It's Getting Serious

By this time, there were quite a few lights and warnings going off in my jet, adding to the stress of the situation. Because our training was so phenomenal, I found myself actually very calm throughout this entire experience, or so I thought. At least, I never felt scared once. I was methodically going through the memorized procedures, attempting to restart my engine to no avail. It was dead.

With my focus buried inside, my peripheral vision caught a mountain peak making its way up the canopy, a sign I was getting low. It snapped me into the next step; preparing for the ejection.

Because the F-16 seat is reclined 30 degrees, it is essential the pilot's back is resting against the seat. If not, serious injury from the initial 30G kick of the rocket motors can cause serious spinal damage. As time neared, knowing I was needing to exit my Viper in dramatic fashion, I zipped off one last radio call: "I'm getting out. I'm getting out." *Still* no call sign.

At that time, I wrapped both hands around the ejection handle between my legs (exactly as taught to do in the simulator), and established a perfect body position. Just before pulling the handle, I had one final thought.

How crazy the mind works. For whatever reason, I thought to glance down at the altimeter so I knew the altitude I got out at. Never was this mentioned in any training. I came up with it all on my own in that instant. So, back straight against the 30 degree reclined seat, I gazed down with my eyes at the altimeter and the dial read 1,700 feet above the ground. Then, I pulled with everything I had—and *nothing happened.*

What is Time?

From the moment I was thrown forward in the straps to leaving the jet, a total of one minute and nineteen seconds would elapse. *Nothing happened*, yet, it did happen in a tenth of a second! Time is interesting.

We have been programmed with solar time, a 24-hour clock since before our birth. It serves us well. But is that what time really is? It is not. Think of your dreams and how we know what can seem to be hours are only minutes of the 24-hour clock.

Time with a lover flies by while waiting in a government office drags on. It's all relative! Back in the 60's and 70's, Milton Erickson studied the human mind extensively in respect to time with some fascinating results.

For instance, one subject under a hypnotic trance thought it took them hours to count 862 individual cotton balls. It was actually just three seconds! If you have ever seen the movie, *The Matrix* where Neo is dodging bullets, then you can perfectly understand what I am about to explain.

After pulling the handle, there was a pause I certainly wasn't expecting! Like the super slow video of today, I can replay this next fraction of a second frame by frame, as slow as I wish.

Following this pause, I heard a pop. It was the sound of the charges releasing the canopy. Next, I could see the front of the bubble canopy rising ever so slowly, frame by frame. As it flew away, I began to feel a gentle breeze (I was actually traveling at some 200 M.P.H.). I had my helmet and oxygen mask on, and visor down over my eyes, but I felt the breeze against the exposed skin and body.

The 30-40lb pull of the ejection handle came with much adrenaline and it only traveled so far. As it reached its stop, I just kept pulling, not even aware I was. Like curling a bar bell locked in its stand, my back began to be pulled away from the seat as my gaze stared lower inside.

A PERSONAL STORY

Black smoke was emerging everywhere from beneath the seat and fire was all around my boots. I actually said to myself, "Oh, my gosh, my feet are going to burn." Immediately after that, I got a serious kick in the butt! It felt like I had bent over and Hulk Hogan swung a 2x4 across my derrière.

Leaving My Jet

As the seat began up the rails, the all-important straight back was no longer. It was curled as the seat began racing out of the cockpit. I fought the G's and got my back straight again (I suffer back issues to this day) and at that point, time went back to normal.

It was just a tenth of a second from initiating the pull to the kick in the pants that seemed like forever. It was another tenth to clear the aircraft; two tenths of a second that seemed like an eternity!

To better grasp what this was like, here is a link to an actual ejection from Viper 6, Opposing Solo, of the USAF Thunderbirds. In this accident, the pilot set the wrong altimeter (human factor) resulting in not enough altitude to complete the maneuver. It is another example of when deletions, distortions, and generalizations lead to a lack of awareness. Fortunately for him, like me, the ejection sequence went flawlessly. https://youtu.be/zD3fdKmMdQM .

As for the rest of my ejection, I had a minor parachute malfunction, followed by another but overcame both. I ended up landing in small trees that actually helped ease the otherwise harsh landing.

Where Did Everybody Go?

Now, what happened to the rest of the four-ship? I expected to hear them overhead, having witnessed a live ejection but there was silence. At this point I had no idea Viper 3 had not been with me and that Viper 2 had experienced VHF radio failure. That all came to light afterwards. I pulled out my radio and quickly realized they had no idea where I was, although by now Viper 3 figured out it wasn't Viper 2 with the problem!

As pilots, we actually perform better under heightened stress. But when it reaches a certain point, as with anyone, clarity is lost and the *computer* becomes overwhelmed, slowing down. As Viper 3 took command of the rescue mission, he sent the assets in the wrong direction by misinterpreting his navigational information. He soon corrected his error, and I was picked up about an hour later.

The Lesson

How much lower would the overall stress have been if I simply added my call sign to that very first radio call? Immense, for everyone, including the outside agencies sent in the wrong direction, for the overall stress level would have been greatly diminished.

What are you possibly missing on a daily basis? What are you *assuming* others should infer from your deletions, distortions, and generalizations? What are you inferring from theirs? Can you relate?

In a flowing conversation of the past, have you thought you were being perfectly clear with your words coming from your map of the world, yet were completely misunderstood by the other individual(s)?

Awareness and language are so vital to all of us—from our family units, work, or in any form of relationship imaginable. Awareness is the key, and opening up our narrow frames to becoming more consciously attentive is the beginning of the solution.

* * *

A PERSONAL STORY

Preparing Yourself to New Pathways

1) When opportunity arises, it's too late to prepare.

2) When we leave out valuable information, confusion, disagreements, and confrontations arise.

3) The more aware you train yourself to be of your surroundings, your language and that of others, the greater overall communication you'll experience.

AWARENESS 16

"With awareness comes transformation and freedom."

ECKHART TOLLE

This is one of the most important chapters in this book. I encourage you to be fully present as you read through it. What you experience in life around you and within you is about awareness.

As we've been learning, increasing your awareness changes everything in and around your world. Becoming consciously aware changes your internal map of how you experience your internal and external worlds. It provides you a wider frame of reference and the ability to maintain greater perspective.

What Do We Notice?

We are exposed to billions of bits of information each moment, yet our conscious mind only interprets a fraction of this vastness: anything more and it would lock up, just like computers sometimes do. Yet, the subconscious mind is continuously receiving it all with little limitation.

Of course, it's all one mind, but this distinction between the two really helps in the discussion for clearer understanding. So, what determines what the subconscious mind allows the conscious mind to be aware of? It's a part of the brain called the Reticular Activating System (RAS). The RAS determines what you are consciously aware of around you.

My good friend, Jeff Senour, is the leader of CTS, a rock band that is all about our youth and veterans. Jeff's amazing creativity developed his signature *Freedom Rock Experience* where he invites high school orchestras and bands to share their stage. Together, they rock out the audience, playing Jeff's music in spectacular fashion. As a leader for the youth, Jeff gets how significant each of them is.

In a world that's so big, it is easy to become unaware of our individual importance. From the stage he shares with them, *"There are 86,400 seconds in a day, roughly 1 million seconds in 11 days, 1 billion seconds in 31 years, and 1 trillion seconds in 30,000 years. Over 7 billion people on the planet and no two are alike, made of just 23 pairs of chromosomes in the human genome. You are special. There is not another exactly like you."*

How Aware Are You?

Right now, on Earth, you are spinning at about 1,000 M.P.H., traveling around the sun at about 67,000 M.P.H., in a solar system hurling through space at 515,000 M.P.H.! Yet, until you just read this, how aware of it were you?

Your perspective, your awareness had you believe you were sitting still, reading a book, as those seconds clicked by, yet, *that is not reality!* Reality is you are travelling over a half-million miles every hour! So, what is perspective? What is time? What is *reality?* What exactly are we missing on a daily basis?

Understanding the RAS

I remember a game we'd play with my daughter in the car called, *I see.* One person would name a color and then anyone in the car would call out and point to that color as it passed on by. Each time a call-out was made that person earned a point.

Let's say the color yellow was picked. You may not think of the color yellow often while you're driving, but you'd be amazed how frequently you'll see it once you bring it forward to your conscious thought. Yellow cars, buildings, signs, and other various objects suddenly appear everywhere!

Now, did more things magically turn yellow or is something else going on here? Those yellow objects were already there, but because they did not serve a purpose or were not deemed important enough prior, your mind naturally deleted their existence from conscious thought.

However, once yellow was deemed important, the RAS was officially directed to begin noticing yellow. And because it was a game, yellow became king!

How about when you are thinking of purchasing a new car or right after you have? All of a sudden you are no longer the trend-setter! It seems you start seeing them on every road you travel. Did they just magically appear, or were they there all along, unnoticed?

Perspectives

We've mentioned individual maps of the world throughout this book. In a commercial airliner, there are two pilots. Following this logic of individual maps, neither is thinking, seeing or hearing *exactly* the same experience. If there is a mistake made by one, the other catches the error, preventing a sort of snowball effect.

I spoke to a surgeon once who said the easiest way to prevent mistakes in surgery is to have two surgeons present, like us on the flight deck, but the costs prevent such. Makes sense, doesn't it?

Although these examples are enlightening, let's push it further to the extreme. This deletion, distortion, or generalization process can make you miss or misinterpret vital information. Somehow, what should have been important information ended up outside the frame of awareness. This is very true in aviation where the majority of accidents are the result of some type of human factor error.

Consequences

I have lost more friends flying the F-16 than I have fingers and toes, and not one of them was due to a mechanical malfunction. Each was rooted in a misinterpretation or something missed all together. One of my favorite instructors during initial F-16 transition was Lou. We were mission planning towards the end of the seven month long training when, out of the blue, he stopped. He looked at me poignantly to say, "Guy, you will have more fun flying the Viper than imaginable." Shifting to a very serious stare into my eyes he added, "But beware, a moment of inattention and it will bite you in a heartbeat." Four years later, Lou lost his life due to a misrepresentation of his flight conditions while flying his Viper over Alaska.

Aviation is safer today than at any other time in history. One reason is directly related to the emphasis placed on educating pilots in the area of human factors. Targeted training greatly increases the RAS in awareness of what is most important in observation and interpretation of all that is going on in the immediate environment. Throughout preparation, briefings, taxiing, and flight, it also includes communications between the pilots in the cockpit, flight attendants, ground agents, dispatch, and air traffic control.

Such training today far exceeds that of the past. The result is millions of passengers are transferred to their destinations all over the world without concern, with most completely unaware that their lives reside in the level of *awareness* the two pilots up front have that day.

Eastern Airline Mishap

There's an infamous accident that highlights this advancement of safety from the past. I share to further emphasize this significance of awareness.

In the world of flying this *awareness* is known as *Situational Awareness* (SA). Being aware of your surroundings and how closely your map is representing *reality* at any given moment. As the saying goes, "How do you know when you've lost SA? When you regain it."

And you always hoped to regain it before tragedy struck.

In 1972, Eastern airlines Flight 401 crashed into the Florida everglades killing 101 of the 163 passengers and crew members aboard. Was there anything mechanically wrong with the airplane? Nope. It was in perfect working order. And back then, there was a third pilot in the cockpit, unlike the two of today. So how is it possible that three experienced pilots could allow a perfectly good airplane to fly into the ground?

Would you believe a tiny light bulb? The short story is that when the landing gear was extended for its approach into Miami, the nose landing gear indicator light inside the cockpit did not illuminate. The pilots now had to determine if the nose gear was indeed not down, or, if it was just the light bulb. As the decision process ensued amongst the tired and fatigued pilots, the Captain inadvertently pushed against the yoke which put the aircraft into an unrecognized decent. Typically, when the autopilot is accidently or intentionally turned off, there is an auditory warning that alerts the pilots. However, there are no such alarms for this situation for it is a design feature of the autopilot that is utilized purposefully at times.

With the aircraft now in this slow decent, the airplane was essentially flying *pilotless*. All three pilots were locked onto that light bulb, like Viper 3 was locked onto Viper 2. In an environment that requires constant vigilance of flight parameters at all times, the distraction of the situation led to the absence of fundamental airmanship.

The crew wrapped their attention around the nose gear situation, **believing** they were in level flight (their map / mind-read / awareness). They were completely unaware that in *reality* they were headed for the ground. They allowed themselves to narrow their focus (channelized attention) so much that even though the nose gear was indeed down, a calamity of errors, especially in SA, led the plane to impact the ground.

Somewhere In Between

Now that we can clearly see the two extremes of the RAS's impact, playful and life threatening, how can we utilize this information to our benefit? When it comes to opportunities in a world of possibilities, it is endless. In Section IV, you will be exposed to Empowering Questions; similar to affirmations, but different and far more powerful. They are a perfect example of opening your awareness through the RAS to recognize and attract that which you desire in your life.

Motorcycles

Here's another example of how I've personally utilized this concept of awareness with riding motorcycles, long before *learning* of the RAS. I rode for years with a specific mindset kept at the fore front of my consciousness (like the color yellow in the game above). Every time I rode the streets, I'd tell myself, "Everyone is trying to kill me."

Knowing what I do now about language, this might not have been the most empowering way to have phrased this statement for it could attract the very thing I wished to avoid! But it did work and it did save my life on numerous occasions.

The concept in riding with this mindset was to recognize (be aware of) a possibly bad situation long *before* it happened. That, without this "awareness," recognizing the situation may have come too late to avoid me becoming yet another statistic.

There is another word for this in aviation as well as on the road and in most situations: *Complacency*—that feeling of security, often unaware of some potential danger. I knew I had to avoid that to survive.

My mindset consisted of this thought as well: "Always be able to see their eyes." Consciously, I rode in a position where I could see the other driver's eyes in their mirror or through their windshield. By doing so, I knew they could see me, and intuitively, I could garner much about *their* awareness of their surroundings.

Elke's Experience

My wife grew up in Germany and rode a motorcycle for many years before we met. She was extremely comfortable on a bike, and we later bought her a Harley Soft Tail Custom, which she road for years in Germany and Italy. Riding in Europe is very different from the States. Not just the roads and rules of the road but in the driver's awareness. A European's RAS is trained differently. Their mandatory driver's education demands much higher scrutiny, including motorcycle awareness, than here in the States.

After we moved to Phoenix, Elke never felt truly comfortable on the roads. At that time, Phoenix had one of the highest red light runner stats in the country! She had a detectable fear which did not belong on a bike. In December of 1998, our friend and neighbor was killed on his way home after a day's ride with his friends. A teenager made a left turn on yellow right in front of him. He never stood a chance. Elke sold her bike soon afterwards. To ease her worry, I did, too, the following spring.*

> *Elke told me upon reading this that what changed after Mark's death was in how she used that phrase, "Everyone is **trying** to kill me." It shifted to a place of lack and disempowerment of, "Everyone **is** trying to kill me." Very interesting; the power of language and a prime example for our next chapter.

Lessons to Learn From

There is much to be pulled from this little ditty about motorcycles. First, I often wonder if my friend rode with the same mindset as me. We had never talked about it, even though we rode together often. Yet, there were a couple of instances that had me wonder, and in hindsight, I wish that conversation would have happened. He was extremely experienced, but what if he had been anticipating that car turning on the yellow rather than trusting she wouldn't? We will never know. Complacency never belongs on a bike or while driving for that matter.

As for my friend's fateful day, what about the awareness of the teenage driver in this case? She stated she never *saw* the motorcycle until it hit her car. This is a case where *her* lack of awareness cost my friend's life. She just didn't see him. Motorcycles weren't present in her RAS at that moment. Like the *gorilla* you'll meet in a moment, it simply was outside her focus when she made that left turn, even though *it was there!*

Another thought is whether or not my friend was looking at *her* eyes as he approached the intersection. Did he notice she never once looked at him? Or had she and still didn't see him? Regardless, it was a tragic case of when lack of awareness cost a life with a spiral effect to all the family and friends involved.

If you've ever had or been involved in a car accident, chances are you asked yourself how could that have happened? What did I miss, or why didn't I *see* it coming? Most likely, somehow your awareness was narrowed: *"How do you know when you've lost SA? When you regain it."*

Today, texting and driving is a large threat. It reduces SA as the RAS is diverted to other tasks away from the road, similar to the Eastern Airlines story. Same goes for driving under the influence. Great strides have been made with alcohol and driving. Now, this legalization of Marijuana across the country raises new concerns in this respect.

Enough of the Drama

My point in bringing awareness to all of this in such dramatic fashion with the RAS is to drive home just how significant it is. I've laid out a few extreme scenarios of what can happen when we *miss* an important piece of information.

Of course, it's not just with flying, motorcycles, or driving. I'm sure you can begin to grasp this concept as it relates to other areas of life. Have details been missed or an oversight occurred that left you wondering, "How did I do that?" Such is actually quite common in our everyday lives.

On a daily basis, what are you missing? What are you walking right past that you've been searching for simply because it wasn't registering with your RAS in a way that would allow your conscious mind to recognize it?

At Niurka's one day events, she plays a short video of two teams, each passing a basketball. The object is to count the number of passes made by one of the teams. And at each event most people in the audience miss three very obvious changes in the video, to include a *gorilla* walking slowly across, even stopping to beat his chest! Why? Because the people have their RAS focused on counting the passes. The video highlights how we miss items of importance every day because our focus is somewhere else. The missing of *"Gorilla Opportunities."*

Here's another one you can find on YouTube called WhoDunnit? https://youtu.be/ubNF9QNEQLA How well did you do?

How many of you are searching for the ideal partner? How many times has he or she walked right passed you and went unnoticed because the focus was misdirected? Or the perfect job? Or the perfect business opportunity? Or that promotion? Or that *thing* which you desire in your life? By opening up your RAS to that which is important to you in a way the conscious mind understands, you greatly increase your awareness, and begin noticing answers and opportunities that *already existed* around you.

The Thermostat

Here is one more characteristic of the RAS that is important to understand. It acts sort of like a thermostat. It keeps you at a *normal* level, if you will. As you set out on some exciting new venture, you take the lever of your thermostat and raise it warmer, representing stretching yourself out of your comfort zone. Your mind, however, will subconsciously bring the thermostat (RAS) back into its *normal* range over time.

This is another reason that without NLP, which creates changes quickly, we tend to fall back into old habits. Without NLP, you have to stay outside your old comfort zone long enough until the RAS does a reset of your new normal, a new habit. Therefore, keeping new awareness present within your RAS is imperative.

For example, you don't see the color *yellow* forever while driving, nor do you see that *new car*. Eventually, it gets dropped from conscious thought. This is why focused training in aviation or driver's education works. It is why *every time* I rode my motorcycle, I reminded myself continuously of the threat. Or, each time I flew the Viper, I remembered my instructor's words of caution. I know for a fact I'm alive today as a result.

Moving Onto Language

Where we are going next is awareness of our language. Now that you understand the significance of awareness, how can you marry this to your everyday experiences? It is in your language. This one facet will change nearly every aspect of your life. In fact, all you've read thus far has been setting up these next two chapters on language.

As you become more aware of the words you use you begin unleashing your true power. The more cognizant of your words, the better you understand what is going on within you at the *subconscious* level. The more you are aware of others' language, the greater you can understand their map of the world. By understanding each other's maps at a more specific level, your overall communication greatly increases. Your understandings of why you and others do certain things or behave in certain ways becomes readily apparent. The mystery is no longer.

In its totality, this awareness of language enhances how you navigate through life. You can notice disempowering language and empowering language. You can catch yourself and others "in effect" or "at cause." You can recognize moving away or towards your desires. And, by doing so, you can immediately replace words and meanings that do not serve you with words of action. The more you do this the more you are reminding your RAS of what is most important to you.

Over time, you raise your *new normal*, your overall level of consciousness, and as you do, more and more opportunities arise. You become more empowered authentically, and yes, you actually begin to appreciate all of who you are, your *Authentic Truth*, even more. You become a better spouse, partner, friend, supporter, colleague, and person in general because you are aware and understand the impactful difference language makes.

But in order to make that difference, you first have to be *aware* of it. It is my sincerest desire you take away from this chapter that importance of being aware.

* * *

Awareness to New Pathways

1) The RAS limits our conscious view of the world.

2) The greater your awareness the grander your perspective and overall understanding of yourself and the world around you.

3) Essential details are missed every day. Importance is in the details. We must raise our awareness of language which is a significant detail.

LANGUAGE - PART 1 17

> *"The single biggest problem in communication is the illusion it has taken place."*
>
> GEORGE BERNARD SHAW

You are three years old, playful, happy, smiling, laughing, expressing your inner joy and artistic side with crayons and water colors as your mom encourages you to play full-out. She gets distracted, leaving you alone, briefly. Wanting to impress her with your increasing creative abilities, you decide in a colorful moment to expand your artwork to the white painted wall behind you.

Several minutes pass and you're feeling so proud, gleefully spreading pure joy of rainbow colors all over that white wall. Your mom returns in horror at the same time your dad arrives home from a troubled day at work. Consequently, you become the recipient of a double dose of wielded anger: Mom upset and embarrassed, while your artwork is the perfect outlet for Dad's day of pent up frustration from work.

And there you are, having gone from a moment of love, peace, joy, and security to utter confusion and fright in an instant! From pure bliss to the unleashing of angry words and possibly even being grabbed and shook. Love instantly transformed to startled confusion, all the while your mind attempts to contextualize this mystery, *without filters at the age of three.*

Although far from your parent's intention, this is how a lasting imprint in your subconscious mind can be created.

The Beauty of Language

What is language?

- "A warm smile is the universal language of kindness."
  ~ William Arthur Ward
- "Kindness is the language which the deaf can hear and the blind can see." ~ Mark Twain
- "If you talk to a man in a language he understands, that goes to his head. If you talk to him in his language, that goes to his heart." ~ Nelson Mandela
- "The language of friendship is not words but meanings."
  ~ Henry David Thoreau
- "Words may be false and full of art; sighs are the natural language of the heart." ~ Thomas Shadwell
- "Language…has created the word 'loneliness' to express the pain of being alone. And it has created the word 'solitude' to express the glory of being alone." ~ Paul Tillich
- "Summer afternoon, summer afternoon; to me the two most beautiful words in the English language." ~ Henry James
- "One advantage of photography is that it's visual and can transcend language." ~ Lisa Kristine
- "The world's most famous and popular language is music."
  ~ Psy
- "Feelings or emotions are the universal language and are to be honored. They are the authentic expression of who you are at your deepest place." ~ Judith Wright

- "The limits of my language means the limits of my world."
  ~ Ludwig Wittgenstein

What Are Words?

Wow! Have you ever wondered what language is and how it affects every aspect of your world? Words create our realities. Words form images in our minds and images are interpreted with our words. Those pictures create a defined panoramic elucidation, further influencing our map of reality.

Likewise, when we experience something, images form in our minds and the panoramic is interpreted into words. These words give meaning to the experience. This meaning is of great importance.

How we interpret these words rests exclusively with our individual maps, which gives them their meanings and thus our way of *experiencing* the world. This also affects how we experience the *other*. Words can express love, joy, and happiness or hateful angry words. Words have the ability to nurture or tear a person down, including ourselves, for we are talking to ourselves *all* the time when consciously awake.

Putting these words into context gives us language. Language is our way of expressing the panoramic experience and is as powerful as the quotes above reflect.

Language is also far greater than *just* words as we will see. There is the deep underlying structure within our subconscious mind: our values, thinking, and behaviors that express our programming. And then there are the non-verbal and physiological aspects as well.

Combined, we can begin unraveling the mystery behind the results we get in life. It is the crust of our discussion throughout this book. As we begin to further unravel this enigma, let's begin with words and sentences, the Linguistics of NLP.

LANGUAGE - PART 1

Uncovering the Structure of Language

Many, especially those in the area of linguistics, for years had been trying to understand why a certain few therapists were able to get quick, effective, and lasting results with their clients, as opposed to others who had ongoing clients for months or years. They recognized a pattern, yet they were still unable to quantify it.

In the early seventies, rather than trying to understand the processes that therapists were using as the linguists of the past, Richard Bandler and John Grinder asked the question, *what are these few doing that is different?* In their search, they uncovered seven specific strategies being used.* It is from this research the NLP model was born.

> *Virginia Satir was one of the primary therapists they studied who attained consistent, amazing results with her clients. She was using all seven strategies but was aware of only five of them until Bandler pointed the other two out.*

In uncovering this vital aspect of the mind, they identified the various ways visual, auditory, kinesthetic, and processing cues are coded within language and interpreted by an individual. They claim this had never been done prior and opened the door to incredible new insights on how the mind formulates and interprets language.

The ways to describe the human experience are limitless. However, Bandler and Grinder determined the "structure" behind our language is actually *limited*. The Black Piano from chapter 13 is capable of infinite ways to create beautiful music but is limited in its structure: body, keys, hammers, and wires.

Although each person has infinite ways to create thought with their words, how each person ultimately sends, receives, and interprets that information, building their own internally represented picture, is quite specific and has structure.

Ultimately, the first model Bandler and Grinder created to understand this structure behind language was the *Meta-Model*.

The Meta-Model

Previously, we discussed the Meta-Model in using questions to dig deeper into the subconscious mind to overcome secondary gain and deletions, distortions, and generalizations (DDG) present in a person's statement. We are going to discuss them in more detail now. For simplicity, I've decided to use DDG as an acronym.

Here are some more examples of DDGs using the Meta-Model to illicit specifics:

- **More is better.** More of what? Better for whom or what?
- **All businessmen are crooks?** *All* businessmen? *Every* single one? How are they crooks? To whom are they crooks to?
- **There are no good men/women out there anymore; they are all taken.** Again, *all men/women? None*, not even one? Have you ever come across *one* that wasn't taken? Is there anyone you know who recently found a good man/woman?
- **I just feel tired all the time.** How so? All the time? Is there ever a time when you do not feel tired?
- **Bad luck seems to follow me.** How so? How often? What happens when it doesn't follow you?

In order to understand what is going on within the person's own map of the world (Deep Structure), we have to dig into the statement by asking questions. Questions that begin with *how, who, what, which,* and *when* are an easy way to begin. *Why* can be used but is not as specific and usually elicits a *because* response (in effect).

Here is the main point of all this: When a person becomes stuck in a problem, part of the problem is a limited view. They see only a *limited* number of choices from their conscious mind. These few choices loop over and over, providing no apparent solution or way to exit their problem. Thus, using a DDG as vital information further entraps the person within the problem.

Recall the Quantum Linguistic exercise with Kelly; questions three and four force the person to go "outside" this current frame, beyond the looping in their conscious mind. (reference page 112)

The goal is to recover the impoverished language, the DDGs, to expand the person's choices. By opening up their awareness from their map of the world to the world's map of the situation, they *step outside their current frame of the problem*. This increases their possibilities and provides incredible, personal insight to their own way of thinking. As a result, the problem is seen differently and new choices emerge. These new choices were there all along but couldn't be *seen* by the conscious mind; they were hidden from it.

Meta-Model Therapy Examples

In their book, *The Structure of Magic*, Bandler and Grinder talk of an experiment they set up between therapists allowed only to utilize this "Meta-Model" technique. By solely using the client's language, they were able to guide the individual into uncovering their impoverished map of the world, their DDGs creating their problem without solutions.

Nothing like this had ever been done in traditional therapy, and there was no shortage of opposition. However, the proof was in the results.

The complete transcripts with the narrative explaining all the options within the Meta-Model are available within their book. They also explicitly state that this technique is not meant to be a stand-alone method of therapy but one to be added to the tool box for the therapist. Yet, their objective was solely to prove we actually do "code" our deep-structured language and that it can be brought to the conscious mind simply through asking appropriate questions.

In a way, this relates back to my earlier statement that the *story doesn't matter*. In working with a person, I am interested in their programming, how did they arrive here in their current situation.

Example One

Bandler and Grinder provide two such examples from the experiment. In the first, the male client initially states (surface structure): *"I don't know how to make a good impression on **people**."*

After the ***forty-seventh exchange*** between the male client and the therapist utilizing only the Meta-Model, we learn that ***people*** actually is about a new girl that's entered his life that he likes but believes she doesn't notice him.

When the therapist digs further with the Meta-Model, the client quantifies the real area of conflict within him: his mother. That, as a child, she would not recognize his efforts.

By the end of this experimental session (93 exchanges total), the client is awakened with new possibilities on how to approach this girl he is attracted to, without the mind-reading of believing he knows what *the girl* is thinking.

Example Two

In the second example, the client is a lady who rooms with two other girlfriends and four kids amongst them all living together. This client uses so many generalizations in the course of the therapy session that even the therapist gets confused at one point! Her problem is initially stated as: *"I want help with…well, my roommates. They don't seem to understand me."*

What unfolds is the client discovering her not wanting to hurt others is actually causing her own pain! Once the therapist successfully navigates through eighty-seven exchanges with the client, she realizes, *"If I let them know when I feel pushed around or want something, then maybe they would be more sensitive."*

Take a look at the opening and final statements again. She has moved from *in effect* to *at cause*, taking responsibility rather than playing the victim. As a reminder, **a problem can only be solved when at cause.**

You Can, Too

Have you ever been called upon by a friend to help them with an issue? How would you navigate to have your friend discover for himself/herself that the issue is *within* their self without building resistance or rejecting you? The Meta-Model is one such way.

This technique is a learnable tool that requires patience with the absence of emotion. When you listen intently to what is truly being said, you already are performing the first requirement in applying this model. Uncovering their DDGs and map of the world, while honoring everything about that person in the process, is then simply a matter of asking the right questions.

Deciphering Language

We are going to spend a lot of focus on the awareness of DDGs, but I wish to clarify that not all DDGs are bad. They also help us to simplify our world and be able to organize the wealth of information we are confronted with constantly. As you have already learned, the RAS can only handle so much. What's important is understanding how DDGs affect our choices and decisions as well as how we hear and interpret our own and other's communication.

The Positives from DDGs

Remember my philosophy about riding motorcycles? "Everyone is out there trying to kill me," and "Always ride so you can see their eyes." These are two examples of what I would consider worthy, ecological uses of generalized information.

By using these "universal quantifiers" of *everyone* and *always*, I was able to be far more consciously aware of more drivers on the road than if I had tried to quantify such. Cars with young drivers would be more specific but not accurate. Not all young drivers are unaware all the time. It would also exclude old drivers with poor vision.

Even though more specific, it is not more accurate. Very conscious drivers who are very aware also share the road. My generalization adds these drivers, too, for anyone can get distracted for a moment. In actuality, there is no way of knowing *who* or *where* the threat would come from, thus, why not be prepared from *all* drivers?

It also distorts in saying *kill*. Of course, I don't truly believe any driver sets out on the road consciously looking to kill me or any other motorcycle rider that day. Overall, this DDG of mine successfully served its purpose for all those years of riding, providing heightened awareness while on the road.

The Challenge of DDGs

Now, let's move on to the limitations of these DDGs. Have you ever known someone entrenched, *stuck in a problem*, a disempowered situation where you could so plainly see what they ought to do? The solution is right there and you can see it clearly!

With great care, you put forward the suggestion of how they can *fix* their problem. And what usually happens? Not only do they not *see* or understand what you are suggesting, they often resist it. This can lead to a wall preventing effective communication, further entrenching themselves in the very problem you were trying to help with. It can be very frustrating for both.

Thus, the key to helping another, or even yourself, get beyond the current way of seeing a problem, is stepping outside the current frame, and recovering the impoverished language and DDGs creating the current map. Doing this through appropriate questions helps recover the deep underlying structure of the problem, providing new possibilities and solutions to solve the problem.

By asking very specific questions, while being fully present and *listening* intently, a whole new world can be opened for the other person. The easiest way to begin understanding how they are seeing the world is to ask that simple two worded Meta-Model question, "How so?" This alone will force them to access some of the missing pieces they have "nominalized" within their mind.

What you are looking for in the other as they describe their plight is generalized statements and/or missing arguments behind their *reasoning*. This applies to your own self-talk as well. *I wish I wasn't depressed all the time.* You can literally ask yourself, *"How so? All the time? What do you mean by depressed?"*

This last question is very important. If I am working with someone, what depression means to me may be different from what it means to the person making this statement. My views of depression are irrelevant. How the person internalizes depression (the panoramic picture) is what matters, and you cannot know that unless you inquire.

In using this Meta-Model, I don't allow them to *go into the story* (drama). I immediately insert a pattern interrupt if they do. My goal is to ask questions that illicit the meaning they have applied to depression. I want to get them to step outside their *old* frame.

Where Confusion Arises

Without filling in the blanks created by the DDGs, more often than not, major communication challenges in relationships, business, education, with the self, and just about any other area you can think of, arise. Why? Because often vital information is not being communicated by the person actually speaking, making it even more challenging for the receiver.

The conscious words expressed in the message are hidden from the deep structure within the originator's *own* mind. And if there are DDGs by the person actually *doing* the communicating, how can the receiver possibly, with accuracy, understand what the communicator's deeper meaning is? It simply cannot happen. The only indicator of the deeper structure at that point may be in the speaker's physiology, a huge aspect of language. These include body and eye movements, complexion, emotions, and tonality to name a few.

When DDGs are present in the speaker's language, you know it represents an incomplete map. These DDGs create a false perception of the world's reality for that person and increase the likelihood of misinterpretations. The perceived message broadcasted is *broadened* to all the choices of possible meanings which actually exist.

Additionally, this leads the listener to further project his/her *own* beliefs, mental map, and mind-reading into what the speaker is saying! **The listener *knows* what the speaker meant, when in actuality, it's most likely a perception** (mind-read).

In a casual meeting or business setting, this can lead to great misunderstandings that quickly escalate and soon depart from the true objective of the conversation; tempers can flare, business deals lost, and friendships shattered.

As relationships deepen, the dynamics change, but the risk is still present in different ways. In intimate relationships, for example, one can almost complete the other's sentences, albeit, incorrectly at times. This can lead to tremendous confusion, especially when one *thinks*, or worse *knows* what the other means.

Adding to the Complexity

Compounding this challenge are the different primary modalities (modes of communication). If one is Kinesthetic and the other Audio Digital (AD), as with Catalaya and Claudia, not only do these DDGs create misperceptions, they create arguments and complete misunderstandings; the message sent is received differently than intended. It's important to understand that once it lands in the receiver's

LANGUAGE - PART 1

map, it can be very difficult to change its interpretation/perception (my poor radio call convincing Viper 3 it was Viper 2 with the problem, not me. He *knew* it was Viper 2 with the problem).

* * *

Understanding Language to New Pathways

1) Words do matter.

2) Our maps drive our language patterns and how we receive messages from others.

3) Understanding language patterns can help unravel the mystery of our current results.

LANGUAGE - PART 2   18

"A client is a client because they are out of rapport with themselves."

MILTON ERICKSON

When I originally wrote out the content on language, it was over 17,000 words long. Each of the chapters you've been reading thus far averages about 3,000. Thus, much thought was given in shrinking the original content down to just two, shortened chapters.

In the end, I intentionally omitted getting into the *technical* aspects of language that can already be found in many NLP books. Rather, I elected to continue in the same style and format for a more practical understanding. If you are intrigued to go deeper into the language of words, a great place to start is the Milton Model. This alone will provide great insights.

Listening IS an Art

Since most people are unaware of all of these simple concepts just discussed in the previous chapter, is it any wonder why there are so many misunderstandings in daily communication? Now that you are being awakened to the significance in language patterns, how can you improve your communication and help others as well? It is in your listening.

I cannot tell you how many times I'm asked a question that requires a rather complicated or at least thorough answer. I'll be a few words into my response when the other person interrupts and says something like, "Oh, I know *exactly* what you're talking about." Of course, knowing this person doesn't have a clue, I just honor their belief of perception and projection (mind-read).

Attempting to prove otherwise would be futile at that point because they've already convinced themselves they 'know' and are simply *not* listening. Also, almost any time a person 'reacts' without a pause, you can ensure they are not truly listening, at least not constructively.

How do you know when a person is truly listening to what you are saying? They will *respond* with a question, repeat back what you've said, or pause while they digest what they've just heard. You will feel it as a sign of being in rapport.

Not Listening

When they are not truly listening, the opposite is true; no questions, never repeat back, and never pause to digest your words. You also feel *uncomfortable* for you are out of rapport with them.

Too often, people are triggered to get out what they want to say. They are already formulating their response, or perspective and usually can't wait for a break from you to spout it out. They may in fact even interrupt you, mid-sentence because they are convinced their message is far more important than what you have to say.

The moment that begins to occur, they cannot possibly be hearing what you are saying fully and completely. At that point, you have a decision to make. Help them become a better listener, or simply become a better listener yourself until they're ready.

When I am in such a situation, I let the other person speak. I'll ask them detailed questions and allow them to go fully into their story until they are exhausted. Usually, but not always, this leads to them eventually returning in kind. If they do, it's wonderful. If they don't, I let it go.

Moving yourself into this type of awareness is so freeing. If I don't let it go, I stand the risk of allowing myself to become frustrated, trying to be heard, and forcing my desire onto the other person. If they are not ready to listen, I'd be wasting my time. Ultimately, in doing this, I'm at peace.

There are instances, of course, when conveying your message is critical when the other is not ready to or will not listen to your message. Simply speaking *at* them does not work. The *best* way to break through that barrier is a significant pattern interrupt; go for a walk with them or *re-enter* the room to start over. Essentially, it is through rapport.

It's About More than Just Words

It is extremely important to understand that "language" is not just the words we use. Much of it is non-verbal in our physiology, the Neuro in NLP. The basics of NLP state that 55% of communication is body language, 38% is the tone of voice, and **only 7%** are the actual words spoken.

How vital would classes on physiology be in our schools then? What would the long-term effects be as generations are taught this significance? I was never introduced to such in my *formal* education. Since physiology alone comprises over *half* of our overall communication, how valuable would this be to high schoolers in preparing them for the *real world*? How about with parents?

Physiological characteristics can be general and very specific depending upon your level of observation. The subconscious mind sees the flushing of the face, changing of lower lip size, rate and depth of breathing, eye and body movements. These are a few of the more common physiological traits to become aware of *consciously*.

It's About Rapport

What is rapport? In its simplest term, it is **trust**. It's getting on the same page of whom you are communicating with. It is closeness with the other person where they develop the *desire* to listen, and you actually *hear* the other person's message effectively.

Rapport is never a solo act. Even with yourself, rapport is created between you and your inner voice, physiology, and tonality. When you are frustrated, angry or experiencing any other negative type of emotion, you are out of rapport with yourself. The opposite of course is true as well. When harmonious with yourself, you are in rapport ,and you experience that inner joy and love fully.

That same type of harmony is what you are striving for in meaningful conversations. Rather than with your inner voice and physiology, you are looking to create rapport with the other in those same areas. Thus, the more natural this becomes within yourself, the more easily harmony can be created outside yourself.

It's like an arrangement of music, with all players on the same sheet of music that makes it a masterpiece. When the *different* instruments of the orchestra are playing from a place of "alignment" (strings, brass, reeds, percussion), the more majestic and beautiful the music becomes. When each instrument is off playing their own thing, there is discourse.

In other words, even if you are Kinesthetic and the person you are communicating with is Ad (flower and computer), you can still make beautiful music together in your communication, **provided you are in rapport.**

I love this statement from Niurka:

"...*rapport is not something missing that we work to gain; rather, it is a natural state emerging from a consciousness attuned to LOVE. When we are in alignment with our true Self, we effortlessly glide into rapport with others."*

I'd add that because rapport is as much about how we communicate with ourselves as well as others, we have just nailed the importance of this book: **Falling in love with ourselves as a natural state of being allows living in a state of rapport with our Self; our Authentic Truth.**

And by doing so, we move through life in flow with others, not resistance.

Aspects of Rapport

When we naturally "mirror and match" the communication of others, we begin building deeper rapport with them. This mirror and matching is not about being overt and making the other person aware that is what you are doing. That will just raise tension. Rather, it is speaking, and reflecting similar behaviors in a more subliminal way.

When done effectively, the other person will begin to relax and open up. Their ego is defused and their fight or flight mechanism hardwired into their brain will no longer sense danger.

The three primary aspects of rapport are:

- Physiology
- Tonality
- Words

Physiology has to do with breathing, posture, gestures, facial expressions, and rates of movements. When in rapport, your breathing matches the others, your posture is similar, and your rates of movements match.

For tonality, it is pitch, tempo, and volume that are primary.

In words, it is modalities and relatable content.

So, effective mirror and matching would have you match their rate of breath, posture, and body movements. You would also speak in their tonality and modality.

Of all three, physiology is most important. It is the quickest way to build rapport. When disharmony is experienced in a conversation, mirror and matching physiology is the quickest way to regain harmony.

You can actually have a better, more valuable conversation with someone where you disagree with them in principle but are *in great rapport*. This is different from *agreeing with them* in principle but *being out of rapport*!

The Significance of Being In Rapport

In Section II, the importance of being in rapport was brought up again and again. Can you begin to conceive why? This concept of rapport is so critical, especially when touching on core values. Principles deep to a person's core can quickly elevate the ego's defense, ending constructive communication.

Take abortion for example—a subject that people will get truly revved up over. One person is for and the other against. Yet, if in deep rapport, a constructive conversation can ensue. If out of rapport, it's gloves on.

Tempo

I believe tempo is also a critical aspect of rapport building. For instance, when stress rises, slowing down a conversation forces the other person to do the same. As both parties do, the overall stress level also diminishes.

In the cockpit of my commercial airliner, there is a fellow pilot and myself. If we are out of rapport, communication begins to falter. If left unnoticed, ignored, or allowed to escalate, mistakes worsen; the checks and balances in place to ensure safety begin to break down.

Rapport is critical in such a constantly fluid environment. Even when all is going well (in rapport), the *unexpected* does happen in the dynamic world of flying. When it does, stress immediately rises. Sometimes one allows their stress to begin *overloading* their conscious mind. It becomes apparent in missed radio calls, increased errors, loss of SA, or accelerated tempo. Their pitch rises and words and actions become more reactionary (same goes for relationships).

The quickest way I've found to bring down that heightened stress in the cockpit is to *slow* my speech. I exaggerate this slowing down of the tempo until the other pilot begins to match mine. Additionally, I'll intentionally speak softer (tonality) and more evenly. As a result, the other pilot naturally comes down to a normal stress level, and we can proceed more logically and productively with the current situation.

Elke often jokes about "pilot talk," meaning when in that environment, we tend to talk in a steady, monotone voice. There is a reason for this. Heightened, emotional voices have no place in aviation. When emotions get involved, stress levels raise, rapport is broken, and effective communication lessens. And in aviation, you sometimes don't get a second chance.

Same is true in the household or whenever involved in a crucial conversation. You may not get that second chance to get your message across in the best way possible.

Being in rapport then is a must. You'd be better off to delay a crucial message until rapport is deepened. Keep in mind **rapport first**, and you'll have far better success of your message being received as intended. Ease your way into a conversation to build rapport. Ask the other person questions relevant to their interests as starters while mirror and matching.

An Example Around Finances

Take a discussion around finances with your intimate partner where one has a mindset of strict budgeting and the other free spending. Can you see how this is a difference in core values? Vital is the language used and the awareness of it from both sides when discussing such a critical subject. Without rapport, a rational discussion is challenging at best.

Take to heart those three components of language: physiology, tonality, and words. Encompass them all and recognize immediately when falling out of rapport. Remember, the quickest way to regain it is in mirror and matching the other person's physiology. If struggling, change the environment. Get moving by suggesting a walk or in some other way to *shake-up* the physiology.

Out of Rapport

What happens when out of rapport? Worse, what happens when one is forceful with their language in all three areas? When I began doing this work, I was absolutely stunned by the number of women who've been adversely affected by the negative emotions/actions of their partner. From verbal abuse, all the way to the most horrific of physical abuse, including attempted murder. It is beyond my understanding how another can treat a fellow human being in such a way—especially the treasured and *delicate* female.

Of course, that is the extreme end of being out of rapport. But how often do the *little events* in our daily lives affect others? Regarding those early developing ages of 0-7, being out of rapport can wreak havoc. At that age, the child does not have the filters or wisdom to understand what is happening. They're minds are total sponges, absorbing everything. They are developing meanings from life's events, creating their map of the world.

A Note to Parents

I went to the bookstore and searched through all the parenting books I could find. Of the hundred or so on the shelves, I found one, maybe two that addressed parenting and communication in the way I'm explaining it in these chapters. How we communicate with our children is so vital.

By now you know the importance of their early stages of growth and their programming without filters. Pia Britto, Senior Adviser on Early Childhood Development based in UNICEF's headquarters in New York stated:

"Neurons in the brain form new connections at the astounding rate of 700-1000 per second. These early synaptic connections form the basis of a person's lifelong capacity to learn, adapt to change, have resilience in case of unexpected circumstances, as well as physical and mental health. While brain development can continue through life, it is most rapid before birth and through the early childhood period of life. As the brain develops, the amount of neurons and synapses peak, and then go through a process of pruning and specialization."

The Four Levels of Brain Functions

As their brain waves evolve with age, more *filters* emerge, meaning, the conscious mind and RAS are more involved. Ensuring their early-on environment is one that promotes healthy thinking and communication that can only benefit their long-term development.

There are basically four levels of brain functions. We move between these, depending on our conscious state. Also of note is that greater learning, even as adults, occurs when we lower the brain waves, such as in trance states.

The important message to gleam from this is that the child does not enter into the adult consciousness until around the age of twelve.

LANGUAGE - PART 2

This is why those early years are so critical—their mind is absorbing everything *without* adult logic to sift through and make sense of it all.

Here is a list of age and associated brain wave development:

- **0-2 Years:** *Delta Waves*; deep sleep, unconscious, pure being, state of oneness (It is your I Am, what I have termed our love core center).
- **2-6 Years:** *Theta Waves*; first state of sleep, hypnotic state, between reality and dreams, intuitions, imagination (where many of the NLP exercises are purposely conducted).
- **7-12 Years:** *Alpha Waves*; awake, but deeply relaxed, meditative state, good for learning, ideas, vision.
- **12 + Years:** *Beta Waves*; conscious, attentive, awakened focus, the logical mind (where we spend most of our waking hours).

A Quick Review

Let's summarize what we have learned thus far. There is far more going on behind the scenes than just the words being said. The words themselves are just a glimpse into the gateway of how a person thinks, how they view the world, and what is important to them in this context.

Our language comprises mostly of our non-verbal cues and tonality. When listening to others, and especially your self-talk, the more you consistently raise your awareness of all these aspects of language, the deeper you uncover the separate, and individual maps that each of us lives with.

One of the most important concepts I'd like for you to pull away from this with a lasting impression is to *PAUSE* in your communication. Really listen to the other person, being fully present with them, and do your best to keep your emotions in check. The emotions are highly ego driven, and they will prevent you from hearing the deeper structure in the other person's language and in understanding your own.*

> *Should your emotions rise, it's prudent to ask what is going on inside of you to create such? Nothing anyone does with their language in a conversation makes you react or behave in a certain way. That comes from within you. So Meta-Model yourself! Ask yourself, "How so? What is it inside of me that is allowing this person to stir up such emotions within me?"*

The less the deep structure is involved in the actual communication, the more the possibility exists for miscommunication, arguments, and overall frustration. Language, and how it is used in communication, is a field all unto itself, and we have only begun to touch on its intricacies here with its relation to communication.

Meta-Programs formulate and develop who we are to the world. Taken to the extreme, such meta-programming can actually deceive the individual from their authentic love, their true essence of their I Am.

The formidable years of the child have tremendous impact on who becomes the class clown, the book worm, the people person, or the recluse. When a traumatic event happens, as in a "significant emotional event," a lasting "imprint" may be created. This imprint remains unless another replaces it or is reprogrammed purposefully through such tools as NLP offers. Think back to our discussion of the Black Piano and the wires going out of tune.

Awareness and Language

This has been a content heavy and involved section, especially the last few chapters. If you didn't absorb all of it this first time, that's okay. I do, however, suggest coming back to it again after you finish the book. Doing so will bring incredible clarity in new ways.

In summary, a prime directive of the subconscious mind is to protect. Outdated programming can be replaced with updated programming that *serves* the person in new, improved ways. All of this is based on our language and how we give meaning to the events of our lives.

Greater awareness to our language patterns allows us to monitor our physiology, tonality, and the words we use. This helps us to recognize when we are moving away from pain or towards pleasure. Likewise, the same allows us to be much more aware of the message being received from the other person. Ultimately, such awareness will allow you to create your desired future with far greater ease.

Moving On - Practical Usefulness

In our final Section, we will discuss ways in which various situations arise in our daily lives and how to begin utilizing these various concepts. Armed with this new knowledge, you will navigate difficult situations with greater awareness and new found grace.

* * *

Language Patterns Leading to New Pathways

1) Truly listening with all senses is an art and essential to supreme communication.

2) Being in rapport is essential to effective communication.

3) Physiology is the most significant aspect of communication. Mirror and matching is the quickest way to gain/regain rapport.

SECTION IV
EVERYDAY USE

Practical Uses

PUTTING IT TOGETHER 19

"Jesus's parables had a clear twofold purpose: They hid the truth from self-righteous or self-satisfied people who fancied themselves too sophisticated to learn from Him, while the same parables revealed truth to eager souls with childlike faith."

JOHN MACARTHUR

In this final section, we are going to connect these language patterns and how they can show up in everyday life. Finally, we will cover the Empowering Questions promised to you from the get go. I've saved them as one of the final chapters so that you fully grasp their power through what you've learned. This section ends with some final thoughts of my own.

Beyond the words themselves, there are also intrinsic meanings and phrases that are cultural and recognized by native speakers to that language. As mentioned earlier, volumes exist on all aspects of language, but here we are focusing on what pertains most in discovering your *Authentic Truth*.

Before we get into the practicalities of all we've covered thus far, there are just a few more general concepts I'd like to share.

What Else is Happening?

Many inferences can be gained from interpretations. Idioms are another example. Elke's native language is German where she lived for 33 years before first moving to Italy and then the United States. Unlike me, Elke is one who picks up dialect with relative ease. Her ability to adapt with languages amazes me. In Italy, she became localized—her accent and the way she spoke sounded like she had lived there her whole life.

Many years earlier, we travelled around the globe in a westerly direction for our honeymoon. We flew from Germany to the States, a quick stop in Hawaii, Asia and back to Germany. My parents were living in Hong Kong at the time, and they added a surprise trip for us to mainland China while there.

During the plane ride over to China, Elke studied one of those travel books with commonly used phrases. By the time we arrived, she was doing pretty well. By the time we left, there were a few occurrences where locals responded as if she actually spoke the language!

In our seventh year of marriage, we moved to the States. Most who have grown up for 33 years in their native country, as Elke had, find it difficult to shake that accent. Heck, I still have a Chicago accent!

Elke quickly adapted and it was soon difficult for a person to believe she was not raised here in the States. But one challenge she had was with idioms. There have been a couple real doozies, but the one that sticks in my head is in reference to the hammer and nail. The actual saying is, "Hit the nail on the head," in reference to the hammer hitting the fat part on top of the nail, dead center. Bless her heart when she said aloud in a group one day, *"Hit the nail on the hammer."*

The point of this is, because we each have different maps and ways of expressing ourselves, no two people communicate exactly the same way, either. For some, the intricacies of language come easily, while others may struggle. Some people have extensive vocabularies and others limited. Add in different modalities of communication and the infinite possibilities that exist in communication, challenges become apparent.

The Infinitude of Language

Words can be arranged in infinite ways and convey almost any thought, build almost any picture, and express almost any feeling. The English language differs from others in that we have many words and phrases which have different meanings depending how they are used.

Take the word Love for example. In Greek, there are six different words for that one word in English:

- *Agape:* soulful love – the love of humanity
- *Philia:* deep friendship, brotherly love
- *Eros:* passion, sex
- *Ludos:* affection, playful towards children and others; includes flirting
- *Pragma:* deep lasting love between partners
- *Philautia:* love of self – what I've referred to as falling in love with myself again.

Often in English, the listener has to infer how the word Love is utilized in order to understand the value in the word Love being expressed. This alone can create much confusion. And this word Love is but one example!

Language truly has an infinitude of possibilities in part because the depths of words are so great and can be combined in so many ways. With such an infinite way of creating thoughts in others through our words, we are given the creation of our own lyrics integrated with our unique music that can move the soul.

We have poetry that activates many senses all at once, fiction writings that take you on a journey into another world, non-Fiction that opens the mind to new learnings and educates, song writing that captures imagination, and of course, intimate conversations with your partner or loved ones – our love connections.

As the opening quotes to Chapter 17 so eloquently portray the varied beauty of language, so do you have such amazing beauty within you. Never forget that. When a person uses language negatively, realize, this is not coming from a place of their higher self, their essence, their authentic truth. Somehow it's been distorted. This is also why what those words stir inside of you is coming from within you, not them.

Be Aware When *Defending*

Have you ever felt you simply *had* to defend yourself? Maybe it is an unexpected outburst that came from nowhere, or a pattern of behavior from the other person that evoked your defensive response. Interestingly, in order for you to speak, the thought first has to emanate from within you, which means it also passes through you, meaning ***it is a part of you***.

What you say out of love or anger is first a part of *you*. That may be a hard pill for some to swallow, but it is the truth. Knowing this, can you see how your language tells so much about what is going on inside of you? How about the other person you are conversing with? When listening with intent (active listening), the words, terminology, and physiology that either you or the other person are communicating is a signpost to the internal maps and programming of each (deep structure).

By not reacting, and adding a pause ***prior*** to responding, you give yourself the opportunity to evaluate from *where* your response is coming: love, hate, ego, or something else altogether. Know there is a loving, caring person within you and the other. **In order to be angered by another, that anger comes from *within you*, not from the other**

person! The more you are aware to this truth, the quicker you begin to understand who you are.

The next time another person quickens you to anger, pause before reacting. *A Course in Miracles* says, "If I defend myself, *then* I am attacked." If you do not *react*, but rather pause and remain in control of your ego's fight response, then the other person is incapable of inflicting anger, or other emotion, with their attack. The issue becomes with *them*, not you.

If you choose *not* to do this, but choose to allow the thought of being attacked to fester, or worse respond in kind (even escalating), **you actually give away your power** to the other person.

With such awareness and practice, you can truly learn to "ground" yourself and maintain a higher state of consciousness. Moving beyond the self, you open up the possibility to help the other person ground themselves. Maintaining rapport is essential of course, and when done eloquently, you can actually guide the conversation to a peaceful resolution while helping them to reconnect and find that beauty within them again.

* * *

Now, let's move on with how to utilize all this collective information you've read in real life situations. Let's put it all together.

An Example From Elke

Here is a great example from a moment of language awareness that ties a lot of what we've already covered. Elke had two appointments in the afternoon set within a narrowed timeframe. She texted the person she had the second appointment with that morning stating, "Can we do 2:15 PM versus 2 PM? I have another meeting at 1PM, and I like to be on time."

Elke pointed this out because she caught herself in a moment of awareness with her language. "Isn't it interesting," she said, "how often we write, 'because I don't want to be late.' That statement comes from a place of being in effect. So, I switched it to 'I like to be on time,' changing that thought to be at cause."

Bravo! That's taking this information and bringing it into your daily living. Catching yourself whenever in effect and changing the language to at cause will change your life because you are in essence changing your thinking.

Here's another benefit. You put the onus on the other person to be on time by putting yourself at cause. It is a respectful way to ensure they receive the message of how you respect time, yours and theirs.

Now, let's dive a little deeper into the impact of language.

The Painter

Remember our little three year old painter from the opening of Chapter 17? Let's carry that experience out a little further. Imagine yourself as that youngster. You are at a stage in life where impressions are made. Desiring to express full creativity without boundaries, the white wall became a masterpiece in your eyes (map).

Mom returns with an expression of horror and Dad, frustrated from work, has just arrived home. You are sitting in a moment of pure bliss, feeling proud just prior to the serious double dose of anger to be unleashed.

"How could you do that?!" your mom exclaims.

"What is this?!" your dad belts out.

The moment stuns you, for you were expecting them to be praising your accomplishment! Instead, they've attacked you in the most unloving way.

Your world, up until this moment, was one of pure love. The moment worsens as you witness your mom and dad engage in a heated argument. You had never before experienced or witnessed such anger from either of your parents, much less both at the same time! You sit there in startled confusion at what is happening as your mind attempts to make sense of it all.

Language is occurring on all three fronts: Physiology, Tonality, and Words. The pace is fast and furious. The volume—loud and obnoxious. And most of all, you are witnessing non-verbal messages in terms of physiology like never seen before. No filters. All is registering.

The intense confusion spirals you into a fit of self-talk, albeit mostly subconsciously:

I know love. This is not love. I know they were happy. They are not happy. I caused them to not be happy. I am the cause of their unhappiness. I have failed. Now, I feel Anger, myself, for the very first time. I was proud of my action. I want them to be proud of me, too. They are mad at me. I'm not a good person. They are fighting because of me.

If I was not so gleeful and enjoying myself in the moment of now with my painting, none of this would have happened. This is my fault for expressing myself, for being who I am. I will change and not express myself again. I will repress my happiness so that my parents don't argue any more. I will never express myself openly again. (limiting belief / limiting decision)

This may seem a bit much for a three-year-old, but the world of the mind is far beyond what we typically give it credit for. The mind is extremely powerful. And this is *just* painting. What about real, significant traumatic events that we do know happens with children -- molestations, consistent physical and verbal abuse, abandonment, etc.?

Keeping You Safe

The possible repercussions from such an event are monumental. Let's revisit one of the primary missions of your mind; protecting and keeping you safe from experiencing past suffering or hurts again.

PUTTING IT TOGETHER

The challenge is that the emotional memory was stored at an age with limited knowing. Life had yet to provide you with great wisdom. At that age, you don't have the same resources as at twenty, forty, or sixty years of age. We change an action into a noun and give it a meaning and that meaning gets stored based on the knowledge and wisdom *at that time in your life*.

When anger was originally stored, as in the example of you as our painter, your mind could not possibly comprehend all the variables in play. It simply identifies the out-of-character responses from your mom and dad and their vehement argument that ensued as a threat to your safety and love experienced previously, or especially, just prior. Other negative emotions could also have been anchored in such as shame and guilt.

In that instant, your "map" as that child was just blown to smithereens. More than likely, you would have held your breath in a gasp as well. Add in any grabbing, shaking, spanking, etc., and this combined effect most likely created new pathways *away* from your *Authentic Truth*, what I call the *clutters of life*. Meta-programs are inserted and core values created that have you move away from pain rather than towards pleasure.

A major adjustment to your map of reality had just occurred. If significant enough, the event can absolutely affect the rest of your life. All created through language; all unintended.

As you age, your life experiences and maturity teach you that some events happen for reasons outside of your control, but that past event is now hard-wired into your mind and cannot be changed by conscious thought alone. It can only be changed by having that event re-contextualize (reprogrammed). Timeline Therapy would be one way to accomplish this.

This is just an example, but as you reflect back to your actual childhood, do you have a conscious memory of some sort of horrific event? Chances are you do, and if you don't, more than likely, there is one stored in your subconscious mind, hidden from view.

Being Aware

In my generation growing up, it was believed *the child won't remember*, or that *such an event isn't that significant*. Without *any* doubt, we now know today that thinking is a fallacy.

Parents, teachers, or anyone that has interactions with children, deserve to be aware of the significance of how their overall language has lasting impacts.

Even in striving to be the perfect parent, there are times we may fall short. Should an out-of-character event happen between an adult and child, the more aware the adult is, the better he/she can enlighten the child to help them comprehend what happened afterwards.

My hope is that those who read this book are at least awakened and mindful of their communication with their children. Be aware of what is coming out of you. If you falter, or witness such behavior from another, immediately adjust to create a more ecological environment for the child. Hopefully, in so doing, we can pass such necessary understanding along to others, spreading the news.

Lasting Impact

How deeply a child internalizes such a traumatic event determines its long-term impact. Years later, this event could show up in various ways, including a person finding themselves falling short of their true desires and not understanding why.

An example I've witnessed of behavioral issues that surface later in life from such traumatic childhood events is the manifestation of an environment void of love, or experiencing lack of love towards others as well as themselves. Another is the inability to express who they are to themselves or others. Not being as creative with their work because they were programmed to *just follow the rules* is also common. This leads to core values and experiences of a person playing life "safe" by staying *inside the lines*.

PUTTING IT TOGETHER

And what type of impact could this have? Take entrepreneurship, for instance, which is all about stepping outside the box. Therefore, should a person such as our painter later strives to become an entrepreneur, they may find resistance, struggling for the desired success, not understanding why the struggle is there.

They know what they are supposed to do, they do it, but their results do not match their wishes. There is a disconnect in their actual core values from that which they wish they were. This is just one example in which these "root causes" can affect our lives unconsciously.

Thus, all of this would be outside the frame of awareness! Yet, the "behavior" and "results" would match the "meaning" stored from that significant moment of the past (Meta-Programming / self-talk). Although the individual's conscious mind has long let it go, the programming remains *in there* (the mind).

There is also that possibility of *no* conscious memory of such an event at all, creating even further discourse between the subconscious and conscious mind. Hence, as an adult, without this awareness, you would have no conceivable way to make the connection between the old event, and the undesired results showing up.

Such trauma can also become the root cause to any of the basic negative emotions of Anger, Sadness, Fear, Guilt, Shame, Doubt and play an associated role in the child's meta-programming. The overall impact can go even further to the person's neurology, and physical actions/reactions: shyness, drooped shoulders, quietness, and other indicators signaling a lack of self-worth. Recall the dagger in Monika's back and black cylinder that penetrated her chest in Chapter 10.

This is what my sister was referring to when she stated, "Why isn't this taught in school?" If language can have such a dramatic impact on a child and into their adult life, wouldn't it make sense to be educated on it while we are growing up? Think about the many emotional challenges that show up later in our lives which could have potentially been reduced through awareness of language in basic parenting skills.

Life Happens

Even when armed with such knowledge, such outbursts or irrational behavior can still occur. Since we are *human* and not computers, our emotional side can get the best of us, especially when we become complacent and allow our *awareness* to diminish.

When this happens, even the best of us can get caught-up in the moment. Emotional outbursts get inflicted upon others; words you cannot take back do happen.

There's a great parable of a Dad telling his boy to take a bunch of nails and hammer them into a wooden fence. Afterwards, he explains each nail represents bad, angry words. He then has the boy remove the nails, explaining that even after the nails (words) are forgotten, the holes they made remain forever.

In the two plus years since releasing my anger at NeoGenesis, I cannot remember once losing control of my emotions as I did in the past. I've incorporated so much of what I've been discussing here, yet, I am aware the possibility always exists. I am human after all. But that I haven't had the *urge* tells me my neuro-programming has indeed shifted.

Of course, most have not had that freedom yet of releasing those deep emotions and are not always in control of their reactions. The next chapter begins with ideas on how to repair the damage of an emotional outburst after it occurs.

* * *

Utilizing Knowledge to new Pathways

1) Language is quite involved. You will begin noticing the positive impact on your experiences simply from this increased understanding and new found awareness.

2) The more mindful you are of your emotions, the more purposeful and positive you can be with your language. Be aware of your words and actions, *especially* around children when easily imprinted or influenced (up to 12 years of age).

3) We are human. Honoring this allows forgiveness to and from others, and ourselves.

AUTHENTIC COMMUNICATION 20

"Enduring trust in a relationship cannot be faked. It is the fruit of regular actions inspired by the conscience and heart."

Stephen R. Covey

We left the last chapter with the lasting damage from ill-fated language. Here I'll cover a couple examples of how to mend such as they occur in our adult life. This format is a model—it will work for most situations beyond the specific examples given. Remaining flexible while coming from a place of love and compassion, and authenticity, can work miracles.

Hand On Heart

Navigating a bad situation can be very challenging. What steps can you take after the fireworks subside? When the bloodletting settles and rational thought returns, how can you repair the damage?

It is imperative that rapport is rebuilt first. There is nothing wrong with a cooling off period, but at some point the issue should be addressed, and the sooner the better. When that time happens, the goal should be to first honor the other person while regaining rapport with them.

Early on, while working with Kelley from Chapter 9, I suggested she do the following with her then, very controlling and verbally abusive husband. This was to be done *in rapport* and face to face, with her hand on her heart (physiology, non-verbal communication):

- Validate him - what do you love/appreciate about him?
- Query his intention – my goal is to have a loving relationship, yet, when you say/act in this manner, this is how it makes me feel—is that your intention?

If yes, continue to ask questions that find the highest intent of his desire to make you feel that way:

- "What does that give you? What else?"
- Keep going, and you will eventually get to love or something similar. Then you can work backwards and introduce other ways for him to express his love and respect that actually serves you rather than tears you down.*

This process is called The Hierarchy of Ideas and known as "chunking up" for agreement and "chunking down" for specifics.

If it's not his intention to upset you, ask his permission to have a discussion about this:

- "Would it be okay if we talked more about this?" And then still chunk up.
- Doing something along these lines may open him up to see his pattern differently. The challenge is he seems pretty engrained in this behavior, and it probably originates from something in his past.
- If the door opens, I'd take the opportunity to go further, asking questions.

- You could even move into the quantum questions like we did on the plane without defining what it is that you are doing. Do it more in a conversational manner.
- Basically, the first step is anything that will get him to step out of first position, his current map of reality. **Continuously monitor your level of rapport. If it begins to break, re-establish before continuing!**
- Be flexible and be willing to change the approach over and over until something happens.
- If he is totally resistant, you then know it is not *your* issue any longer. If he is unwilling, for whatever reason, there isn't much you can do until he is ready.
- Remember Kelley, the one who is most flexible is the greater influencer.

Kelley never had the opportunity to give this a go for the dynamics were near violent and her safety mattered most. Her now ex-husband, as it turned out, simply would not seek counseling or any outside help with or without her.

This format, however, is a great starting point for those who truly are looking for something better and are willing to do what it takes to make it happen.

How About the Child?

What about with the child, though? Their world may have just been turned upside down. The imprinting of a major negative emotion may have been implanted, so now what?

Love.

Love is the answer for love is the most powerful, emotional force on the planet. As soon as possible, sit down with the child and speak utilizing their modality (Kinesthetic, Auditory, or Visual) and ensure they know they are loved. They may be too young for a NLP "process," but they need to know they are loved by those they've always known love from, even if you believe they don't understand.

Love & Communication

This process of love and communication sets up a very important future model for the child. It is my strongest belief that foundational to raising children by parents, or anyone having influence over them, that a solid grounding in love and open communication is present.

With love and communication present, they will figure out the rest as they journey to adulthood. Remove either of those two ingredients and suddenly, uncertainty is created as many other variables enter the mix. Love and communication is their shield, their armor against the woes of the world.

Additionally, following an emotional event, be on the look-out (aware) for personality/behavioral changes that could be related. This will be your first indication as to how deeply the event impacted the child's programming. If noticeable, make sure to have that conversation with them. If it surfaces later as the child ages, you can address the event again as well.

It is also vital for the adult to dig deep for learnings as well. **Take a moment to imagine how different this entire experience for our painter** *could have been* **if the child had been met with encouragement, not for painting on the wall, but for expressing his or her creativity**. What if instead of Anger the child was met with Love? What if the parents calmly handled and disciplined the situation with the loving care of a Mother Theresa? Can you begin to see the difference?

The damage to the wall was done. Yelling or not yelling would not change the wall's appearance in any way. The wall has to be cleaned up; the choice becomes, *"Does the immediate family environment come from love or expressed anger?"*

The outburst that occurred was about the adult(s), *not* the child. The more you keep the child's interest at the forefront, the better you can keep yourself in check as well. This is not to say discipline is unwarranted, and as kids grow, adjustments to discipline have to be made. What it is saying, however, is to be *mindful* and *aware* of your words, actions, and language in the process of disciplining.

When Two Maps Meet

The Meta-Model Bandler and Grinder created aids in decoding the underlying structures behind the language. What I personally have found fascinating while learning the greater depths of language is just how much we *do* delete, distort, and generalize constantly *without any awareness at all*.

Because no two people see the world exactly the same way, ambiguity quickly arises in the basic communication structure. Additionally, this is the sort of double whammy we covered in Chapter 17.

As a quick review, first, the person speaking has often omitted the deeper meaning through DDGs. When the person conveys their message, they are doing so from their unique map of the world—from the way their values and experiences form the representation of the original thought in their own mind.

Second, we have the receiver, with his or her own unique map of the world, values, and experiences. **We now have a message communicated with certain DDGs being received with another set of DDGs**: two maps, two sets of interpretations. What was said, and what the other person heard, can quickly become two different things (like Bob and Sue whom we'll meet in our next chapter).

Without going into great detail, suffice it to say, the more you pause and investigate, the clearer and more precise the speaker's intent becomes. Being aware of when mind-reading may be occurring, by either the speaker or the listener, allows for greater clarity to surface.

When unrecognized, confusion or something catastrophic can more easily unfold.

The quickest way to sense something is not right is when rapport begins to break. That is a *red flag* that something didn't land in either your map or theirs as intended. That is the time to pause and ask either yourself or the other person directly what just happened.

The sooner you catch this, the easier it is to rectify. If instead, this disconnect is allowed to gain traction and momentum, the challenge of overcoming misunderstandings increases significantly. As negative emotions elevate, true communication is reduced.

Mind reading

When a person projects to know *what* the other person is thinking or meaning, it is called "mind-reading." Bandler & Grinder state:

> *"In mind-reading, the clients have little choice as they have already decided what the other people involved think and feel. In mind-reading, clients may systematically fail to express their thoughts and feelings, making the assumption that others are able to know what they are thinking and feeling. In our experience, the client's assumed ability to read another's mind is the source of vast amounts of inter-personal difficulties, miscommunication and its accompanying pain"* (Structure of Magic).

Here's a short example of mind reading from *the Structure of Magic* where C = Client and T = Therapist. Take note of how 'digging' reveals DDGs to the client:

C: *Henry is angry at me.*

T: How, specifically, does Henry make you angry?

C: *He never considers my feelings.*

The therapist has at least the following choices:

a) What feelings, specifically?

b) How do you know that he never considers your feelings?

C: *Because he stays out so late every night.*

The therapist now has at least the following choices:

a) Does Henry's staying out late at night always make you angry?

b) Does Henry's staying out at night always mean that he never considers your feelings?

Here are some other examples where the deliverer is mind-reading:

- I'm sure she liked your present.
- I know what makes him happy.
- I know what's best for you.
- You know what I'm trying to say.
- You can see how I feel.

In each of these examples, there is at least one assumption in knowing what the other person is thinking or feeling. How often does this occur, especially when speaking with a friend or intimate partner? Whenever there is mind reading, the potential for misrepresentation rises quickly.

If - Then

One other area of language structure, of the many that actually exist, is Cause and Effect, or, *IF this THEN that*. Here are a couple of examples:

Example 1

I want to go out tonight for dinner, but I have to watch my finances.

The hidden structure behind such a casual sentence is IF I did not have financial concerns, THEN I would go out. How often do we give ourselves and others such ultimatums in various contexts? Here is how we can break this down to find the underlying structure, i.e., what is going on in the subconscious mind driving such a statement? In this case, let's say it was a thought you had.

First, we can switch it around and ask our self: *Do you always have to watch your finances when going out for dinner?*

We can also dig for more specifics: *How, specifically, do you have to watch your finances in order to go out for dinner?*

From there we can ask: *If finances were not an issue, then you would go out for dinner?*

Getting even clearer, we can add what is called a "Model Operator of Necessity" which is something that necessarily must happen: *Are you saying that your finances, necessarily, prevent you from going out for dinner?*

This provides insight into how a person is creating this casual sentence.

Example 2

Let's say your fifteen-year-old daughter comes to you and says, *"Dad, there is a party tonight I'd like to go to."*

You ask standard questions like where the party is and who is going to be there. But one thing you didn't ask, and she didn't offer is that most of the kids there are spending the night (deletion).

So far the conversation is going very well, and your daughter seems pleased you are open to letting her go. Sensing your approval, she goes the extra step, *"Dad, most of the kids are spending the night. Can I, too?"*

Suppose for various reasons this was not acceptable and you decline her request. And of course, you receive from her the frustrated, *"But, Dad? Why can't I? All the other kids are!"*

So here we have a classic cause and effect situation: IF the other kids are spending the night, THEN I should be able to as well.

Let's fill in some more details. It's boy/girl party. There have been issues with alcohol in the past with some of those going. Recently, you have gotten whim of sexual activity amongst some that will be there.

Now, from her point of view, her map of reality, it makes perfect sense for you to allow her to spend the night. She knows she is a good person who follows the rules, doesn't drink, and isn't having sex.

However, from your map, you do not choose to allow your daughter to be put in such a situation. You know your daughter is a *good girl*, and you trust her fully, which is why you initially agreed to let her go. However, you are also aware going that extra step in allowing her to spend the night exposes her to an environment that is not conducive with your parenting. You disagree with the behavior of some of those attending and the unnecessary temptation or *threat* to a fifteen-year-old.

You are appreciative for her honesty in asking and wish to honor that, but you feel it necessary to deny her request of spending the night. Rather than just saying no, which would violate her map and possibly have her leaving the conversation upset or angry, how can you open her fifteen-year-old mind to seeing a different picture?

Without knowing all the family dynamics, family rules and history, this becomes quite hypothetical. But let's see what comes out of it.

You say something like, "Darling, you know how much I love you?"

"Yes, Dad."

"Well, I want to make sure you know that you mean the world to me. And I greatly appreciate you coming to me and asking if it's okay for you to spend the night at this party."

She looks at you, defeated, knowing she's being denied (physiological communication / feedback).

What mind reading may she be doing at this point? *Dad, you don't understand. But I will behave. But I'm a good girl. But you don't trust me. But, but, but...* all sorts of justifications and DDGs creating an entire narrative separate from your own map.

AUTHENTIC COMMUNICATION

Your objective at this point is to honor her, yet also help her understand the wisdom of your decision to say no, that staying overnight at *this* party is not appropriate. There are several approaches that could be taken; some we've already covered.

One option you could effectively use is questions to bridge her possible mind-reading (what is she thinking?). Rather than *mind-read her*, why not ask her directly?

"So, what are you thinking right now?"

"Dad, you don't seem to trust me, otherwise you would let me spend the night."

Another, IF/THEN, statement. Based on what we've covered thus far, how could Dad respond? He could get argumentative and say "Yes, I do! But I'm your father, and you will do as I say."

Yet, how would that land in *her* world? More than likely it will be met with resistance and true communication ends for the moment. As their emotions heighten, each of them walks away frustrated, *even though there is love between the two.*

An Alternative Approach

His daughter threw a spear, and it would be easy to allow Dad's ego to defend. But, what if instead, the dad paused, and simply responded with, "How so?"

Now the daughter has to expand upon her statement, which deep down, she more than likely knows is false; her dad truly does trust her. *"How so"* is the easiest way to reel her back in and make her think about what she just said. Being a simple question to ask, it also provides the dad more time to listen intently to her response, understanding better her map through her eyes (second position).

If she holds to this mistruth (Dad doesn't trust her), the next logical response from the dad may be, "Is that really true? Is there ever a time where you have felt I have trusted you?"*

> * Note the word 'felt' in this sentence. Recall our discussion of speaking into the modality of the other – especially during crucial conversations. Felt would be great if the child's primary modality in this case was Kinesthetic. What if she her primary modality was Auditory? What word could you use instead? How about "heard?" Or if Visual you could use? How about "seen?" This may seem trivial, but it is an incredibly subtle and often missed opportunity that can make a huge difference in communication and rapport.

Some examples can help if she stumbles, like, "How about last week when you and your friends went to that concert?" or, "...when you slept over last weekend at...?" or any other time trust was present?

And if the dad has trouble formalizing a response, there is another infallible method to question a "quantifier" like you *never* trust me. The dad could simply respond with "Never?" "There has *never* been a time I didn't trust you? Not even once?"

Of course, whatever methodology is utilized in the conversation, the more playful and the deeper the rapport, the more positive the outcome will be. Remember to always honor and respect the other with love and compassion (understanding).

This hypothetical situation presupposes a respectful relationship between the dad and daughter already exists. Of course, not all such relationships enjoy such. Yet, it is never too late to start. Honoring, while maintaining authority through posture, will provide a win-win in the end.

Wise Words

One of my favorite author's is Norman Vincent Peale, author of the acclaimed, *The Power of Positive Thinking*. His sequel to that book is lesser known, but it had the biggest impact on my life about ten years ago when I first read it.

I was helping Janna with her dad's estate sale of the home she grew up in. Her mom, who had passed, was an avid reader, and I was pouring over these books of wonder. In there was this second book of Norman's

I had never heard of, *Stay Alive All Your Life*. It was an original from 1957. Janna gave it to me as a gift. I treasure that book and it has more red underlines and notes than any other book I've ever read. Here's a quote that relates to this as well:

> *"Unconsciously, parents project their own fears and children, like sensitive antennae, pick them up. Your present fears may have their roots in your childhood experience. When the original source of your fear is determined* [Timeline Therapy], *it is easier to eliminate it. Always remember, in dealing with fear, that it may owe its existence to some old, vague, memory, and has no present substance."*

The same is true for Anger, Sadness, Guilt, and Shame.

* * *

Clarification to New Pathways

1) Active listening is the number one way to improve your communication.

2) There is power in the pause. Utilize questions while in rapport to clarify the true intent of the other's language (verbal and non-verbal).

3) Remain flexible in your approach. If one way is not working, adjust and become creative – think outside the box while knowing the structure of language is coded (limited).

RELATIONSHIPS 21

"The missing link in all forms of education may be found in the failure of educational institutions to teach their students how to organize and use knowledge after they acquire it."

NAPOLEON HILL

As we continue on this journey, I would like to introduce you to a few more concepts of NLP that often occur in conversations. Since this is a book about reconnecting with your *Authentic Truth*, it is important these are addressed. These often show up in relationships, *including in our relationship with our self.* Therefore, understanding these will help you understand yourself even better.

Presuppositions and Lost Performative

Presuppositions and the Lost Performative are fancy words…so let's simplify them. A presupposition is where a thought, concept, emotion, feeling, is pre-supposed in a statement such as:

If you knew how much you hurt me by behaving this way, you wouldn't do it.

In this causal, If-Then statement, it presupposes *I am hurt* and that you are responsible for it. This may or may not be true, but identifies how I am internalizing or representing the story. This gives you a reason to pause and analyze if this is indeed true or if something else is in play.

Same basic formula applies: You would ask, "How specifically am I hurting you?" or "What specific behavior of mine is it that is hurting you?" The goal is to elicit more information to help close the gaps of my DDGs in this instance. Don't forget being in rapport is a must for effective communication to evolve!

A lost performative is where a person generalizes the world in their internal map and mistakes this *for* reality. This includes judgments of others:

- *It is wrong to hurt anyone's feelings* (says who?).
- *It is best to be kind to everyone* (according to whom?).
- *College is necessary to become successful* (are there other ways to be successful? This also presupposes several things, including a generalization of success).

You want to be able to recognize these generalizations a person presents about their model of the world, for **they are ultimately generalizations about the person's beliefs, not the world itself**. There may be other possible solutions which they simply do not see.

These lost performatives are often found in discussions around religion, politics, human rights issues, abortion, etc., and thus often show up when deep core values are involved.

Because of the DDGs involved, lost performatives are likely to appear with "moving away from pain" values. Thus, the person is aware of only a limited number of possibilities or options.

There are a number of cue words you can listen for to help you identify the lost performative: *good, bad, crazy, sick, correct, right, wrong, only, true, false.*

Physiological and Other Ambiguities

There is so much to language patterns and effective means to navigate a situation. Is it any wonder why miscommunication is so common? We are communicating beings, verbally and non-verbally. Whenever we are in proximity with another, we are communicating. Although we've been discussing verbal communication, can you also see how this pertains to the non-verbal as well? A little look here, a little look there, a wink here, a wink there, a sneer, a smile, eye contact, or no eye contact.

How about that cell phone? Putting it down, or even better, putting it away all together when someone else is talking or asking for your attention in some way. And then there is the whole plethora of physiological (body language) possibilities. Whether or not we are speaking, we are communicating constantly and the human mind is registering it all, albeit, mostly subconsciously. The question becomes, how are these non-verbal messages being received? When a DDG occurs, how can the message be conveyed with far less ambiguity?

* * *

Language and Relationships

Relationships are one of the more common areas I find myself helping others with. Obviously, there are many books written on the subject. It is one of those areas of life that each of us has to personally re-learn the lessons of those who've gone before us. In hopes of creating some short cuts to this *re-learning* experience, I'd like to bring together concepts covered already and how they relate specifically to relationships.

Taking what we've learned up to this point, let's see how we can apply this to a hypothetical but realistic exchange between a married couple. This is presented as another model that can be applied across the board to any relationship, including children and teenagers.

Here's the objective of this discussion: I wish for you to pull away the *framework* of the language patterns, as well as the deeper structure behind the DDGs involved, within the minds and maps of these two individuals. This will allow you to take this knowledge and apply it to any ongoing challenge or possibly one that may arise in the future.

Bob and Sue

Bob and Sue are a married couple. After several years, they find themselves arguing more than either would like to be.

Bob tells his friends, "Sue is always arguing with me."

Meanwhile, Sue tells her best friend, "Bob is always arguing with me."

Who is right? Well both are, aren't they? You cannot argue unless another is also participating, otherwise it is not an argument but a venting if only one is expressing their displeasure. To argue, two people need to be involved. Here, in their own minds (maps), Bob and Sue each feel it is the other creating the argument, not themselves.

This example is designed to help you identify these different maps and how, through language it's possible to arrive at a peaceful resolution. The answers are revealed from the "Deep Structure" and DDGs from of their language.

What's Missing?

First, let's break this down a little further. What story is Sue telling herself about Bob and vice versa? Let's say I'm a good friend of Sue's and she comes to me with this statement:

Bob is always arguing with me.

Have you ever experienced something similar, where a friend unloads on you? How have you, or how would you, handle this? What

I am going to ask of you is to begin shifting your awareness from the statement itself and start looking at the underlying structure of what is and what is not being said. To do this, you have to be *fully present* with the other person and in rapport.

First, we know there is a "Bob," there is a "me," and supposed "arguing." There is also this generalization of "always," also known as a universal quantifier, like *everyone, all, never.*

Now, what don't we know? What DDGs exist in this statement? What constitutes arguing to Sue? What is Bob arguing about—who or what? Is there ever a time when there is not arguing?

Since we know it takes two to argue, what would happen if you took the sentence,

Bob is always arguing with me, and shifted from "in effect" to "at cause?" *I am always arguing with Bob.*

Ouch! Try that on! Of course, that may not be the best approach, and I am certainly not recommending it right out of the gate. It is, however, presented to demonstrate how the individual's mind interprets and communicates within him or herself. For in actuality, aren't they the same? There is a Bob and a Sue and they argue – supposedly, a lot. But this shift in thinking is significant.

An Effective Response in Rapport

So how could you respond to a friend like this in a loving, compassionate way that builds rapport and gets true communication moving? To ultimately have them step out of first position and uncover new possibilities?

By now you know we have to help the person grasp the DDGs within their communication. For instance, you could respond to Sue with something along the lines of, "Oh, I am so sorry to hear this, Sue. What specifically is Bob arguing with you about?"

Using questions such as "how so, what specifically, who specifically, where specifically," requires the person, Sue in this case, to search for the deeper structure of her statement...those items deleted.

Sue responds with, *"Well, he is just not happy with the way I look."*

"Really? How so?"

"When he comes home from work, after I've been cleaning and cooking all day, he thinks I should look like we're going out on a date."

Discovering Missing Details

From here, an entire host of "Meta-Model" questions can be asked to dig further into Sue's map:

- Does this happen all the time?
- What specifically does he say to you?
- What does "looking like we are going on a date" look like to him? To you?
- How is his tone of voice when he greets you?
- What is his physiology saying to you?
- When he says this or that, how does that make you feel?
- What would you like him to say instead?
- Has there ever been a time when he came home from work and said something differently?
- How about when he did not go to work and was home all day - was anything different?
- How stressful are things at work for Bob? Could that have an impact in this regard to when he comes home?
- If you were to look in the mirror before Bob comes home, what do you see? Do you like what you see? How would you like to look instead?
- Is how you look important to you?

- Have you ever asked him if how you receive his message is his intent, specifically?

With each question, a host of new information will surface from Sue's subconscious mind. In asking these types of questions, Sue is forced to go outside of her normal thought processes, her conscious looping. She becomes more aware of her own DDGs than in simply stating, *"Bob is always arguing with me."*

Connecting to the Deeper Structure

Are you seeing why being present and in rapport is vital? You have to be an active listener unconcerned about your own thoughts, opinions, or views. With each of her potential responses, further inquiries can be investigated regarding Sue's statement.

For example: "Does this happen all the time?"

"Well, it has become more and more common for him to come home and say something to me about my appearance."

"So, there are times when Bob comes home and does not address your appearance?"

"Well, yes."

"So, Bob doesn't *always* come home and say something about how you look?"

"Well, I guess not always."

"What does Bob say when he does not say something about how you look?"

"He sometimes will ask how my day was."

"How is his tone of voice when he asks how your day was?"

"Well, I'm not sure? I never thought about that."

"So, when Bob does come home and says something about how you look, what specifically does he say, and how does he say it?"

"It varies, but usually he will say you look tired, or you don't look as pretty as you usually do. He knows how sensitive I am about my appearance, and I want to look good for him."

"Is it possible, Sue, that Bob is not upset with you as you are receiving his words? Is it possible he is concerned for you in some way? What would happen if, *before* allowing yourself to get upset, you paused, took a breath or two, and then simply asked Bob something like, 'How do you mean, Bob?' or simply ask, 'How so?'"

By doing this, Sue is gaining options to breaking the old pattern of how she internalizes Bob's message. This *opens* dialogue rather than shutting it down through reacting emotionally to a repetitive trigger, in this case a negative anchor: *Bob comes home and we argue.*

It's About Refinement

Without gathering more information, is it possible to actually know what the other person is thinking? The true intention behind something said can so quickly become convoluted and land negatively in another's map.

Have you ever had this happen to you? Everything is moving smoothly with your partner, and you give a well-intentioned compliment. The next thing you receive is the wrath of anger, cold shoulder, or silent treatment. And you stand there, stunned, wondering what the heck just happened?

From my experience, this is one of the first major breakdowns in relationship communication and with communication in general. We don't listen closely enough for the subtleties of the language and that which is a DDGd. Rather, we hasten to react emotionally, believing we *know* what the other person's intention was (mind-reading).

Sifting Through the Quagmire

Let's continue with Bob & Sue playing this out with three possible scenarios:

- Scenario 1) How Sue responded in the past.
- Scenario 2) Sue is right and Bob is truly upset with her appearance.
- Scenario 3) Sue's initial interpretation is missing vital information that, when investigated, changes her interpretation.

Certainly, there could be far more possibilities and complexities, but for the sake of clarity, let's explore these extremes.

Scenario 1

Bob walks in the door and upon seeing Sue says, "Hi. So what have you been up to all day? You look exhausted, not like your normal self." (Note how this could also be *said* in different tonalities, pacings, pitch, etc., each invoking their *own interpretation* based on the receiver's map).

Sue reacts with, *"Why are you always getting on my case, especially right when you walk in the door?"*

"I'm not getting on your case! You just don't look good."

"You are always putting me down, and I'm sick of it!"

"I'm not putting you down, Sue. You just don't look yourself."

"That's right. And you're not helping me either. I take care of this house and you, and all you can do is tell me I don't look good."

"That's crazy! Why do you always take things the wrong way?"

"I'm not taking it the wrong way. That is exactly what you said!"

"No, it isn't! Why do you always have to argue the moment I come home?"

"Me, argue? - It's you who comes home and starts in on me!"

RELATIONSHIPS

* * *

Ugh! Enough of that.

How many times have you been involved or seen another couple in such a situation? With such a repetitive, habitual "negative anchor," misunderstandings can quickly escalate. In short time, all true communication is absent and emotions have taken over, creating havoc within the relationship. Should the negative anchor strengthen, it can reach the point where neither is looking forward to seeing the other upon Bob's arrival at home. Next, he finds reasons not to. Sue finds reasons not to be there or encourages him to delay his return home.

This *type* of exchange, taken to the extreme over and over, especially around areas like finances and other similar stressors, can soon evaporate what little romance was left, leaving the couple headed for separation or divorce. Keep in mind, this isn't just couple related. This relates to any situation—kids, business, friendships, etc., basically, anywhere DDGs occur in communication and one person projects or mind-reads into another without full understanding.

Scenario 2

Let's move onto scenario two where Sue elicits more information before reacting:

Bob walks in the door and upon seeing Sue says, "Hi. So what have you been up to all day? You look exhausted, not like your normal self?"

"How so?" (Meta-Model)

"Well, I have to be honest with you, Sue. Ever since you left your job, and are home all the time, you just haven't been yourself. And when I come home, I want to see the Sue I fell in love with…happy and vibrant, the way you use to be."

"How specifically do you see me, Bob?" (Digging further into his map)

"Well, your hair is not put together as it usually is. That ragged t-shirt and old shorts you wear are not flattering. And you never have make-up on."

* * *

Okay, I'm stopping there before spears are thrown in my direction! In this case, I would agree: Sue's interpretation of Bob's presented response is negative, *even if that was not his intention.*

But she would not have known this specifically without asking those questions. It provides clarity with details she did not previously have and **allows an opening** to further *discussion* rather than arguing to arrive at a solution, provided, Sue keeps her emotions in check.

Scenario 3

Now, let's play out the possibility where Sue discovers she did *not* initially interpret Bob's intention as he meant it:

Bob walks in the door and upon seeing Sue says, "Hi. So, what have you been up to all day? You look exhausted, not like your normal self?"

"How so?"

"Well, I have to be honest with you, Sue. Ever since you left your job, and are home all the time, you just haven't been yourself. What's going on?"

"How do you mean, specifically, Bob?" (Rapport is vital in these next exchanges).

"Well, you know how when you used to work as a realtor, you were always ready to put on your best? Now, you don't look as happy. And maybe I see that as a reflection of how you are feeling about yourself. It pains me to see you like that, and I want to make sure *you are* happy."

"What do you mean by saying 'not happy' and 'pains you' how?" Note the shift outside of herself. This is significant as she digs for more

RELATIONSHIPS

information with a response *before* providing her own perspective. She is detaching from a typical emotional reaction. This does several things as well: It lowers the defensive ego from both, builds greater rapport, and invites a constructive conversation.

"Sue, I love you. You mean the world to me, but you don't seem to smile as much as in the past. And you don't seem to be taking as good of care of yourself. I'm concerned for you."

"Oh, Bob! I love you! No, I am totally okay. Yes, I miss getting out there at times, but I'm happy being home with our baby girl every day and caring for her. What if we planned a date night once a week where we remind ourselves of who we are together?"

"That's a great idea, Sue!"

* * *

Although hypothetical, there is truth to these three scenarios. What I wish for you to gleam from this is that, yes, your intuition could be right about another's spoken word, or, such mind-reading can lead to grand delusions and broken rapport. You cannot know for sure the intention of the other without exploring the DDGs present. Ambiguities exist in our language and navigating through them, defining them more clearly, is essential to true effective communication.

Where Else Does This Apply?

And guess what? ***All of this applies to your self-talk!*** With greater awareness, you can catch yourself doing this very thing with your own DDGs and negative self-talk. Get curious about your thoughts! You can then actually Meta-Model yourself. It becomes a very interesting, enlightening journey, and leads to an even greater understanding of your *Authentic Truth*.

Communicating to New Pathways

1) Ambiguous language leads to misunderstandings and misinterpretations. The more precise you are with your language the better overall communication will be.

2) Listen for DDGs, universal quantifiers, and similar language leading you to *interpreting* (mind-reading) the intent behind a message received. If unsure, ask, "How so?"

3) When you feel that knot in your stomach, something has gone adrift and rapport is breaking, it's time to pause, regain rapport and then Meta-Model.

INTIMATE RELATIONSHIPS   22

"When we are inwardly free we can honor and love others; you can love others in ways that seem impossible."

EMMERSON EGGERICHS

The core of this book is about your Authentic Truth from a position of love and compassion. With relationship struggles being so common and creating so much pain, I wish to include a short discussion on what it takes to have a healthy relationship, and for those who are searching to find one.

This opening quote is from my favorite book on relationships, *Love & Respect*. There are many great books out there, but this one is biblically based, and as such, the truths within stand the test of time.

The central theme of that book says it is natural for the woman to love on the man and the man to respect the woman. But God says, for the woman to respect the man and the man to love on the woman. This is the very truism I've found to be absent with broken relationships. The absolute quickest way for a woman to lose her man is to disrespect him. For the man in losing the woman, it is forgetting the romance.

Statistics

There seems to be infinite books and resources available by professionals in the field on how to attract and make intimate relationships work. From experience, I can say healthy relationships among flight attendants and pilots alike are often challenging. The demanding schedules and time spent away from home exasperate the communication challenges that confront all relationships.

With half the marriages ending in divorce here in the United States, it seems unusual when I meet a fifteen, twenty, thirty-year-old plus marriage amongst my peers in the airline industry. Yet, the *statistics* state the divorce rate for airline employees is much lower than the national average. Statistics are a funny bird. Although studies may say otherwise, to encapsulate all the variables is not simple. Numbers can be skewed in different directions.

> *"Marriage and divorce are both common experiences. In Western cultures, more than 90 percent of people marry by age 50. Healthy marriages are good for couples' mental and physical health.* [Yes, for those paying attention, that is a "lost performative"]. *They are also good for children; growing up in a happy home protects children from mental, physical, educational, and social problems* [another lost performative]. *"However, about 40 to 50 percent of married couples in the United States divorce. The divorce rate for subsequent marriages is even higher."*
> ~American Psychological Association http://www.apa.org/topics/divorce/

It's More Than Just Communication

What's absent from this American Psychological Association quote above is how many people *remain* in marriages (or relationships) that are *not* happy. How many feel compelled to stay because of their kids, a sense of obligation, financial, security (the feeling of nowhere else to go), or the fear of being alone?

Studies again and again make the claim from successful marriages of twenty-five years and longer that communication is the number one key value. I agree, but why? Is this the only major key element in play?

Of course, as we've been learning, communication is quite involved and encompasses "language," going to greater depths than typically discussed. And let us not forget the "awareness" piece to this puzzle!

However, I believe the real secret to relationships is when couples respect one another's *core values* in an honorable way. Quality communication, a willingness to learn from one another, and the thirst to seek understanding in order to maintain a place of harmony, are essential to a long lasting relationship.

Whether stuck in a relationship or separated from it, differences in core values are a primary reason the cycle of conflict began. With the addition of poor communication, listening skills, and awareness, can you see how things can quickly get out of control?

In my *listening* to others talk about their relationships, a difference in core values is the underlying theme I hear again and again. And when I explain it to them, almost always I get this sort of, "That's it!" exclamation.

Deeper Communication

Core values are even deeper than beliefs. They are part of our *Identity*, just above our *I Am*. When any discussion arises that attacks or stirs a core belief within you, the nervous system kicks into high gear and emotions rise, sometimes to a boiling point.

Ensuring your voice is heard, because you *know you are right*, becomes more important than the actual meaning of the conversation. Without rapport (trust, which includes respect), should a core value be encroached, the ego gets fired up, and will do whatever it can or needs to do to defend its value system.

Brian Tracy, in his book *Focal Point*, makes this statement:

"When you are treating other people in a manner that reflects your highest values, you can feel it inside. You feel happier and more confident. You experience higher levels of self-esteem and self-respect. You feel greater peace and contentment within yourself. As a result, you live and work in greater harmony with the people around you. When you are living consistently with your values, every part of your personal life flows more smoothly."

Regardless of the length of time together, when conflict arises, it most always goes beyond a difference in beliefs. At the deeper, soul level of core values, your identity exists. This is why I have repetitively brought up the *I Am* throughout this book. Even though your identity is the beginning of the layers of life, to know thyself is the greatest gift you can ever give yourself.

The *clutters of life* cloud the vision to the inner soul. Peeling back the layers of the onion built from this journey of life is so important and requires diligence. But when this is done, what is left standing alone in its true essence is your true identity, followed by your true *I Am*.

Much of the deeper Evolved NLP work with Niurka is directed at helping a person discover themselves again. It is why I so clearly state that what her Neogenesis course did for me was to guide me back to my *Authentic Truth* and had me fall in love with myself again.

The Value Elicitation exercise is one way to begin peeling those onion layers. When accomplishing this VE exercise with others, words emerge from their subconscious mind, attached to their core values. But even without this VE exercise, just *listening* to another unveils so much about them: how they think, why they do what they do, what their beliefs are, why they get the results they do in life, and ultimately, their core values.

An advantage of the VE exercise is eliciting the "strategies" behind a person's behaviors. Upon finishing, the person is always amazed at seeing on paper how they are actually programmed and the strategies behind their decision processes. They, often for the first time, *see* why they keep attracting the same negative relationship, if that's the case.

These listening skills are different than just causally listening to another speak. They are looking at the deep structure of the sentences, modalities, and neurology, to name a few. It is a skill that develops into an art of seeing into a person's mind to gain a deeper understanding of who you are attached to at a soul level.

This is different than the mind-reading discussed earlier; it is, in fact, the very opposite. Rather than imparting the listener's map onto another, the listener is delving into the speaker's actual map of how they see the world.

How powerful could all this knowledge we've covered thus far be for intimate relationships? Not that each is *dissecting* the other all the time, but in the depth of communication? If, according to the experts, communication is the key ingredient to lasting relationships, wouldn't it make sense that increasing the skill set in communication would increase the value of a relationship?

Back to Core Values

What are your core values? They are what you hold most dear. When aligned in your life, you are at peace and in harmony at the soul level. They drive your behaviors which drive your actions which drive your results.

Core values include God, character, integrity, family, conscientiousness, discipline, authenticity, success, honesty, service, kindness, loyalty, fulfillment, forgiveness, honor, respect, and many,

many more. Do you know what your partner's are? Are they aligned with yours?

Let's see how differences in values can play out. For example, you are out with your partner for dinner, and you both witness something at a nearby table that to you seems very disrespectful. Let's say this other couple is treating each other kindly, but the man is treating their waitress very unkindly for no apparent reason. You have the same waitress and find her very pleasing. It bothers you deeply.

You mention this to your partner who apparently does not value this experience as you do and dismisses it with a "whatever" comment. Of course, it is not just a "whatever" to you, so you strike up a conversation, expressing why it bothered you so. It quickly becomes apparent that *respect* in this context is simply not as important to your partner. Conversely, your partner cannot understand why you are making such a big deal about it.

You begin to wonder if your core value around respect is not aligned with your partner's connotation of respect. You begin reflecting over your relationship, and for the first time, begin putting the pieces together. You feel a dis-ease within you. You feel a lack of peace. You feel out of harmony inside because you just realized something significant in regards to your partner (a different map of the world). Yet, because of your awareness, you have also just discovered new-found clarity around the subject within yourself.

Now What?

The depths of this pseudo relationship will often govern the significance of the misaligned core value and subsequent direction of the conversation. A decision will be made as to whether or not it is worth the potential conflict to continue the conversation or not. Another factor will be your core value surrounding the *need to be right* in a conversation.

If the relationship is healthy, in deep alignment, and harmonious with proven communication skills, a conversation around this topic could easily unfold. Great insights for both can be gained that will strengthen the relationship even further.

However, if communication is poor, or often absent, the "you" in this story may choose to ignore it all together, knowing it will only lead to *another* fight. You dismiss it and allow it to fester, adding to a list of other topics that are un-talked about. In time, more frustration builds and you may not even understand why you begin losing love or respect for your partner.

Discovery

Here is a quick exercise you can do with your partner or any friend. Pick a subject area, say family, work, vacation, a hobby, music, religion, etc., and ask yourself what you value most about that topic.

As an example, let's say *family* is chosen as the topic and we are witnessing a husband and wife. Each writes down their answers privately first and then they compare notes. The wife's top three answers are *communication, loving, encouragement*. The husband wrote, *decision maker, fun, provider*. Important to keep in mind, there is no right or wrong, just different maps. And remember the map is not the territory.

Now, can you see the different maps? The husband doesn't even mention communication, the wife's number one core value in family. She didn't mention fun, his number two core value. This is so significant. I would go on to say that even if the top three values are the same, but in a different order, there is the potential for conflict to develop.

Can you see the importance in understanding the other's value system? Had you thought about this before? How could this simple understanding change your relationships or those of your friends'? With this out in the open, a real dialogue can ensue. We mentioned earlier that a healthy relationship can absolutely evolve with differences in core values provided there is effective communication present. This is one way to understand how that is possible; and there is a constant flow of love and respect throughout the process.

Parenting Issues

When effective communication is not present, and there is a difference in core values, conflict will show up again and again. Now let's take this conflict to parenting styles, especially when the parents are experiencing challenges between them, or are divorced.

Children get caught in the middle between conflicting signals from each parent. *They* have to be the appeaser, wanting to satisfy both sets of out-of-sync values, and behave appropriately. When around both parents, if the core values differ enough, they will often recede and remain quiet, not wanting to negatively affect either.

Or, it can also have them choosing sides, leaving one of the parent's demanding respect or love from their children. That never works and creates yet another spiral drift into deepened misery.

In divorces with a displaced family that involves children, this type of complex behavior becomes even more prevalent. The parent's divorced because of their differences. If these differences were a direct cause of incongruence in core values, especially the most treasured values including parenting styles, it is the kids that have to make sense of it all. And how often do the courts mess this up? I've heard way too many stories.

When divorced parents get caught up in hurting each other emotionally and financially, it is ultimately the children who suffer most. If a child happens to be in his or her formable years of 0-7 and all the way to twelve, the height of their meta programs and behaviors being developed, long-term, adverse effects could result. Words, behaviors, and actions can uplift or destroy. Be mindful of how you are communicating.

There Is Hope

I have thus far focused primarily on the negative aspects of misaligned core values because our divorce rate in this country and pain amongst relationships is so common. But there is a bright side to all of this as well.

When core values align, there is magic: love, companionship, honor, and respect flow naturally. Conflict is minimal, and when it does arise, it can be aired constructively and easily discussed in a natural flow. The family has congruency and the kids are given the absolute best opportunity at developing into healthy teenagers and beyond.

Here is my "lost performative" on parenting and believe it to be true to my soul:

Provided there is open communication with your children, and they know you love them unconditionally, they will figure the rest out on their own.

If they know without a doubt that they can come to you with anything, and they know your behavior is not to "react" but rather *pause* and "respond" with the maturity the conversation demands (Meta-Model), they will open up to you. You will not be guessing as to what they are *"up to"* and a deeper level of trust between your child and yourself will be enjoyed.

The other key is they have to know they are loved, truly, always, and unconditionally. Speak their love language and their primary modality.

Remove either of these two ingredients of open communication and love, and it becomes a crap shoot. Actually, although different in context, these two basic principles also apply to all relationships.

What to Look For

Today, when listening to another person's woes regarding relationships, I key in on this area of core values. If a woman is looking for the *right guy*, for instance (or vice-versa), I encourage her to first know her *own* core values clearly. I suggest she forgets about the attraction piece, income, or other behavioral qualities when searching for a man initially, and concentrate on knowing her *own* core values first. This is so important.

I encourage her to sit quietly (meditate, if familiar) and soul search about what she values most in life and to write those thoughts out. From there, I suggest she moves on to what values she is looking for in her partner and write those out.

If this is all new to you, why not give it a try and do some inventory? Also, I am not saying or suggesting that you can only have a healthy relationship if all values are aligned. That would be panacea (possible but not necessary). It is to say that understanding this concept around core values by each partner opens the communication pathway that is the cornerstone to healthy relationships.

Remember, according to the experts, in order to have a lasting, healthy marriage, communication is the key. When conflict arises, you can discuss, in a healthy manner, how such relates to the core values of each individual. This leads to better or improved understanding and communication.

You will be surprised at how quickly a negative dynamic can switch into a constructive conversation provided both parties understand this concept. If it is only you with this understanding, then you are at least aware of why conflict is possibly arising and can get curious. You can begin asking yourself questions, Empowering Questions, as to how to resolve and guide the other into understanding. Of course, you could also have them read this book. ☺

The Take Away

Here is what I wish for you to take away from this thought: You can meet someone you fall in love with that differs in your values. You are overjoyed and *blinded* by romance, love, euphoria, companionship, etc., possibly obscuring the mis-alignment of core values.

But over time, as the emotions become more familiar and *life* situations develop, these core values begin to surface and become of greater importance. With this exercise of first discovering what your authentic core values are, what you value most in a partner, and utilizing Empowering Questions to attract them, he or she will show up exactly as they should, and the draw will be natural.

He or she will possess the qualities you desire and, as a bonus, you will be sexually attracted as well. The long-term health of the relationship has a solid foundation because the values are more closely aligned than just going for the *look, prestige,* or the *money*. If you are already involved in a relationship, this methodology and knowledge can strengthen it or at least begin a path towards greater understanding.

Your Gut Knows

Lastly, your subconscious mind (your gut instincts) will unconsciously send you signals and provide you guidance when meeting someone new. Even when the attraction piece is overwhelming, most often, people in a broken relationship will mention that there was something in their gut warning them, but they ignored it.

Believing you can *change* someone is another red flag. Unless you can change their core values, there is little hope of *changing* them as you may desire. Core values *can* be changed as we have seen; however, the person has to *want* to change! If you are hoping they will come to seeing things your way, it may be a very long, tough road.

I often wonder if this is in part why I've met many people with successful marriages that connected through an online dating service. In filling out the personal history and details, in essence, core values are being elicited, uncovered, and displayed (maybe subconsciously). This brings to the forefront their individual maps before actually meeting.

In the past, such details may not have been brought out so quickly before attraction takes over. It provides a more direct approach rather than the common initial niceties.

Regardless, knowing one's core values is essential to living your joy with your partner both mentally and physically. It also develops a long-lasting, happy family unit.

Passing on Guilt

I'm closing out this chapter with a discussion on "Guilt," for it can be a huge *negative* driver with some people in how they communicate. Have you ever been made to feel 'guilty' by someone? Many grew up in an environment where guilt was used as a form of parenting. As the child grows, using guilt can become a natural way of communicating for them with others. But is it effective?

Guilt usually comes in the form of an "If – Then" as discussed in Chapter 20. But it is so prevalent in relationships I decided to add it here (this actually applies to all communications – and especially with children!).

There are infinite ways to throw guilt onto another. It may work in the short term but in the long term it only brings pain and despair to all involved. For instance, in regards to partnerships, have you ever used yourself, or had used on you, something to the effect of, *"If you don't stop this 'behavior' then I'm leaving for good."*

The ego is an interesting creature and as already mentioned, it loves to be right. This may seem empowering to the person delivering such a message, but how does it land in the other person's map? How does their ego respond? Defensively of course, and thus, any subsequent *effective* communication is absent.

Even if said in a loving way, such language makes it **all** about **you**, not the other person. For example, your desire is in helping someone, say an alcoholic from drinking. You say, "If you don't stop drinking you'll never see me again." Or, how about with your child, when they misbehave and you threaten them with a guilt ladened response?

Language of this type is in effect, satisfying an egoic position. It is not about the other person even if you mean it to be. And the other person's ego will most likely interpret this as an *attack* against them from *you*. Regardless, it will not be received with the intention of their best interest in mind.

Making the Shift From Using Guilt

So how do you shift the emphasis? Probably much the opposite of what you might first think. Look at this from a problem frame perspective. Since a problem cannot be solved while in effect or stuck within the frame of the problem, the objective is to somehow shift the person you are addressing out of their current frame, without inflaming their ego.

How can you do this? Believe it or not, **you put the apparent focus on you, to shift it from being about you**. In so doing, the other person has to think differently about their thinking. Allow me to illustrate with an actual conversation that prompted this discussion on Guilt.

A Conversation About Guilt

I received a text message from this person we'll call Samantha. She was upset with her boyfriend who is an alcoholic. She hid a bottle of Vodka from him in the middle of the night. She then texted me:

Samantha: *I'm going to tell him it's my last weekend here, and I want to spend it with him "not drunk," and I'm going to tell him if he doesn't stop, I'm not going to come out here anymore or see him anymore.*

Me: May I suggest making it about him and not you - in other words, by saying the same thing but phrasing it in a way that it is about him, it is more powerful. You can do that through questions.

Samantha: *But I'm not going to let him sneak it, and hide it, then act like I'm an idiot or get mad at me when I say, "he's drunk."*

Me: You could start by asking him, "What is it about me that you enjoy?"

Samantha: *Yes, you're right*

Me: How long have you felt that way?

Samantha: *Yes, that's good! :)*

Me: What is it about me that makes you want me around? How would it feel to have me around more? What would happen if I were to leave? If you were here all alone, without me around, or in your life, what would be different? Why do you believe I would not want to be here? What would make me leave? What would allow me to stay longer?

That's the idea - makes sense? You shift it from you by making it about you, but where he has to think of it from his position. How it affects him; not how it affects you—that's the magic [this is a type of Reframe as well].

Samantha: *I can see! I need to start doing that more often! And with my daughter, too!*

Me: Yes. Very powerful with your daughter because it shows you are concerned about her not you. It's a total shift in thinking.

Samantha: *My mother used to tell me things so harshly, I would just end up feeling bad about myself. And I don't want to be like that. I know she loved me and was trying to tell me things out of love, but it didn't sound loving the way she would say it. If it had I probably would have taken it to heart more instead of feeling broken-hearted.*

Me: Yes! Now take a look at your text and what you were going to say to your boyfriend: *"If he doesn't stop, I'm not going to come out here anymore or see him anymore."* Can you see how that is about you? Even though you wish for him to be healthy? Guilt, Guilt, Guilt.

Samantha: *I see the difference; HUGE difference! I can see that now. This is so good and powerful!*

Me: Now think of how often that type of negative language pattern possibly comes out in regards to your daughter. It is a habit. In changing this thinking on how to express yourself, your language towards others, including your daughter, will contain less projection of guilt. This is very powerful; it can change everything between you and her.

Samantha: *Yes, I'm sure it did in the past. Sometimes I would even catch myself. But I guess I just didn't know how else to say it at the time to reach her. It's amazing at how simple the shift is once aware, and I can remarkably see the difference! I'll start doing that immediately! Thank you, Guy!*

Me: When you push guilt onto someone it is selfish and all about you (I'm speaking generally for all of us). But when you truly make it about the other person, they welcome what you have to say and are more eager to satisfy and please. We are pleasing individuals but guilt is nasty. It works - for a time, but never in the end for it is absent of true Love; it is a misdirected form of it.

Samantha: *Yes! I agree...I had a LOT of that growing up.*

* * *

How many of us have?

Remember to Pause

The lesson is once again in awareness. Laying guilt onto another person is ego driven. You may feel powerful in the moment when communicating in that old way, but doing so pushes people away because it doesn't come from a place of authentic love. It is another aspect of the great deceiver that the ego can be.

So once again, we can observe the power of the pause. Allow time to respond, and if in doubt, go with a question to illicit more information. If this is new to you, and you incorporate this shift, you will be amazed at the results you receive from others, and for yourself – for your communication now comes from love and is authentic.

* * *

Understanding to New Pathways

1) The quickest way for a woman to lose a man's love is to disrespect him. For the man to lose the woman, it is to not love on her.

2) Open communication is vital to the long-term success of a healthy relationship.

3) Our Core Values tell the story.

THE CHALLENGE WITH AFFIRMATIONS 23

"As the plant springs from, and could not be without, the seed, so every act of a man springs from the hidden seeds of thought, and could not have appeared without them."

JAMES ALLEN

Ultimately, this is a book focused on helping you discover more about yourself. In this light, any problem you may find yourself stuck in can often be traced back to a limit within your own deep structure of your thought, and how you are using your language. In *listening* to your own self-talk, you awaken further the secrets to your current results in life.

When stuck in a problem frame, the barrier exists in your language and DDGs. The quickest way to investigate what those are for you is through questions.

Allow your subconscious mind the power to be the friend who sees clearly the solution, and allow it to free you by expanding your language by asking yourself, *"What are my current DDGs?"* The more you do this, the greater your awareness into your own thinking and the resulting choices become, bringing you closer in touch with your *Authentic Truth*.

The Challenge with Affirmations

Why questions? In her book, *Supreme Influence*, Niurka teaches her magical creation of Empowering Questions. Allow me to explain what these have come to mean to me, and how I (and others I've taught) use them over these next two chapters.

For many years, I was drilled with the necessity of affirmations. Affirmations are positive, visionary statements, which often, but not always, begin with the words "I am…" Such as, *I am financially free. I am earning $10,000 per month in residual income. I am living my dream aboard my private yacht.*

There are thousands of examples online you can find, and they have proven to work for some people (they wouldn't still be so popularly taught and used today if they didn't). Literally, it is a method to reprogram your mind. However, because it is working more at the behavioral level and not at the depth of core values, the process is very slow. It requires diligence and incredible repetition.

The other major challenge I've personally experienced is that in saying an affirmation, there is a direct disconnect between the conscious and subconscious mind. Since affirmations are stated in the positive and present tense of a future goal or desire, you are basically attempting to trick the subconscious mind into believing it is true.

But the subconscious mind cannot be *tricked* in such a way that is efficient. In other words, you say, *"I am financially free,"* yet at the deep structure and core value level, it knows you are not. Your self-talk says, *"Yeah, right…"*

This misalignment between the conscious and subconscious mind creates dis-ease. The intent of the affirmation is not fully embodied, which is a necessity for such an affirmation to create the change desired.

Affirmations, done long enough and with the right intensity, belief, panoramic imaging, and so on, can create the desired shift in programming sought. Each person is different, and for some, this shift happens quicker than for others who may never allow the *lie* to be believed.

What I have found through studying, using, and researching the mind is this lack in authenticity can hinder the very experience the affirmation is attempting to manifest. In fact, it can increase resistance to actually attaining it!

Affirmations in Action

The conscious mind knows you are not *financially free*. (In actuality, you would want to be far clearer in the affirmation, such as what dollar figure would require you to have complete and absolute freedom for your desired lifestyle after all expenses, in residual income or savings. In other words, what income flow would allow you to no longer have a *job*? I am simplifying in this example).

Sunday night arrives and you studiously say your affirmations aloud while your conscious mind *knows* you have to get up early Monday morning to go to work. This misalignment can negate the effectiveness of the affirmation itself.

Is it a waste of time? Not necessarily, for at least it causes you to look forward and image, picturing possibilities that actually can exist. However, if the disconnect is too great, over time it can create more frustration than inspiration. If this is the case, then maybe the affirmation is not being contextualized in the best way.

I have journals filled with affirmations, written out over and over and over again, thousands of times that have never manifested. I have 3x5 note cards I'd recite and carry with me throughout the day that have never manifested. Yet, I continued doing them, believing they would assist in driving me towards my desired goals—my desired direction in life.

In his book, *The Slight Edge*, Jeff Olson drives home the importance of doing the little things consistently over time to create the difference,

THE CHALLENGE WITH AFFIRMATIONS

"Only 5 percent, 1 in 20, achieve the level of success and fulfillment they hope for. The only difference is the slight edge. The secret to the 5 percent's success is always in mundane, easy things that anyone can do. **They are easy to do and easy not to do** [emphasis mine]. *They seem insignificant, like they don't matter, but they do."*

Simple decisions, versus errors in judgment, over time produces the slight edge. My long-term exercise in affirmations is an example of a simple, disciplined effort which has produced some results in the areas I desired to manifest but definitely aided in moving me in my desired direction overall.

Even though most of my affirmations did not come to fruition, there are those that did. More importantly, *the consistency in the discipline required did not go unnoticed in my evolution.* I most likely would not be sitting here, writing the pages of this book, if it hadn't been for those affirmations begun over seventeen years ago. But what if you don't have to wait seventeen years to begin manifesting astounding change in your life? That's where Empowering Questions make the difference, and I promise, we will get to them.

Development of a Traditional Affirmation

In order to create even greater value and paint the full picture of how Empowering Questions differ from affirmations in manifesting that which is desired, let us return to the simplified affirmation of, *I am financially free.*

In true affirmation format, it would be more like, *"I am enjoying the life of my dreams living financially free."* Even more specific would be, *"I am enjoying the life of my dreams earning $10,000 per month in residual income,"* or, *"I am enjoying the life of my dreams today, earning $10,000 per month in residual income as I rest upon the sandy white beaches of Maui."*

Using this as a hypothetical example for discussion (and inserting a dollar figure and projected date that would work for you), let's say this is my affirmation, and I do believe it is possible. It is the desired direction, and ultimate achievement I am striving for. However, I do not *feel* comfortable in saying this for I *know* it is not yet true. I know it is possible, but I do not yet embody it at the soul level. Rather, I am willfully attempting to program my mind into manifesting the law of attraction in my favor to produce the desired result.

What I have found happens with such a disconnect, is a focus more on the *lack of*, rather than the abundance of the desire, in this case, financial freedom. My mind gravitates more towards something along the lines of, *Well, I want financial freedom because I am tired of not having it.* This sets up more resistance than attraction by the universe in terms of energy.

The Law of Attraction

The Law of Attraction is about energy. Rather than struggling to make something happen in your life, the Law of Attraction brings it to you naturally.

To be effective in attracting that which you desire, you must be in positive vibrational flow of, rather than resistance to it. For me personally, and for others I've spoken with as well, affirmations, when disconnected from the self, often create more resistance than attraction.

Any time a *want* enters the equation (in effect), lack naturally follows: *I don't want to be fat*, presupposes that I am fat and wish to be skinny. Said, or just thought in this manner, means I first have to think of being fat in order to be skinny! *I want to be rich* has the mind contextualize my current financial status as lack of being rich but *wanting* to be (in effect). Remember, ***A problem can never be solved while in effect.***

Regardless of the format, *want* is *want* and *lack* is its cousin. If you have ever been told time and again to do affirmations and have not seen

THE CHALLENGE WITH AFFIRMATIONS

results, I believe this is what is happening even if the word *want* is not used. Now, as stated earlier, for some people, affirmations are effective. I would attribute this to the way their minds are already wired in a way that bypasses this want. They are able to clearly allow themselves to *be* the living embodiment of the affirmation's promise.

For affirmations to manifest in their purest essence, a person has to say them from *and remain* **at cause**. Bottom line, the Law of Attraction towards your desired direction only works when you are at cause.

However, the Law of Attraction is **always in play!** But, if in effect it **isn't** going to attract that which you are striving for in your desired, positive direction! It will attract exactly what you are putting out; **more lack of**. Here again is where you being **aware** is so important.

If you are emitting lack as your energy, more lack is exactly what you are going to attract! This is why people find themselves convinced bad things *always* happen to them. They may be right, as they are living in effect, but it doesn't have to be. They may be attracting such, but once **aware** of this little fact, they can *immediately begin shifting* the negative into positive energy, the *lack* into *desire* and from in effect to at cause.

James Allen, in his powerful little book written in the late 1800's, *As A Man Thinketh*, sums it up best: "…the outer world of circumstances shapes itself to the inner world of thought…man is the causer though nearly always unconsciously." *Thoughts become things* is this books credo:

> *"Every man is where he is by the law of his being; the thoughts which he has built into his character have brought him there, and in the arrangement of his life there is no element of chance, but all is the result of a law which cannot err. Circumstances does not make the man; it reveals him to himself."*

Empowering Questions are incredible to raising your level of unconscious awareness and shifting to living more at cause.

Moving Into "At Cause"

How can you bypass this *want*, change your circumstances, and move into at cause? What if you changed the format of the affirmation from a statement into a specifically designed question to completely bypass any thought of *want*? This is what Empowering Questions do. By taking the affirmation and creating a question styled in a specific format, that *want* disconnect magically disappears.

No longer are you *lying* to yourself. A direct gateway to the subconscious mind is opened, and the Law of Attraction is activated in an exact way that is conducive to manifesting that which is desired. You are now creating an image of the future event from an ***at cause*** mindset.

In the next chapter, we are going to cover how to build your Empowering Questions step by step. These questions are quick, easy, and are more productive than affirmations of the past. In working with these for two years with many people, I would say their format is magical and aid dramatically in creating the environment for extraordinary results in a specified, desired direction.

It's easy to do and easy not to do. The choice is all yours. But before leaving this chapter on affirmations, I would like to express how they can be used effectively as reinforcement to daily living.

Affirmations Today

Today, I use affirmations, but in a different way like, *I am Amazing! I am powerful and loving. I greet this day with love in my heart. I am a worthy individual who loves people. I am grateful for all in my life. I honor and respect others.* In fact, my personal mission statement, my personal mantra, my *I Am*, which evolved after my first NeoGenesis course with Niurka, is in itself an affirmation:

I am a loving, evolving human being
Embodied with character, wisdom, and meaning

THE CHALLENGE WITH AFFIRMATIONS

Harmonized to be a good and faithful servant to my Lord and Savior, Jesus Christ
Spreading peace, love, and joy into the hearts of my fellow man
Guiding them to love and believe in themselves
More than they ever thought possible
Ultimately making this
A better world for all.

Affirmations designed this way definitely have validity because of belief. In the above statement, I know each word to be true. This *is* my *true authentic self*. My Identity. My *I Am*, unearthed through a process of deep inner reflection. There is total alignment within my body, mind and spirit. I feel whole and complete and this mantra serves as a reminder of who *I Am* on a daily basis. It provides support when life *attacks* me today, allowing me to remain grounded in my true essence.

Now, let's get to the power of Empowering Questions!

* * *

At Cause to New Pathways

1) Affirmations are powerful, but can leave a person stuck in effect.

2) The Law of Attraction for your *desired* direction works best when you are at cause.

3) Thoughts become things.

EMPOWERING QUESTIONS 24

"Questions are the answer."

NIURKA

Now let's see how we can uplift your powerful words of desired manifestation to the next level with Empowering Questions. If you commit to these for at least two weeks, I can almost guarantee your awareness in *all* aspects of your life will significantly open.

For truly, what is happening here is a retraining of your RAS to be more aware of that which you most desire to attract into your life. In this process, you are also training yourself to be more aware of all that is around you and within you; especially with your self-talk.

There is also one other extremely significant advantage to these questions: They are the quickest way to shift from being in effect to being at cause that I know of; taking any problem you're facing, stuck in victim mode, and turning it into an Empowering Question. Immediately, you take responsibility for it and remove the *reasons* and blame game. You give back to yourself your power instead of giving it away to someone else. Remarkably, because no problem can be solved while in effect, you open the door to fresh possibilities and solutions.

At the end of this chapter, I'll add some ideas for you to use when teaching these Empowering Questions to others. For parents, teachers, councilors, etc., the power in these for kids is beyond measure. They can be developed around *friends, testing, homework, sports,* or even being a *better son* or *daughter*. They can teach adolescents to teenagers the skill of problem solving in a unique and fun, effective way.

Creating Empowering Questions

Niurka explains a simple three step formula in the formation of Empowering Questions in her book, *Supreme Influence*:

1. Begin with *What, How, or Who*
2. State in the affirmative
3. Build Momentum with words like, *right now, even more, while*

So simple: *What can I do right now to attract even more happiness into my life? How can I add even more value to my life right now? What more can I be doing right now to increase my personal finances?*

What I have found in practice, however, is many people are actually timid in creating these empowering questions, at least initially. I'm not sure exactly why this is, but chances are it comes back to some aspect of self-worth. Maybe they feel they don't deserve what they are asking for; *It's okay for someone else, but not me.* Or, I've tried something like this before and it never happened.

Whatever the reasons may be, it is bunk, and they just need a bit of encouragement to get them in the groove. Through the practice of working with others, I've discovered a few easy steps proven to be very helpful in getting a person in action to create their Empowering Questions.

Taking Action

These additional steps begin by having the person take out a blank sheet of paper and across the top write out three columns. Why not follow along? Grab a notebook or blank sheet of paper and pen/pencil and let's work on this together, *right now*.

Of course, you may be reading in a place where that is not possible. Certainly, continue reading. I will admit from experience there have been many occurrences I never came back to do an exercise the author recommended doing at that time. Don't let this happen to you here. Come back and do this at least once. Trust me, there is more involved in the *process* than just *writing* words down.

However, if you even had a thought of doing it later rather than now out of **convenience**, get curious and ask yourself, "What's my *resistance*? What's the *secondary gain* by *not* doing this right now?"

"Why, Guy? Why, not right now? What would doing this right now give me? What does not doing this now give me? What would happen if I did this right now? What would happen if I didn't do this right now? What wouldn't happen if I did this right now? What wouldn't happen if I didn't do this right now? Wouldn't it just be easier to grab that piece of paper than answer all these questions?"

This is how to create the curiosity within you to learn more about yourself: your self-talk, your self-awareness, your internal programming, and your core values moving away from pain or towards pleasure. Questions truly are the answer.

Regardless, the above paragraphs should have given you *pause*, in one way or another. Carry this concept of *curiosity* with you throughout your life. It will repay you in monumental proportions.

Being Specific

These steps will make getting started with these questions easier and with greater focus. Keep in mind with each of these, specificity is so important. The more your mind hones in, the greater you can expand the Sub-modalities (the pictures, sounds, and feelings of the imaging). By doing so, your Empowering Questions become even more impactful.

If I were to put you twenty feet out in front of a huge soccer goal with no goalie or other players, would you be able to kick the ball into the net? Almost assuredly. But what if I blindfolded you before you walked onto the field? That ball could be kicked wildly in any of 360 degrees.

The more specific you are, the more you get to creep that blindfold from your eyes, making the goal easier to see. Each time you add specificity, your mind is seeing that empty net more clearly, just wanting to score.

Column 1

Across the top of your blank sheet of paper, you will have three columns. In the first column, label it *Desires* and write down 3-5 desires which you would like to manifest in your life. Do your best to quantify, being specific.

This is true for any area you choose. For example, personal finances is more specific than simply finances; understanding my children is more specific than just parenting; being more *present* in my relationship, rather than just being a better spouse, is more refined.

Column 2

In the second column, list 3-5 things you *do not want*. Why? Because doing so accesses a different part of your thinking. We filter/categorize these differently from our desires.

Once you have the *do not want* written down, change it to its opposite and it now becomes an additional desire that was already within you but hidden from conscious thought. Amazingly, you will come up with at least one, if not more, ideas not listed in Column 1.

Column 3

In the third column, list 3-5 qualities you love about yourself; aspects that you value highly about you. Some examples might be *I am driven, I am loyal, my character is very important, I am tenacious, I am giving, I am creative,* etc. See if you can get even more specific: *I value myself* is a great start, yet, it is not as specific as, *I value my punctuality.*

If you happen to struggle with this column at all, get curious. There is absolutely something about you that you do value—even if it may seem benign in this context, there is something. Write it down!

An Example

Putting these three columns together we then have an example of something like:

Desires

- Earn $10,000 per month
  Specifically - Job, residual, investment, business
- Travel more
  Specifically - travel to Aruba next year in September
- A new car
  Specifically - a new Tesla Model S, red w/tan interior and larger batteries
- Earn my advanced degree
  Specifically - in family psychology by [date]

You Don't Want

- Failure
  Change to: Success/Achievement (publish a book by [date])
- Unloved
  Change to: Loved. Attract the right partner with aligned values
- Fear

Change to: Confident, self-worthy, valued, courage (add specificity)

Positive Attributes About You

- Honest
- Character / Integrity
- Family orientated
- Resourceful

From here, you can now begin formulating the structure of the empowering question.

Creating an Empowering Question

Let's develop one from the above information starting with the first desire of earning $10,000 monthly. For some of you this may seem like an extraordinary amount. For others, this may seem too low. What we do know, is that there are people earning this or much more on a consistent monthly basis, so we know it is possible. Since it is realistic and possible, it is a perfect example for an Empowering Question, especially if not yet believed. Feel free to insert any dollar figure you wish based on your individual circumstances, ensuring it is above what you currently are earning and there is a definite, specific purpose behind the figure.

What opportunities surround me right now to easily earn $10,000 per month in total personal income?

Note some of the key language here: opportunities, easily, earn, total. And now say this same question aloud but as a statement (affirmation): I am earning $10,000 per month in total personal income. Can you *feel* the difference? That difference is what we covered in the previous chapter, that feeling of being disconnected.

As for setting a date for accomplishment, let's assume it is currently the month of January.

What opportunities surround me right now to easily earn $10,000 per month in total, personal income by December of this year or sooner?

Or sooner tagged on is important. Why would we want to limit ourselves (typical in affirmation style) to a specific date? Why not allow the Universe to be flexible and deliver it even sooner?

Let's build upon this same question further. Let's throw in one of the attributes from Column 3:

What opportunities surround me right now, where I can tap into my resourcefulness that will easily allow earning $10,000 per month in total personal income by December of this year or sooner?

One step further would be to add in the reason for the increased income:

How can I best utilize my honesty, character, and resourcefulness, to attract and increase my monthly income to $10,000 or more on a consistent, monthly basis, allowing for even more quality time with my wife and children by December of this year or sooner?

What about outside resources available to you (the *gorilla* from Chapter 16) you aren't currently aware of? Let's begin the question with Who:

Who do I know that can best help me utilize and expand my knowledge and skills, increasing my monthly income to $10,000 per month or more, further validating my confidence, self-worth and value? (Note: you could add specificity to exactly what knowledge and skills).

More Than One

I like to teach a person to create at least three empowering questions around the same desire, a What, How, and Who question. *What* elicits content, *How* elicits process, and *Who* elicits resources. If you look back, I've done just that with these examples. Therefore, by developing all three questions, you are maximizing the potential for its manifestation by expanding your overall awareness.

EMPOWERING QUESTIONS

Say this affirmation aloud followed by its empowering question equivalent:

- I am enjoying early retirement at my beach house earning $30,000 per month.
- How can I best utilize my honesty, character, and resourcefulness, to attract a $30,000 or more monthly residual income allowing for peaceful relaxation wherever I choose to be?

Do you feel, or hear, or see, or process the difference between the two?

Your Turn

Create one or two empowering questions right now for that which you desire. If you have a pad and pen, even better, but at least take a few moments in thought and begin to play around with these. There is no right or wrong, per se.

One gotchya in creating these questions is in not being aware of disempowering presuppositions that can sneak in. As talked about in the Language chapters, presuppositions pre-suppose or claim something to already be true within the question. You want to avoid negative, or disempowering states, or that which is not desired.

For instance, "How can I procrastinate less so I achieve my goals?" presupposes you procrastinate. Because this is moving away, it is not empowering. Simply switch around the negative behavior with something like, "How can I more quickly and easily achieve my goals?" This slight difference puts you at cause, allowing for solutions to be recognized.

Unlimited Uses

The beauty of these questions is that they can be tailored to most anything a person desires in their life. Students can use them for homework and tests. I've used them to make smoother landings for my passengers. They are powerful in relationships, too.

These Empowering Questions used regularly will change your life. From greatly improving communication in all types of relationships to problem solving of any sort, creating expansion through these questions will provide you new possibilities from seemingly out of nowhere.

Recently, I helped a woman who is a professional free diver develop her Empowering Questions to increase her depth from 41 meters to her goal of 60 meters. The application to our lives is endless! They are easy to do and easy not to do. Armed with this knowledge, the choice to incorporate them into your life becomes yours.

Don't "Answer"

Here is the other aspect of these questions to keep in mind; **they are not meant to be answered**, or at least not as a conscious-minded question. Of course, if you can, well then excellent! But chances are, if they were that easily solvable, the Empowering Question was not necessary to begin with. An answer may indeed arise in the process simply because you are widening access to your mind and opening your awareness, raising your level of consciousness around the possibilities that already exist!

Yet, these questions are most useful for areas where the answers cannot readily be discerned (where you do not know how to bring the solution about, or are in a position of feeling stuck). Once spoken into existence, the subconscious mind has no choice but to seek the answer.

This is how the Law of Attraction truly works. It is vibrational energy in the world of quantum physics. This also completely relieves all the pressure from a typical affirmation. In other words, **you are not**

required to know how this will manifest in your life! You give it up to your subconscious mind, the Law of Attraction, Spirit, God, Angels, Source, the Universe, etc.

A Real Life Example

I recently worked with an individual just being introduced to Empowering Questions. He was very familiar with affirmations, and so I asked him to say aloud an affirmation of his desire.

As he did, his entire physiology changed. The Neuro aspect of NLP was in full swing. As he spoke aloud his affirmation, he felt a lump begin to manifest in his chest. He pointed to it as his breaths became shallow and quickened. Then, a paleness overcame his face. He shifted quickly into a disempowered state simply by thinking of this desire and echoing it from within.

This was hardly conducive to manifesting and tapping into the Law of Attraction toward his desired result! By the time we finished putting his affirmation into an empowering question, he felt and looked completely different. His color returned, his breathing deepened, and his posture was more erect, and yes, the lump in his chest was completely absent.

He was amazed how something so simple could have such a profound affect physiologically. It certainly begs the question, if the physiological is that observable, imagine what is happening within the mind and results of the past versus what's possible?

Additional Examples

Here are some more examples I've helped others with:

- *How can I honor myself even more while fulfilling my life's purpose and pleasures with greater awareness and joy?*

- *How can I increase the value of my message and communication even more effectively through questions to elevate the conversation I am having right now?*
- *How can I best elevate my higher awakening right now, perceiving everyone including myself, in the higher planes of unconditional love and oneness?*

Usefulness of Empowering Questions

In summary, once spoken into existence, several ascendancies are activated in various ways. First of all, you have widened your awareness simply by creating the specific question modeled in a specific way. You have eliminated some filters within your RAS, actually opening it up, allowing more conscious awareness of vital information which will aid in the achievement of the question's desired result.

With this increased awareness, suddenly you become alerted to conversations that may have gone unnoticed before. For instance, you are in earshot of two people talking at a coffee shop when a key word associated directly with your Empowering Question reaches your conscious mind. Rather than missing an opportunity, you now seize the moment, and bring into your life a contact that can provide exactly what you were searching for, or vice-versa.

As another example of the usefulness of these questions, when forced to make the many decisions we do throughout the day, your subconscious mind is in full awareness. As a result, it will better guide you towards making decisions that allow the manifestation of your desire.

And the amazing part of all this? Outside the formulating and occasional conscious thought of the question, most of the process will be *outside* your conscious awareness. The Law of Attraction exercised in your favor!

Final Thought

One last thought…be **playful** with these. Make it more about *doing* them than attempting to word them perfectly. Just start. The more you exercise them the easier and more natural they flow. You can begin simply with, "How can I be even happier right now?" and build upon it as you get more comfortable.

They don't have to be graduate-level questions when first starting out. In time, as you become more comfortable with them, they will naturally include more accurate and expanded information that will broaden even further your awareness and activation of the Law of Attraction in a way that works for you.

It almost seems magical when experienced, for done correctly, they absolutely work. Get courageous and creative in developing your Empowering Questions. Make them a part of your life. Teach them to your children, other family members, and friends. You will be incredibly rewarded if you do.

My dear friend, Gail Kraft, recently wrote an entire book dedicated to Empowering Questions, *The Empowering Process*. It is a phenomenal resource and guide to getting even more out of life!

Teaching Empowering Questions to Others

Lastly, if you are teaching this to someone, you want the person to utilize their own verbiage, not yours. However, a person may find themselves a bit stuck.

Go step by step and ease them into the structuring of an effective Empowering Question. If needed, help guide them to creating the first one or two. After that, they take control and get creative in developing their own. If known, guide them to utilize their primary modality: Auditory, Visual, Kinesthetic, Audio Digital. It makes the questions even more powerful.

If they are serious about learning how to use these Empowering Questions to attract their desired results, have them write out at least three a day and share them with you. Text or email works great for this as well. Ensure you have their permission for your feedback. Then together, you can adjust, if necessary, to make them even more empowering. After a couple of days of this, they've got it.

* * *

Empowering Questions to New Pathways

1) Questions provide answers where none seem to exist.

2) You are not looking to 'consciously' answer your Empowering Questions. You are making yourself available for the answer to appear.

3) Be playful and have fun with these! They can change your life!

FINAL THOUGHTS 25

"Why do you stay in prison when the door is wide open?"

RUMI

One of our greatest treasures are the various enlightened souls who have walked this planet and left behind their gifts for all of us to learn from. These great poets, philosophers, scientists, artists, inventors, authors, and sages magnificently contain deep truths in simplicity, just like Rumi's quote above.

For all our advancements, technological, medical, scientific, etc., isn't it amazing the power that these greats understood without any of that? Quantum physics today is proving what these great men and women have been teaching us for thousands of years; everything is energy, popping in and out of existence. How we interpret the world is truly that—an interpretation.

Yet, their truths to navigate life are steadfast. What was spoken and written long ago by many, holds as much value today, if not more, than the moment those thoughts were first recorded. Learning from these greats proves that we don't have to reinvent the wheel unless we choose to (unless we are unaware such wisdom already exists). Today, their words live on for all of us to learn and grow from.

FINAL THOUGHTS

The Evolution of Life

The day I wrote this out, I had just finished an amazing morning visit with my daughter and granddaughter in Philly. My daughter Ashley is married, a mother of two beautiful children, and now a nurse. She and I live thousands of miles apart, and any time afforded together is a pure blessing.

What made this short August visit extra special was Natalie's 7th birthday. And how incredibly ironic this visit aligned, as I was finishing the original content to this book.

If you remember, in the Author's Note, I asked you to treat this like a conversation, as if we were sitting together on a flight from L.A. to New York, getting to know each other's stories and sharing what we do. Last night, I flew from Phoenix to Las Vegas to Philadelphia, and now I'm closing this book after this special day on the East Coast. Isn't life fascinating? Completely unplanned, I just had to pause in this moment at the wonder of it all.

I sat across from my granddaughter at the Green Eggs Café near Independence Hall, in awe, knowing the content for this book was already complete. Knowing how *significant* that age of seven is, the majority of her imprinting now complete.

Her meta-programming was mostly established and will forever affect her future. One can already perceive how her behaviors are going to play out. She has already decided her likes and dislikes at a deeper level. She was so adorable as I watched her navigate those Silver Dollar pancakes in front of her. Between those delicious bites she was enjoying, I listened to her express favorite memories from this past summer.

And there sat Ashley, deservedly proud and more beautiful in my eyes than ever. She is an absolutely amazing woman who completed college with a Nursing degree while raising two kids who were often ill, and a husband deployed with the Army and away from home for half the time. None in our family could understand how she managed it all, but somehow she did.

Ashley is so aligned with who she is. She is living her passion, following her dreams and creating her life of happiness. If you ask her if the challenges were worth it, she will tell you, "Absolutely!" Knowing first-hand the constant obstacles thrown her way as she ventured on, there is no way she would have been able to pull it off if not in alignment. This is the advantage of living your Authentic Truth. Work and effort become a part of the magical and joyful journey with ease and grace.

Living Your Dream

Ashley is a testament to the slight edge principle. She also fully embraces the concept of, *"If it is to be, it is up to me."* No matter the outside forces that negatively attacked her, Ashley found a way. She is so resourceful and adaptive to any situation thrown at her. She is a true model of possibility for anyone.

In regards to pursuing her Nursing degree, it would have been so easy for her to throw in the towel at least a dozen times that I know of, and no one would have faulted her for it. But she would have. She had reached a point of maturity where full realization of her dream was about her own desire to accomplish this goal, serve others, and to better support her family financially.

Ashley had a dream and that vision pulled her to where she is today. Rather than moving away from pain, she was pulled by a vision so strong, she plowed through any and all obstacles; like the plow of a freight train drives through the winter snow drifts along the tracks.*

> *If you care to see this in action here's a great visual: https://youtu.be/uvbgq2Ni2uE*

Obstacles showed up and redirections happened, but in the end, it was her vision that pulled her to goal achievement. Today, her dedication

FINAL THOUGHTS

to herself and family is rewarded with her dream nursing position, delivering new life to our planet.

There is a wonderful book entitled, *The Dream Giver*, by Bruce Wilkenson. The book is divided into two sections. The first section is an allegory of a young boy's journey to achieving his dream, and the second is a teaching by the author of the learnings from the story.

The young boy first receives his dream from the Dream Giver. He then deals with all the naysayers, questioning himself if his is a worthy dream.

He then ventures out and encounters all sorts of obstacles like Giants, Doubt, Bullies, Wasteland, etc., but in the end, he does achieve his dream.

The second section explains the process, utilizing the story to describe what each of us goes through in achieving a Big Dream. The author involves the reader into understanding the worthiness of every step taken along that journey.

That book reminds me much of my Ashley today. She had a dream and no matter the obstacles, she stayed on course and made it happen.

What's the Goal of Life?

Isn't pursuing a vision the ultimate journey for any of us? To discover your passion and go for it with everything you have? There is music within you that no one else can play. That is what lives at your core center. If you have not yet unearthed your definitive purpose, it is awaiting your self-discovery.

We each are gifted with something unique that no other can bring to this world. Discovering your *Authentic Truth* is as much about falling in love with yourself again as it is pursuing your ultimate passion in life; being in total flow, and in complete and absolute alignment with your Identity and your *I Am*.

This is not something anyone else can decide for you. Yet, in the process of discovery, there is great wisdom to draw from and teachers and guides to help you navigate to your truth. That is what Niurka did for me, and it is my mission to be doing for others now.

Your journey in completing this reading should have you realize that all the answers are contained within you. It is only a matter of unlocking them from your subconscious mind.

By understanding better how your mind behaves in this world of infinite maps of reality, you now know yours is truly unique. The greater your awareness in how you see and interpret the world, the more clearly you will see who you are and your significance within it. Your language creates your world. Change your language, change your world.

Love – A Way of Living

Love is such a powerful force. My wife and I adopted many years ago awakening in the morning with this mantra:

- *I greet this day with love in my heart.*
- *If God is for me, who can be against me?*
- *All things are possible through Christ who strengthens me.*

The latter two are from the Bible, Romans 8:31 and Philippians 4:13, respectively. The first line is from Og Mandino's epic book, *The Greatest Salesman in the World*.

The book is a story about a young man who wishes to be financially free after seeing it in another. He is graced with Ten Scrolls passed on from the wealthy salesman he admired. It was explained that should he invest his efforts to memorize and put into practice these scrolls, his dream would happen.

The first time Elke and I read this book many years ago, we paused with the Scroll Marked II. It touched our hearts, resonating deep within us, reaching our souls. Years later, I chose to memorize the 983 word scroll that begins with, and repeats throughout, *"I greet this day with love in my heart."*

Today, I still use it as a daily mantra, reciting the entire Scroll to myself from memory. What I've found is its truth surfaces again and again in my life in different ways. For instance,

"When I am tempted to criticize, I will bite on my tongue, and when I am moved to praise, I will shout from the roofs." Another is, *[My shield of Love] will uplift me in moments of despair and calm me in times of exultation."* One of the final lines says, *"If I have no other qualities, I can succeed with Love alone."*

I have found with the daily repetition of this entire Scroll, there is an inner peace created. Similar to an affirmation, it's more a resolution and grounds me to what is most important in my daily living—the love and care for others.

It has also created for me that all-important *pause* in critical situations. Rather than reacting in stressful situations, I can close my eyes and allow those words to soothe and calm me. And that provides greater access to the resources of my subconscious mind, creating even better results.

Our Thinking

What we program our minds to think will have dramatic effects on how we live. *"As a man thinketh, so is he."* More great wisdom passed down for us all. It's also Biblical: *"Above all else, guard your heart, for it is the wellspring of life."* (Proverbs 4:23)

Yes, we have deep levels of programming from our early childhood that can be addressed. But we also have the ability to alter how we interpret the world, a level above programming, by addressing our behaviors.

Even though I mentioned this earlier, I believe it so significant, I am writing of it again. One of the greatest and easiest choices you can make in creating a positive shift in your life is to turn off the television, or at least be aware of what and when you are viewing your programs. I cannot stress this enough.

News is important, but so is your mind. TV shows are entertaining, but so is a good book.

We have created a culture that does not promote, as in the past, the creativeness of the mind. Music programs have evaporated from many schools, electronics have replaced outdoor play, texting has replaced verbal communication.

In a book, your mind calls upon more faculties than simply watching a screen where the images are already created for you. This also programs you by the vision of another: what they wish you to think, feel, and see. This is not to say all TV is bad; it means monitoring how much and what sources you allow yourself to be programmed by.

If you didn't know, your brainwaves begin to slow (Theta/Alpha) prior to going to bed at night and in those first few waking moments. When they are low, more *direct access* to your subconscious mind is the result. Much of the filtering utilized by the mind during waking hours is bypassed. How many people fill their minds with the negativity of the news or a crime/drama TV show just prior to going to sleep?

Think about this: You have an open channel to your subconscious mind where it will be programmed. You can choose to program it with inspiring language, authentic affirmations, Empowering Questions, visionary images, thoughts of what I did right today, gratitude, the promises of a better tomorrow, **OR**, you can watch the news, a reality show, or sitcom that does nothing towards building your future, and actually creates negative thinking. It is the ultimate contrast and it is a choice: easy to do and easy not to do. The choice truly is yours. What value do you place on your future? What do you wish to leave behind to this world? As a man thinketh, so is he.

FINAL THOUGHTS

Develop a Ritual

Empowering Questions, affirmations, resolutions, and mantras are powerful and most efficient during those times right before bed and right after waking up. If you make the decision to believe that the day begins in the evening, it will change your entire perspective of going to sleep at night. Set the intention the night *before* of what your day *tomorrow* will be. Fill your mind with gratitude for the passing day, and ask how you will make tomorrow even better. Just this one little change will have a dramatic effect in your life.

Formulating this habit, allowing it to become a way of life, will slowly reprogram your mind to think more positively, more objectively, broaden your awareness, see more possibilities, relieve emotional pain and stress, and help you connect with your soul.

If you believe in God, these are precious moments of the day to connect your soul with Him. If you are not a believer, it is still a moment to be savored, and will aid in aligning you with your core center.

Be Curious!

I'd also like to encourage you, especially the non-believer, to never stop asking questions about God, faith, science, history, and the future—all of it.

As your awareness grows, continue to listen objectively, and be open. The result is living a life filled with far more love, joy, and happiness—something we addressed earlier as a known challenge in today's world for many.

Over time, you will notice significant, consistent positive shifts in your state as you go about your daily life. You will begin to see the world in a new light. Develop your own ritual for every evening and every morning. Set the intention and the positive mindset will follow. Eventually, it will become a natural way of being.

Life Is Precious

Life is precious. You are on a journey, and you have the choice to choose your direction of travel and destination or to travel rudderless and adrift. No one is able to predict what a particular day will bring. Travesty can strike in an instant, as can absolute joy. So, why not prepare yourself to handle either with love and compassion?

The closer you allow yourself to align with your *Authentic Truth*, your core, your heartfelt, love center, the greater the armor you will have to ensure you ride the storms with grace and relish the joys of life with controlled exultation.

Remember, how you talk to yourself will directly impact every area of your life. The primary difference in successes amongst different people resides in how they interpret the world through their language, programming, and self-talk.

Science and visionaries working in this field continue to provide us with new insights into genetics, the mind, and consciousness. We are learning more and more about the effects of programming on our overall lives. What you have immediate control over right now is how you allow yourself to talk to you. I implore you to adopt some Empowering Questions, affirmations, resolutions, and mantras, and journal them.

My friend and mentor, Susan Walsh, suggested many years ago starting a "What Did I Do Right Today" journal. (Remember I was pessimistic and very hard on myself in the past) It's magical. Many of us spend far too much time focused on what we did wrong throughout the day and not enough time on what we did right.

The first time I began such a journal (and I've done this multiple times), I kept it going for over a year's time. Every night, before retiring, I would add several items of that which I did right throughout the day. In time, it became a habitual way of thinking.

FINAL THOUGHTS

Meditation

In *Super Brain*, the authors, Deepak Chopra, M.D. and Rudolph Tanzi, Ph.D., clearly state of all the possible ways to improve and sustain one's health, the most effective is meditation. It is so powerful, yet largely not understood or practiced in America.

What is meditation? Here is how Adyashanti states it in his book, *Falling Into Grace*:

> *Letting go of our conflict with life, dropping the struggle with who and what we are. Through resting in this way, we enter a state of nonresistance, where we'll be able to have a taste of what it is like to live for a moment without judgment or conflict.*
>
> *The most essential aspect of meditation, what meditation really is or can be, is a relinquishing of control...it is a state of discovery. Sitting in quiet and stillness and just being in a state of openness gives you a clear opportunity to watch what happens internally when you stop judging your experience, when you stop judging your mind for being busy, or you stop judging yourself for having a particular feeling.*
>
> *With this foundation...we've had some taste of what it's like to let go, of realizing for ourselves the futility of trying to control things...we can much more naturally develop a wider perspective on our experiences, even the difficult ones. In this way life itself becomes a meditation, and a whole new relationship with existence starts to unfold.*

I suggest you explore exactly what it is and give it a try. There are plenty of books, web sites, and YouTube videos to learn from. Once you practice meditation, and there are many different kinds, you will find *you* connect with *yourself* on deeper and deeper levels.

A great place to begin is with a grounding meditation. This is my go-to mediation, especially whenever I am feeling a bit *off*. It places me back on firm ground, while bringing clarity to whatever is troubling me. As mentioned eariler on page 54, Niurka's has a version available on YouTube: https://youtu.be/ZexwyMvAceI

Setting an intention and going into a meditation will also allow greater connection with your subconscious mind. The time spent there will connect you with your higher conscious, providing expansive possibilities where none seemed before. This will lead to more choices and possibilities and a better life overall.

A Final Thank You

My main goal in writing this book is to awaken within you, and the greater population, alternative solutions to approach life's problems and to be aware they exist. Life is often made far more complicated than necessary because our tools to cope with issues and behaviors as they surface appear limited.

Now, you know viable, proven methods do exist, and that it is okay to seek help. If every person understood even the basics presented here, I believe our world would experience far less pain. Too often we become subjects of the *machine* of life rather than evolving our *Authentic Truth*.

As you complete these last few words, I wish to thank you sincerely *and* congratulate you for investing your precious time in yourself. This book reaches far more people easier than I could ever meet with one on one. That is a gift of leverage. Because you put forth a willingness to explore, you are also the better for it. With its end, you have an awareness today you didn't have before you turned its first page. Now, you have the ability to be consciously aware of the choices you make and why you make them.

You have the choice to stop and *think* about your *thinking*, allowing for, *and* creating new choices from the get-go. You also know it is possible for you to live authentically as your true self. My hope is that you take your journey seriously and to the next level. Join me in my quest to pass

FINAL THOUGHTS

along this vital information by sharing this book with a family member, friend, colleague, or organization.

My goal is to get this into the hands of teachers, counselors, prisons, clergyman, professionals, parents, teenagers, and anyone with influence or just needing to hear this message. Help enlighten another, pay it forward, and let's make this a better world for all, one person at a time, one community at a time, and beyond.

You truly are precious; a precious gift for the world to know. Someone today will be touched by your love, moved by a deed you do, inspired by words you say, or enlightened just with your presence. Raise your level of awareness to the beauty of it all. Get out and fly—your spirit will enrich another's life today.

AFTERWORD

Their Words

I will be the first to admit writing this book was one tremendous learning curve. More importantly is the journey it created for myself, my closest friends, and those I continue to work with. This excursion brought to light new ways of seeing the world...my very own *map of the world* changed in some ways.

I'm currently re-reading one of my favorite books of all time, Norman Vincent Peale's book, *Stay Alive All Your Life*, mentioned in Chapters 5 & 20. The values, truths, and wisdom contained within are far beyond the cost of the words or the investment in time to read them.

My mom often tells the story of her dad carrying Dr. Peale's books around with him. She talks about her dad's gracious and kind heart and how others loved him so dearly. Although he passed way too early from cancer, and I never had the chance to meet him, I know my mom inherited much of her dad's gift of giving to others. She truly is one of the most giving and serving people I've ever met. She accepts no accolades or thank yous, she simply gives from her heart.

As I reflect, maybe that is why I am who I am today? I love people, and I love watching them attain their full potential so often hidden from themselves. We are living in interesting times. The world often seems lost, as does our country pitting itself against one another. What

AFTERWORD

a waste. Life is so precious and we only have a limited time here. We live in a world of *Infinite Possibilities!* If you're feeling there is still no hope, may I also recommend the books, *Abundance* and *Bold*, by Peter Diamandis and Steven Kotler. You are ultimately in control of how you think! Strive to get the most out of all that life is, in all ways.

As for God, after years of contemplation, Tolstoy came to the conclusion of this simplistic truth: "To know God is to live." I so agree. And that is my map. Even if not yours, I do encourage you to explore the possibility. I do not understand this new value system our country, as a whole, has seemed to adopted of turning away from God. We forget history and often do not know or understand it. Seek knowledge from wherever you can as often as you can. As Dr. Peale says, "Seek inspiration in books, friends, music, art, travel. Interest is a measure of aliveness."

This Afterwordss is about how life never stands still. It is constantly evolving whether aware of it or not. This section is dear to me for each of these individuals are now a part of my soul. Sharing in their experiences and realizing even more of the details than presented in this book, each has overcome major hurdles in their lives. It is a joy to share their words with you.

Let's Hear From Them

Following are the stories from those in Section II. Part of this journey has been learning that life never stops moving and new challenges constantly arrive. NLP, and Evolved NLP, provide brilliant insights that can create amazing enlightenments into the self. But, they are not a panacea.

For true connection to your Authentic Truth to continue, it is a daily practice. The blessing is that this daily practice can be far more easy and natural with the initial transformation from working with a professional. But if complacency is allowed to sneak in without awareness, maps can be changed in ways that do not serve you. Stay vigilant. Remain involved and become a better you each day. Apply the slight edge principle knowing that you are whole and complete. The answers are within you.

* * *

Catalaya Afterword

What more can I say about this precious friend? She is forever attached to me at a soul level. Over the course of time we've spent together, on and off working and just hanging out, Catalaya has never once lied to me. She has never "misspoke" or had to take back something she said. Everything that I've experienced about her is authentic. That is how I see her map. She is brilliant, genuine, funny, and creative. And in there possibly resides some of the issues she has with others; she cannot be fit into a box. It's not that she is a rebel, as I've said about her in the past. Now, I realize she is simply an extremely Kinesthetic Free Spirit. Attempting to confine her with rules and 'normalcy' goes against her core values as to who she is. As she explores this further, she is overcoming old challenges in new ways. The more time I spend with her the greater my belief grows in her. I have a clear picture that she will continue her expansion and create tremendous success all around her.

* * *

As you read in this book, I attempted to take my own life at sixteen years old. I know exactly what drove me to that point [supreme awareness]. I now understand that no matter what I go through I will eventually succeed at being at the happiest point I can be.

After working with Guy, I can understand day-to-day problems better without feeling like I can't get away from it. That there *is* always a way.

AFTERWORD

What I find now is that people look up to me for they see me as strength for surviving; and that in turn gives me more strength from them. The thoughts have arisen of cutting but there is just not the want. I could not work myself up to it. I feel safe from it unlike in the past. So, even though I still face challenges, I now have the confidence to work through them. That is the biggest difference I now have. I trut myself.

In fact, six months after my attempted suicide, I achieved a tremendous accomplishment. Elke trained me to a fourth-place trophy in my first bikini contest. I used working out as a beneficial pain instead of hurting myself in a non-beneficial way.

My words to anyone who is in the place I once was: Don't beat yourself up. It's not wrong to ask for help. You're not bad because you feel this way. Hope only works if you're wanting it.

Claudia Afterword

An interesting phenomena I've noticed in doing this work with others is the challenge to see exactly how their life was before the transformation took place. For Claudia, beyond the immediate concern for her daughter was this issue around finances. It showed in our first meeting at their home and afterward. However, she, for the first time after being on her own, is now gaining control. I do believe this was a direct result of her Value Elicitation around finances. She has become an enlightened student bettering herself constantly in this regard.

* * *

I have had the pleasure of meeting Guy off of Facebook. I had posted a prayer request for my daughter who had just attempted suicide. Guy reached out to me and the way of his wording caught my attention. I opened up myself and two daughters to meeting him. This was a huge step for me, being super protective of them and not wanting any added trouble, pain, drama, and was worried that it would be another financial setback. I hadn't met anyone that offers to give their time in their craft for free.

I am a single mom of three kids. Safety, protection, and providing the best for my children and finances are a huge part of my life, they are my life. I hadn't seen it at the time but I was super protective and controlling because of the fear I had in becoming financially harmed any further than I was already. I had married young and my ex-husband was in total control over finances.

When we divorced, I had no idea how to budget at all. I had no credit in my name and had negative things on my credit. I was totally ashamed, hurt and scared by that. I didn't want to lose my children and would just ignore the credit ratings and bills.

The anger over finances played in every aspect of my life. I was afraid to allow the kids to have certain freedoms, because, what if something happened requiring expenses to remedy and I was unable to pay for it? That played on my mind in every aspect of my life and weighed me down in ways that I hadn't realized.

Guy met with my daughters and I, and then with each of us separately. I was open and willing to listen and learn everything he had to say. We had decided to work on my biggest fear. At first I was like how could that be finances? I mean, the area of finances wasn't what I wanted help with; communicating and understanding my daughter, who had just attempted suicide, was.

I decided to trust Guy and the process and we started with finances [VE exercise]. Incredibly, it totally opened my eyes to the pattern that I had created in so many aspects of my life. Finances was controlling me, my communication, and my behavior with my children. This proved eye opening in how it affected my life in every negative way possible. Guy opened my eyes to seeing this, and guided me to take steps towards facing it and overcoming it.

Afterwards, I signed up with my bank for a credit monitoring company and that day I looked at the financial controlling factor as a

AFTERWORD

positive. The flood gates of emotional happiness happened when I got my first credit card in my name at 39 years old.

The amount of relief I have felt and continue to feel is amazing. I am less angry, more patient, more open to my children's adventures and I am more relaxed than I have ever been in my life. It is a very refreshing, rejuvenating, uplifting feeling and I feel in control in a positive way. Every day that this positive increase happens, I think of Guy and smile. God sent me this amazing, knowledgeable man that took my negative situation and turned it into a positive way of life. That effects not only myself but my children's lives.

Kelley Afterword

Throughout this book, I've done my very best to be truly authentic. Of the individuals mentioned in this book, Kelley's transformation is maybe the most profound. She has truly blossomed into her Authentic Self with a freedom unmatched before. Her successes continue to pile up. It truly has been an absolute blessing and joy to witness.

* * *

You should know you, Guy helped change my entire life for the better!!! Forever grateful for the role he played!!! Since I met and began working with him, I have accomplished so much in such a short amount of time beyond what I even had planned. The most amazing part of it was it was coming to me at the perfect right timing. The problem I was having pertained to a newly formed self-doubt, low self-worth, feeling alone and not enough again. I was in a relationship where I was constantly controlled. In the event something wasn't exactly to what they wanted, I would be yelled, sworn at, and called names.

I went thru thinking everyday there was something wrong with me to be treated like this again. Because of these emotions, I was not living a full life and productive days as I should have been. My mindset had changed over the prior year from where I felt like I could accomplish anything I put my mind to, to feeling completely stuck and helpless.

One day a mutual friend of Guy and mine posted information about Sociopaths, Egotism, and Narcissism. I asked a question under comments asking what to do if the person you are with was just entirely described. I honestly stared at the post in complete awe that I had never heard these words and it was exactly what I was dealing with on a daily basis. I had lost my spirit over the year because of it and knew I needed a greater understanding and help.

Guy sent me a message with a lot more information about it and I replied back asking if he could help me. He proceeded to ask me what I was seeking? I instantly responded and I had so much passion wanting my old self back. He agreed to meet with me and the next week began the process of returning back to me.

The greatest experience memory for me is when we spent the first weekend in June experiencing all my emotions I had and what I wanted. That week I left the man I was with. Upon the following week, I again met with Guy and he proceeded to hand me the sheet [the words written down on several pages from the Quantum Linguistic Exercise accomplished on the airplane] and I didn't take it. I said, "That's not me anymore!" and I said it with full confidence.

I had gained the courage to take the first step and leave a really bad situation. The following month I attended a [Niurka] conference in LA with Guy and Elke where I took in more knowledge about the power of my words and mind. My confidence in who I am came full force without any question; I was again unstoppable and empowered.

Today I am not just back to where I was previously but *in an even happier place than I thought imagined*. I have been published in multiple magazines, both in writing and photos, made it into a 2017 calendar, featured photo on the cover of a romance novel, am almost complete with my own book, website about to launch, and currently working

AFTERWORD

with some other individuals putting on a conference in order to inspire others.

Most importantly, I have become a better mother by putting my children in a better situation. I am utilizing key learnings and applying it to my children and teaching them a better way. I have also found an amazing man who is beyond measure. He is what I expected. Our dynamic together is deep and meaningful, and impacts my soul on a level that helps create the best version of me. Thank you again Guy for being you.

Kelley – www.fitintransit.com

Monika Afterword

Monika and I have not had much communication since that time in her kitchen. We talked a few times, and she called once when she found herself in a confusing family situation and needed clarity. She is a powerhouse in her own right—especially when she is on top of her game. We met recently, and I can see she still is struggling at times with certain issues. I reminded her that we haven't continued the work and we only released Anger. There is much more we can do when ready. I also mentioned to be aware that the more you involve yourself in an ongoing, daily practice in awareness, the greater the overall evolution will be. Knowing Monika's full story, I can say from the heart that she is amazing.

* * *

I didn't know Guy but saw a post of his about personal power through a mutual friend on Facebook. I was stuck in a self-sabotaging state and didn't know how to escape it. I decided to send Guy a private message through Facebook and he responded.

Over the course of several months he agreed to help me remove my self-doubt and fears around my own success. For whatever the reason, whenever I'd begin to experience successes in my life, someone or something seemed to drag me back down and I'd have to start all over again.

In working with Guy, I discovered things about myself and family I hadn't known – at least not consciously. But as we delved deeper it brought new awareness to my past in new ways. The results have been amazing.

Although I still suffer physical pain from a neck injury, I am free of all the other pain that plagued me for many, many years, still some 8 months after this experience of release through working with Guy. Turned out, much of that pain from the past was pent-up emotional pain.

I have recently gained a greater connection with my family and this has turned out to be a true blessing. Even my work has seen dramatic explosions of growth at times. Yet, what Guy also writes is true – our ongoing awareness is so crucial for old habits can arise so this is not a one-time thing but a practice. I thank him from the bottom of my heart for all he has graciously done for me. He is an enduring friend that I'm glad I reached out to.

Lexi Afterword

When I first considered taking the initiative and reaching out to Lexi, I was hesitant. From all appearances, she seemed to be the biggest challenge of anyone, outside of Catalaya, I'd worked with up to that point. I asked myself if it was in my best interest to take on such an unknown. We all need checks of our blind spots, so I first reached out to a fellow friend who knows this work and me well for her advice. Her response after seeing some of Lexi's Facebook posts was, "That's going to be a project, do you really want to take that on right now?" But Lexi was hurting inside. Anyone with any sort of discernment could see that. It was her well-being that mattered more to me at that moment than the project it might bring. I understand we cannot save everyone. There are only so many hours in the day, but I wanted to at least make the attempt with Lexi.

AFTERWORD

*I only work with a few people at any given time, and I had the opportunity to give her some attention. The fighter pilot in me looked eagerly at the challenge and potential learning as well. Funny thing is, I spent less time with Lexi than **anyone else** I've worked with before or since! You just never know where a person is in their stage of evolution, how ready and willing they are, and where that connection will go.*

* * *

A while back I was very unhappy with my situation living with my grandparents. I was so stuck in this life and couldn't see how to get out and move forward.

Guy reached out to me through Facebook and offered his help. I face medical challenges and had suffered a lot of abuse growing up. I wanted to change but just couldn't figure out how to do it.

After a certain point, I'd get lost in working with therapists in the past. The therapist would lose me and I'd get anxious. Cutting to the point was essential. Guy listened and made me feel heard. At that point, helping me to feel understood allowed me to accept his wisdom.

The best part was how he helped me to redirect my venting. My frustration was sometimes taken out on others when it wasn't always them who caused it. I learned how to release this through a filter to calm down. He asked me questions that helped me think about what it was that upset me so bad.

Prior to changing my ways, I had no self-respect at all. I was completely attracting the wrong men and lowering my standards. Now I'm focused on my goals and achieving self-respect and have mastered saying "No."

I feel in control of my life now and responsible for who I am. I am accomplishing what I knew I could but in the past was unable to make happen. Now I do. I see myself being financially fit with an amazing husband and a child.

Connie Afterword

Connie is a genuine soul who has faced her own demons and won. Anyone who has personally experienced or been around addicted behavior knows the challenges are anything but easy. What I find so uplifting in Connie still today is that she makes her life better because she truly desires it. I believe she hit her bottom soon before reaching out—and now she lives with a new-found hope that has her striving towards her vision of a continued path towards a better life.

* * *

When I first met Guy, I had just learned of my son's wedding, and that I was not welcomed. Today, because of this work with him, the repair with my family is slowly reuniting. I am excited to say that I am now invited to this most special occasion. There have been many such victories, however, not everything has been resolved as of yet.

The problem for me was that I had been raised Catholic, one of 7 children with a father who was a domineering force. We were told how to worship, what to think and feel, and what to value in life. This carried over into adulthood and ultimately led me to substance abuse.

I was able to raise my children and have a successful career as a nurse. All the while, I never questioned who I was, what role God played, or what I valued in life.

After many attempts, I was able to achieve sobriety in my mid 50's. My parents had both passed and my children were on their own. I had just me. All my friends were gone too, alcohol, parents, and children. My world was gone. I did not have a 5 year plan. The unease and pain started to set in. It was a gnawing, hollow hurt in my chest and it left me feeling so ALONE.

Additionally, I had several failed relationships. Someone once asked me what I liked to do??? What I valued??? And that led me to start questioning who I was????

AFTERWORD

While browsing Facebook one day a picture of a lion with a blue background and Guy popped up. The article talked about CORE VALUES. I was so confused and hurting so much that I decided to comment, "How do you know what your core values are?" To my surprise this man answered and offered to help me. Thus began my journey with Guy…

My personal experience with Guy has been one of self-awareness and much personal growth. It has not been an easy road. There is a constant fight between my conscience and subconscious mind, but, I am aware of this and the battle lessens every day. Guy has been a joy to work with, mending my brokenness with real hope of a better life. He is always positive and making me aware of the battles won. Coming back into the fold with my family is amongst the greatest victory.

About four months after my story ends in Chapter 12, I met Guy in person for the first time and we got to accomplish some additional work. Today I remain sober in part to Guy's devotion to my healing.

Some of the original pain is still there but greatly lessened. It serves to remind me to remain vigilant. I remain consciously aware of the work I will continue with. I am mending relationships with my family and most importantly my sons. For me it is progress in daily baby steps. Guy enabled me to start the journey of discovering ME and WHAT I VALUE. I will continue to work with Guy until I feel that complete freedom I know is possible within me.

ADDENDUM

Ariel's Transformation
(Including Her Words)

This is such a powerful story that I felt compelled to add as an addendum to this book. Now that you are fully aware of what is possible and have an understanding as to how such transformation can happen quickly, let's explore one last example of a phenomenal awakening through this work that recently unfolded.

I feel this so important because it is so common with so many women who are **stuck in abusive relationships or situations!** For Ariel, it was a twenty-five year, unhealthy pattern, that is now broken. It provides hope of what's possible when a person is able to step outside their problem frame and see their situation from a new perspective (similar to Kelley).

Meeting Ariel

We are born, and then life happens. When negative aspects are allowed to fester and grow without awareness, we become more and more disconnected from our Authentic Self. If this disconnection becomes great enough, and we lose touch with our very love core center and tragedy can strike.

ADDENDUM

Allowed to go without a pattern interruption or reprogramming, this disconnect can reach the point of taking one's own life as with Catalaya's attempted suicide. Fortunately for her, she broke through this wall of separation and is now more aligned with who she is than ever before.

But tragedy can strike in other ways, too. For instance, in Ariel's situation, her disconnection began at a very young age. Thrust into her family's religion from birth, she was born into an environment she had no control over. This refers well to the opening of Chapter 11's discussion that we do not have control over our environment at birth.

Ariel and I were casual Facebook friends, she posted mostly happy thoughts and we never had a conversation but intuitively my gut was telling me something was amiss. We eventually began communicating and her story touched me deeply.

Ariel is attractive and beautiful on the inside and out. She is loving, caring, funny, intelligent and outgoing. And unfortunately, there are men in this world who take advantage of such youthful innocence.

As Ariel grew up, the family's religion taught her life to be a certain way. As she looks back on it now, she sees how much it controlled her and disconnected her from herself.

Searching for solid ground, she married at eighteen to what would develop into an abusive situation. By nineteen, she developed Rheumatoid Arthritis. It took the medical professionals an extended period of time to diagnose because it isn't something common in a nineteen-year-old!

What would cause such an auto-immune disease to manifest? Could it possibly be a disconnection from her Authentic Truth? In my opinion, the stress of the religion and abusive marriage took their toll, and Ariel's subconscious mind allowed it to happen as with my niece in Chapter 2.

This is what is so challenging to understand about the mind. Our thoughts are so powerful; they seemingly can create even more pain when so disconnected from our self.

In Ariel's case, she had thought about suicide but what she turned to was alcohol and men. In her mind, it was a way to regain love and value in herself. After three failed marriages and a string of boyfriends, many of which turned out to be abusive, a repetitive pattern emerged.

Ariel eventually left her family's religion, which also left her alone. All those she'd known her whole life, friends and family, shunned her as the religion taught them to do after one leaves.

Eventually, all of her life events culminated to her and her seventeen-year-old daughter ending up homeless. Having nowhere else to turn, she went back to two of her former abusive boyfriends. First the one until she couldn't handle the abuse any longer, and then the other, where she is at the time of her writing you will read below.

What's so significant about Ariel's story is that it is all too common among women. I hear way too many stories of abuse making me wonder how can this happen again and again? And from the man's point of view, what drives them to such behavior to treat another soul in such a way? I believe the answer is at an early age, something significant happened in their life to create this disconnection from who they truly are.

This was the state Ariel was in when we finally began talking; fragile, broken, feeling lost, and hopeless. She was living in a state where believing in trust and support were absent in her life. Here was an attractive woman in her forties, that from outward appearances one would assume she had it all together. She certainly is loaded with potential, but how she had interacted with life was based upon her programming, and she deserved the chance at a new perspective.

Because Ariel lives out of state, our work was mostly phone calls and Facetime. She began as an eager student, so ready and willing. She continues to play full-out today, improving herself with greater and greater awareness and drive to heal completely. She is exhibiting the exact formula I laid out in Chapter 5, the Secret to Happiness.

I began simply by explaining the process and understanding how the mind truly works. The first tool I taught her was Empowering

ADDENDUM

Questions. These alone began shifting her entire emotional state. Her awareness so greatly increased in such a short time, it amazed even me.

However, one night about three weeks into our work, Ariel reached out via text, and I could tell something was off. I called her and instantly recognized she was in a black out. This is a condition common to an alcoholic, drinking in excess, often alone, to the point they have no conscious memory of the event.

The next day, I got serious with Ariel. Her progress was going well but this was a show stopper for me because of my experience with Janna. We had a serious and quite direct conversation. She was receptive, but it wasn't that easy.

About a week later, while driving back from California, we were again talking about her drinking. She had admitted a couple of times her desire to quit but unable to. During that phone call, completely spontaneous, I did a hybrid of both a Reframe and New Behavior Generator. As you will read in her own words, it worked solidly, allowing us to continue working together, moving forward.

Several weeks later, we met for the first time in person during one of my overnights in her hometown. We accomplished a New Behavior Generator, a Swish (a powerful exercise to break a habit where a specific trigger is involved. For her it was time management—with phenomenal results), a full-up Value Elicitation Exercise, and Timeline Therapy releasing her Anger.

The outcome? Ariel felt lighter and began seeing her life in new ways. She is falling in love with herself and gaining new found strength in many ways. The impact from the exercises has created a true transformation back to who she truly is at her core. Now, she clearly sees **how** her pattern of abuse showed up as it did in the past; how her behavior actually attracted and allowed it to dwell in her life. And this morning, a few weeks later, I received from her a revelation so profound that it inspired me to add her story here. It is in her "language" that makes this so significant. It is absolutely "at cause," meaning, a transformation has happened.

Her story encapsulates so much of what this book is all about to include stepping outside a problem frame with new awareness, falling in love with one's self again, transformation, and reconnecting with one's true love core center. This can be you, too.

I wish to be clear regarding her religion discussion. This is about Ariel and her personal experience with this religion. I am unfamiliar and am not advocating this to be true of the religion. It does, however, highlight the damage that can be done via any belief structure that creates dis-harmony without awareness.

I purposefully am not naming the religion for it is *unimportant to the context of the actual transformation*. The religion relates more to the *story* than understanding the *how* she ended up where she did. Also, keep in mind, she had already left the religion before we began talking. As with others, it is not my place to subject my own personal beliefs upon a person's transformation.

Enjoy her words now unchanged except the removal of names:

Ariel's Words

I can see what you were trying to tell me about my boyfriend being manipulative in an abusive way now. I can so clearly see it...even looking back into the past how he's done this all along to keep me right where he wanted me...

Being mean, hurtful or accusatory which in the past I would just get angry and be mean back...then I'd feel guilty because I could have quite the temper I guess from all the anger that I had inside me in the past making me like an explosive time bomb when something would set me off...not proud of that but realize it was my way of trying to protect myself and was largely tied in my subconscious making it difficult to control or handle such matters differently. Sooo happy to be free of

ADDENDUM

feeling like that Guy, you have nooo idea!!...I just wish I could go back in time and erase all the damage I caused by it. Especially any that effected my daughter.

It was difficult with her sometimes because she, like me has a very strong spirit...which could roll over into seeming "stubborn" when you're in a parent-child relationship trying to teach and "parent"... especially when you both have different modalities!

I know I should view the past...even mistakes as gifts I learned from and gained strength from...even more so now...but with the depth of my heart it's so difficult to not be saddened when you can see how badly you handled things and how, because of the way you did, you played a part in why your child has some of the issues she does. [*my sister Lia's point in Chapter 1*].

My daughter's also very much like her father...I mean I was a tad stubborn and hard headed and temperamental as a child as well... well at least according to my mother anyway...but what's funny is my grandmother who I loved sooo much...she was always so sweet, generous and kind...she used to always tell me "You were so sweet and gentle when you were little"...She used to say how I would love on my brother and sister and caress them...even at a very young age. We lived with her for a while till I was about five.

But...her father...

He's one of these "thinks he knows EVERYTHING" types and you could never persuade him otherwise...he's also very cold and apathetic about other's emotions and feelings for the most part...not sure what I ever saw in him except he was funny and attractive. And I guess coming out of an abusive relationship and all I had been through, to laugh felt good. He also happened to be partially raised in this same religion as I which made me feel we could relate and that he could understand me in ways others couldn't.

Outside of us both having a bit of a stubborn streak..(him more than me of course) haha...My poor daughter didn't stand a chance

NOT having one. Even when she was a baby close friends would tell me..."Wow, she's going to be strong willed"...which with the right tools can be a good thing as I am now learning.

But once she got to be 10 neither of us seemed to understand the other very well and that's when I left my third husband...her step dad of almost 5 yrs...that I was practically forced into marrying by my mom and the religion...to this day I wish I would have dashed out that side door I kept looking at wanting to run....wanting to run so fast and so far that I could be free of it all.

And here I am trying to help my alcoholic boyfriend when SHE needs me more than anyone!...That was my thought this morning around 3 am when he was acting like a jerk to me as he often did...that or rough with me...using he was "tired and grumpy as an excuse"...saying the next day..."I'm sorry Baby, I shouldn't have 'said that'..or 'acted that way'...or 'been so rough' I was just tired and grumpy"

Several times it's even been because he happens to get up in the middle of the night he'll down a bunch of alcohol then goes back to bed...that's usually when he's been really rough with me and ends up hurting me. Then, when I tell him he hurt me he gets mad "AT ME" for it. So, I leave and tell him he's acting like an ass and go sleep on the couch at which the next day he kisses me and tells me how "Sorry" he is and the whole cycle begins again. And oh yeah, sometimes even leaving his credit card and tells me to go buy something nice or get my nails done.

Speaking of being rough...he hurt my back really bad the night before last...it's another reason I haven't been feeling very good. He had fractured my back about a year ago when we got into an argument and he pushed me...I did slap him beforehand though. He was hiding another girl that he was flirting with while in a relationship with me and asking her out. I lost it and slapped him...twice.

Again...not proud...but that's when he pushed...well...more like shoved me into the ground and it fractured my lower back and hurt one

ADDENDUM

of my lower discs...since then if I move it just the wrong way or pushed too roughly it will start hurting extremely again. As a matter of fact, after he just acted the way he did and I came up here to sleep on the couch I gave in and took a muscle relaxer/pain pill because I couldn't stand the pain any longer.

I didn't want to tell you about that...I mean, about him hurting me... He didn't mean to last night, he's just really rough when he's drunk and doesn't realize his own strength. But still...I'm tired of it and deserve better than that.

Now I'm going to have to try to do all the things I need to get done and can hardly move...while "I was wanting so badly to help HIM" and while "I was caring for HIS needs" and he so little about mine...I'm done with these types of relationships once and for all.

I'm just in another abusive relationship...Not as severe as my first husband and one of my other exes...but only by comparison. And still nonetheless abusive. [*this may seem obvious to the outsider, but not necessarily to the person within the problem*].

Which is probably why my arthritis has been worse since I've been here. I've been wanting to help him at the expense of my own mental and physical health and that of my daughter, who I need to be there for more!

I guess I just stayed with my boyfriend because I felt he was all I had...another reason I've decided to write that book on the religion. EVEN NOW it's effecting mine and my daughter's life!!...If we were any other family I would have the support and help of my mother and step-father and friends I've known for years when going through such a difficult time like I've never been through before...yet they ALL turned their backs on me...that's what the "religion"...what THEY call the "TRUTH" teaches them that "GOD" WANTS them to do!!!...Can you imagine??!! I would NEVER turn my back on my daughter! And I can't imagine God would EVER want me to!

[*The Transformation*]

You're so amazing Guy, how you have such a kind way of helping me to see the whole picture; myself without brow beating me about it or making me feel stupid for not seeing it before. You have a natural loving way of directing others and getting them to open their subconscious mind to see it themselves with their own eyes so that it's a lesson that hits straight to the core and makes you want to get away from it and never make that mistake again.

You did the same with me and my drinking...I've had alcohol here all around me since I've been here and I've had one glass of wine last night for Valentines, and one the first night I was here [*recall Bandler's form of pacing after working with an alcoholic at the end of Chapter 12*] and here's why: As soon as I got here I felt my body tensing up and I didn't know why...now I do...my subconscious was trying to tell me what I already knew but was allowing myself to be blinded to because of what I had previously been conditioned to think "love" was.

Also, too, the more you show me what "Love" is, the more aware I am of what it's not. I hope that's not wrong for me to say. I mean it in an almost "supreme kind of way"...if that makes sense. I don't know how to explain actually. But I know I can see the difference so hugely and easily I'm like "**HOW could I not have seen this so clearly before?**"

Thank you once again for waking me up and opening my eyes.

Just saw how much I texted...Well, as always, thank you for listening to me...it helps to say these things out loud...or rather "text" them out loud, lol. It's almost as if as I'm saying them the picture becomes even more and more clear in my mind. When I tell it to you I can more easily take myself out of it and see it from a 3rd position and that makes it even MORE clear!

Yes...I feel even more free...I've felt more peaceful. I finally released all that anger and emotion I was carrying and holding in from the past with my ex right before getting arthritis. Thank you!

ADDENDUM

* * *

In the six weeks that have passed since this writing from Ariel, her transformation has truly blossomed. She is utilizing the tools and increasing her awareness to her full advantage. She even found a way to attend the Niurka 1 Day event in Los Angeles. New possibilities and opportunities keep coming to her - the Law of Attraction - a result of raising her inner vibration and shifting her overall state to living at cause.

* * *

There is Hope!

For anyone suffering in such a situation, whether it is you, a family member, or a friend, know there is hope. It is a matter of finding the right guide to unlock the answers within. There are many professional therapists who do incorporate NLP. Even though NLP may not be "recognized," how can one argue with the results? Evolved NLP is real and it works.

And with that, we finally do bring this book to a close. I wish you the very best life has to offer. May you experience the grandest aspects of this world, in all of its true wonder.

Blessings my friend...may your journey of awakening continue to enlighten your discovery into your *Authentic Truth*.

APPENDIX

Secondary Gain:
Guy (Ch 4, p. 49)

Timeline Therapy
Guy (Ch 4, p. 51)

Representational Systems Test:
Claudia, Catalaya, and sister (Ch 6, p. 75)

New Behavior Generator:
Catalaya (Ch 7, p. 85)

Value Elicitation Exercise:
Claudia (Ch 8, p. 97)

Quantum Linguistic Questions:
Claudia (Ch 8, p. 100)

Circle of Power Exercise:
Kelley (Ch 9, p. 110)

Quantum Linguistic Questions:
Kelley (Ch 9, p. 112)

APPENDIX

Timeline Therapy:
Kelley (Ch 9, p. 113)

New Behavior Generator:
Monika (Ch 10, p. 124)

Value Elicitation Exercise:
Monika (Ch 10, p. 122)

Perceptual Positions
Monika (Ch 10, p. 123)

Timeline Therapy:
Monika (Ch 10, p. 120)

Reframe:
Lexi (Ch 11, p. 134)

New Behavior Generator:
Connie (Ch 12, p. 144)

Value Elicitation Exercise
Chapter 14, p. 174

Quantum Linguistic Questions:
Chapter 17, p. 209

Hierarchy of Ideas:
Chapter 20, p. 244

Value Elicitation Exercise:
Chapter 22, p. 272